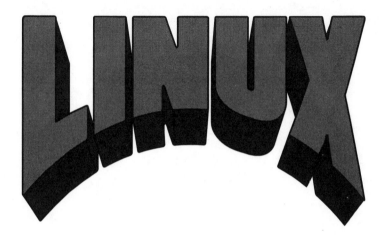

CONFIGURATION
AND INSTALLATION

PATRICK VOLKERDING,
KEVIN REICHARD, AND
ERIC F. JOHNSON

A Subsidiary of
Henry Holt and Co., Inc.

MIS:Press
a subsidiary of Henry Holt and Company, Inc.
115 West 18th Street
New York, NY 10011

First Edition—1995

Printed in the United States of America.

```
Volkerding  Patrick.
   Linux configuration and installation / Patrick Volkerding, Kevin
Reichard, Eric F. Johnson.
      p.  cm.
   ISBN 1-55828-426-5
   1. Operating systems (Computer)  2. Linux.  I. Reichard. Kevin.
II. Johnson, Eric F.  III. Title.
QA76.76.063V64  1995
005.4'469--dc20
```
                                                                95-18598
                                                                     CIP

10 9 8 7 6 5 4 3 2 1

MIS:Press books are available at special discounts for bulk purchases for sales promotions, premiums, fund-raising, or educational use. Special editions or book excerpts can also be created to specification.

For details contact: Special Sales Director
                         MIS:Press
                         a subsidiary of Henry Holt and Company, Inc.
                         115 West 18th Street
                         New York, New York 10011

Editor-in-Chief: Paul Farrell   **Managing Editor:** Cary Sullivan
Development Editor: Laura Lewin   **Copy Editor:** Melissa Burns
Production Editor: Anthony Washington

Table of Contents

Section II
Using Linux

Section III
Linux Communications and Networking

Section IV
Linux Programming

Introduction

Welcome to Linux

Welcome to the Linux operating system! If you're looking for a version of UNIX that you can run on an inexpensive PC, we think you'll get a lot out of this book.

In these pages, you'll be guided through a Linux installation and configuration process from beginning to end. You'll also learn about the many unique tools offered by the Linux operating system, as well as how to use these tools in a variety of situations.

What is Linux?

Linux (pronounced *lih-nux*) is a 32-bit operating system designed for use on Intel 80386 (or higher)-based PCs. Technically, Linux is a UNIX workalike, which means that it responds to standard UNIX commands and will run UNIX programs. You might see some references elsewhere to Linux as a UNIX clone, but that's not strictly correct. (If it were, Linux would be a lot more expensive than it is, due to the additional overhead of licensing fees.)

Linux began life as the project of a single man, Linus Torvalds (then a student at the University of Finland at Helsinki), who wanted his own alternative to another UNIX alternative—namely, the Minix operating system. He designed Linux to be similar to Minix (the original Minix filesystem was incorporated into Linux), yet more stable and freely available.

For a long time Linux was an operating system under development, as many beta versions of Linux circulated throughout the computer world—and mostly distributed through the Internet world. Version 0.2 was released to the world in the middle of 1991; in 1994, version 1.0 was finally released. A ready and willing group of volunteers helped Torvalds finish Linux; additionally, these volunteers (which included one of the authors of this book, Patrick Volkerding) helped create the add-on software that has made Linux so popular.

The CD-ROM that accompanies this book is based on Linux Kernel 1.2.8.

Linux is actually a rather trim and fit operating system. You could install Linux from a three-disk set (the *a* series, which you'll learn about in Chapter 2). So why do you need a CD-ROM, filled to the brim with bits and bytes? Because the core Linux operating system, as such, doesn't do much more than offer a command line and respond to the core UNIX commands. You'll also need the additional software—ranging from utilities like **diff** from the Free Software Foundation to compilers and editors. Because this additional software is different from distribution to distribution, there are differences between Linuxes (Linuci? Linuces?) available on the market. On the accompanying CD-ROM, you're using the highly regarded Slackware distribution. (For example, the installation program—so critical for many users—is unique to Slackware.) And Linux also features its own graphical interface, based on the X Window System.

This also leads us to one essential truth about Linux (something also true about UNIX): Linux is a series of tools. You use one tool to do one thing, another tool to perform another function. As a set of tools, the Slackware distribution is more than just Linux.

Why Should You Use Linux?

Since it runs UNIX programs—most notably through compiling original source code written for the many UNIX variants across the world— Linux is the ideal platform for many potential users:

- **Users** who want to learn more about the UNIX operating system and the X Window System.
- **Internet surfers** who want a powerful platform for cruising the 'Net.
- **System administrators** who want an alternative to expensive UNIX workstations, either in their workplace or at home.
- **Programmers** who want a cheap home or small-business platform for developing software that can be used on other, more powerful UNIX systems.

There are many features to Linux that you should find attractive:

- **You've already paid for it**. By purchasing this book, you've purchased a full implementation of Linux, complete with scads of useful programs.
- **Linux follows standards**. For the most part, Linux and its tools follow various standards, such as POSIX compliance. As a programming platform, Linux can be used to develop and test code for a wide variety of platforms.

Linux can be used for most of your everyday needs. True, Linux lacks the wide range of applications found in the PC world. However, for most of your daily tasks (particularly if you want to use Linux for programming or the Internet), the accompanying CD-ROM contains enough tools to satisfy most of your needs.

Will Linux replace more popular operating systems, like DOS and *Windows*? That depends on your needs. For many basic computing tasks—word processing, spreadsheet, telecommunications—Linux and the Slackware distribution is a perfectly adequate alternative to other PC operating systems. As a development platform, Linux is more than adequate. Since Linux is freely available, it attracts the attention of many programmers and developers who release their software to the computing community—meaning that there's a decent selection of software in the computing world, even beyond what's available on the CD-ROM. The one drawback to Linux—which, admittedly, is a major drawback—is the lack of robust applications for everyday use. True, you can do work with **emacs** and **groff** for document creation, but this process is awkward at best. Given the track record of the UNIX industry and the robust growth enjoyed by Linux, you can expect to see many more applications down the road.

Of course, this isn't to say that you won't get use out of the applications on the CD-ROM. For many, the usage of Linux as an Internet tool will alone be worth the price of the book. Programmers who want to code for other UNIX and X Window platforms will also find this book and CD-ROM extremely useful.

Linux, Slackware, and this Book

LINUX Configuration and Installation focuses on the version of Linux included on the accompanying CD-ROM. We made this decision because the world of Linux is so wide and varied, and despite what some people think, there are differences among Linux distributions.

If you own another Linux distribution, there will be things in this book that will apply to your distribution (particularly in Chapter 5 and beyond). However, be warned that we're sticking to the Slackware distribution of Linux for the particulars in this book.

What is Slackware Compared to Linux?

Linux, as distributed by the many good people who work on it, is only a kernel, and without additional utilities, can't do anything .

The Slackware distribution of Linux builds on this core with utilities, programming libraries, and ports of other UNIX and X Window programs, under a unified whole. Many of the setup utilities on the CD-ROM, for example, are unique to the Slackware distribution of Linux.

The Free Software Foundation

Many of the utilities and programs contained in Slackware (as well as most other Linux distributions) come from the *Free Software Foundation* (FSF), or are licensed under the general terms of the Free Software Foundation. Since so many of the utilities are connected with the FSF, we urge you to check out the group (via its many Usenet newsgroups) as well as read through its general license, which is contained along with its programs (for example, **emacs** gives you an option to read through the general license). For more information about the Free Software Foundation, write:

> Free Software Foundation
>
> 675 Massachusetts Av.
>
> Cambridge, MA 02139
>
> 617/876-3296 (voice)
>
> 617/492-9057 (fax)
>
> *gnu@prep.ai.mit.edu*

Resources on the CD-ROM

The CD-ROM includes a rather robust set of UNIX utilities, as well as a complete implementation of the X Window System.

A full implementation of the Linux operating system can be found on the accompanying CD-ROM.

In addition, we've included a set of documents, called the Linux **HOW-TOS**, in the **docs** directory on the CD-ROM. These are text files that examine a portion of the Linux operating system in great detail. Occasionally we refer to these documents throughout the course of this book.

Conventions Used in the Book

To make this book more usable, we've incorporated a few conventions that should make it easier for you to find what you need. These include the following icons:

 The **Note** icon indicates something that you should pay special attention to.

 The **Warning** icon warns you about actions that could be hazardous to the health of your computer or your Linux installation.

 The **CD-ROM** icon refers to items found on the accompanying CD-ROM.

In addition, we've used some specific formatting commands in the text:

- **Bold** type refers to a command
- *Italic* type refers to a new concept
- Monospaced type refers to a command line entered directly at a prompt and ending with the **Enter** key, as in the following:

    ```
    gilbert:/ elvis
    ```

How to Reach the Authors

You're free to drop us a line via electronic mail at:

reichard@mr.net

However, we must warn you that we can't promise you further guidance to Linux than what's printed in this book. Between the three of us, we receive a lot of electronic mail, and at times it's impossible to keep up with it. Therefore, don't assume that this electronic-mail address will bring you instant help.

Section I

Linux Installation and Configuration

Welcome to your brave new journey with the Linux operating system! This section covers the installation and configuration of Linux:

Chapter 1 is an overview of the Linux operating system, explaining its components and other facts you'll need to know before installation. If you're not a past or present Linux user, you'll want to read this chapter carefully.

Chapter 2 guides you through a Linux installation from beginning to end. In many ways, installing Linux is one of the more daunting tasks you'll face, since Linux runs rather smoothly once it's installed and configured correctly. Again, this is a chapter you'll want to follow *very* closely.

Chapter 3 covers the installation of XFree86, the implementation of the X Window System, designed for PC-based Unices. It's a lead-in to

Chapter 4, which covers XFree86 configuration.

Linux and PC Hardware

This chapter covers:

- The hardware needs of Linux
- PC configuration requirements
- Processor needs
- RAM needs
- Supported hard drives
- Supported SCSI cards
- Supported network cards
- Supported mice
- Supported CD-ROM drives
- Linux and laptops

Preparing for Linux

An ounce of preparation is worth a pound of cure, goes the old (and cliché, some would say) saying. This is one case, however, where there's a kernel of truth to the old saying—particularly when it comes to installing and configuring Linux.

Before you rush into a half-baked and ill-conceived Linux installation, there are a few things you should do, mostly relating to your PC's setup and configuration. In this chapter, we'll guide you through the steps you'll need to take to prepare your PC for Linux, as well as warn you as to whether your PC is even capable of efficiently running Linux. In the next chapter, we'll run through a typical Linux installation.

Preparing Your PC for Linux

Like all PC-based Unices (including SCO UNIX and UnixWare), Linux is pretty fussy about the hardware it runs on. By fussy, we mean that Linux does a lot of interacting directly with PC hardware. DOS, by comparison, is a very forgiving operating system, pretty much able to run and function on almost any PC. It will ignore some small flaws in the PC architecture.

Linux, however, will expose those flaws. As a PC UNIX, Linux interacts *very* closely with PC hardware, writing directly to various PC components. If there's a problem with your PC—however small—Linux will find it. The problem is somewhat lessened if you're using brand-name equipment; remember (as mentioned in the Introduction) that Linux is a product of a virtual army of volunteers, and they're just like everyone else when it comes to computer equipment—if half a million people bought a particular PC model from Compaq, chances are good that a Linux developer (or two) will be among the half million buyers. This is how hardware gets supported under Linux; the most devoted make sure Linux works fine on their systems. It's certain that someone out there will have experience with Linux on popular hardware—it's less likely that someone out there will have experience on your spanking-new hardware from NoNameClone Corp., located in the strip mall on the outskirts of town.

However, if you do buy a PC from NoNameClone Corp., this puts an additional burden on you, as you'll need to know more about your PC than you ever thought. The ideal situation, of course, would be to not actually own a PC yet and to put one together expressly to run Linux. (This is the way we approached it, in one instance.) A bad situation is buying a no-name clone from a local vendor and having no idea about its components. The worst situation is buying a no-name clone, and being a UNIX workstation user, fairly ignorant of the quirks surrounding the PC architecture. A middling situation is buying a clone from the likes of a CompUSA or Best Buy and having decent documentation regarding the components.

Since we don't live in an ideal world, we'll assume you know little about your PC and need a primer on its components. We'll run down both the minimal and ideal Linux PC configuration, followed by a compatibility list.

When buying a PC, the temptation is to spend as little as possible, or try to squeeze by with lesser or inferior components. We understand the need to live on a budget—we certainly don't have thousands of dollars worth of computer equipment sitting around our home offices. But there comes a point when you need to make the necessary investment if you want to run Linux effectively. Too often, we see people complaining in the Usenet newsgroups about Linux not running properly on their PCs, or that XFree86 won't run in higher resolutions on their unsupported graphics cards. You can avoid this by either taking an inventory of your PC before installing Linux (which may mean actually taking off the cover and physically poking through the components) or making sure a new PC meets the compatibility guidelines. Either action is a real pain, we admit; but by spending some time upfront, you'll avoid a ton of problems later in the installation and configuration processes. You may be pleased with yourself after saving some cash buying a new graphics card from NoNameClone Corp., but in the end you're better off paying a little bit more for hardware that's been thoroughly tested by the huge number of existing Linux users.

Table 1.1 Linux PC configuration guidelines.

PC Component	Minimum	Ideal
Processor	Intel 80386 or equivalent	Intel i486 or equivalent; Pentium; Intel clones
RAM	4MB (8MB for running X Window)	16MB
Graphics card	VGA graphics	SVGA graphics; card explicitly supported by XFree86
Hard drive	100MB	275MB or more
Bus	Anything but MCA	Anything but MCA
CD-ROM	Double-speed drive	Quadruple-speed drive
Mouse	Microsoft, Logitech or compatible	Microsoft, Logitech or compatible
Network card	None	Supported model (if networking)

If you're not sure about your particular hardware setup and Linux compatibility, check out the **HARDWARE-HOWTO**.

Bus

Linux has been found to run on all the major bus architectures—ISA, VLB, EISA—except for the nonstandard Micro Channel Architecture, found on most IBM PS/2 models. (Luckily, not every IBM PC features an MCA bus; the ValuePoint and PS/1 models feature an industry-standard ISA bus.)

The PCI architecture isn't universally supported, however. Be sure and read the **PCI-HOWTO** before attempting a Linux installation.

Processor

Linux needs at least an Intel 80386-based processor in order to run efficiently—period. Don't bother with a 80286-based PC. If you've got an older PC sitting in the closet and you think it might be neat to recycle using Linux, leave it there, donate it to your local charity, or give it to the kids to bang on. It won't be useful in your Linux adventure.

Pentium users may note that there's no explicit support for the Pentium processor. However, when monitoring the various Usenet Linux newsgroups, we've never run across anyone complaining about problems with Linux running on a Pentium platform. Similarly, we've discovered few complaints about running Linux on any of the Intel-compatible CPUs, such as those from AMD or Cyrix. (The exception was an early release of the AMD 486DX, which would occasionally fail; these problems were not limited to the Linux world.) While nothing in this world is guaranteed (especially not in the Linux world), you can feel pretty comfortable about using Linux on any Intel or Intel-compatible CPU that's a 80386 or better.

RAM

Random-access memory is one of those sticky issues when it comes to the PC. If you're a workstation user, you're probably used to working with scads and scads of RAM. (Then again, most workstation users have someone else footing the bill, as the costs of that RAM can add up rather quickly.) In theory, it would be great to work with scads and scads of RAM on a PC. Linux, like any 32-bit operating system, loves to work with as much RAM as possible.

In the real world, however, there are bills to pay, and the reality is that RAM is one of the most expensive parts of a PC, both upon the initial purchase and if you ever want to upgrade. If you're a workstation user, you'll want to read through the following section, which explains RAM and the PC. If you're a PC user and are comfortable in your knowledge of RAM, you can skip to the following section.

The PC and RAM

If you buy a PC these days and aren't too attentive to details, you can very easily end up with a PC that has 4 megabytes (MB) of RAM, as this is a popular figure with packages offered by the likes of CompUSA, Best Buy, or Computer City. In this day and age, 4MB isn't a whole lot of memory, even when running Microsoft *Windows* and MS-DOS. It becomes even more confining when running Linux.

The following from the Slackware FAQ should illustrate problems associated with low memory.

Q: I can't get anything to work at all! What's the deal?

A: If you seem to suffer catastrophic failure (!), then check the file FILE_LIST on *ftp.cdrom.com* in **/pub/linux/slackware** against the contents of your disks and make sure you're not missing any files.

Also, I've noticed that most of the reports of kernel panics and system hangs have come from people with 4MB. If you're running into these types of problems I'd suggest forking over the money for four more megs. I have 8MB of RAM and never have crashes. (Well, only when I really push my luck.) If you don't want to do that, then go through your **/etc/rc.d/rc.*** files and get rid of any daemons you don't use, like **crond**, **lpd**, or **selection**.

If you've got 4MB and you're getting "virtual memory exceeded in new" warnings, make sure you set up and activate a swap partition before running **setup**. If you're hard up on memory, type this at the boot kernel's LILO prompt:

mount root= /dev/fd0.

This will allow you to mount the rootdisk instead of loading it into a RAM disk, saving over 1 megabyte of memory for LINUX to use for the installation process . You'll have to install from the other drive or from the hard drive. You will also not be able to create any kind of boot disk, so you'll have to install LILO and take your chances. I only suggest using this approach if a swapfile will not work.

Linux will boot and run on a PC with 4 megabytes of RAM. However, you'll be running into memory constraints very quickly, and chances are that you won't be able to run the X Window System at all. In fact, 8 megabytes is barely enough to run X and Linux. We've used the combination on an 8MB machine, and the results weren't too encouraging; in fact, we were strongly encouraged to ramp up to 16MB of RAM right away.

This is why we recommend you upgrade and buy as much RAM as you can afford. Before you do so, you should know how today's PCs handle RAM and how you can buy it.

Almost every new PC supports Single Inline Memory Modules, or SIMMs. Additionally, almost every new PC has four SIMM slots on the motherboard, and most SIMMs are sold in multiples of two or four—1MB, 2MB, 4MB, or 8MB. The less memory on a SIMM, the cheaper the SIMM, obviously.

If you bought a PC with only 4MB of RAM, you probably ran into a situation where there were four 1MB SIMMs installed in the four motherboard slots. When you upgrade your PC's RAM, these 1MB SIMMs will be relatively worthless, unless you bought a PC from a vendor that allows you to trade in old RAM when buying new RAM. (The trade-in price depends on the vendor. Typically, you'll get a credit for half the price of the old RAM when trading it in, provided you bought a PC from a vendor that assembles their own PCs. We've dealt with some cloners that give you full credit on the old RAM when trading it in, providied the PC was bought within the last year.) The same would be true if you bought a system with 8MB of RAM, and the SIMM slots were filled with 2MB SIMMs.

The best-case scenario is if you have a PC and only half of the SIMM slots are filled; in our case, we lucked into purchasing an 8MB PC that had 4MB SIMMs. (Contrary to popular belief, not every PC needs all the SIMM slots filled in order to function properly.) In this case, we needed to buy two more 4MB SIMMs to stick in the empty slots, bringing the total to 16MB.

Depending on the motherboard configuration, you may have to play with the SIMMs and their order in the slots. In the case of the 8MB PC with two more SIMMS added, we needed to stagger the SIMMs (old SIMM, new SIMM, old SIMM, new SIMM) before the system would recognize all 16MB of RAM. Normally this isn't something that's documented, so you might need to call the customer-support line of your PC manufacturer for advice when adding new SIMMs.

Graphics Card

Dealing with a graphics card has been one of the most problematic areas of Linux—or rather, XFree86, which serves as the X Window System graphical interface to Linux. XFree86 deals directly with the graphics card and must know everything about the card in a configuration file (such as the amount of RAM it has, the chipset it features, and what modes it supports), putting more stress on you than does the average software. Because of the work connected with this issue, we've devoted two chapters—3 and 4—to the subject of installing and configuring XFree86.

Hard-Drive Controller

Unlike most PC-based Unices, Linux isn't too fussy about the hard disk or hard disks it supports; basically, if a hard disk is supported by a PC's BIOS, it will also work fine under Linux. This goes for IDE, EIDE, MFM, RLL, and SCSI hard drives.

Regarding how large a hard drive you'll need—as always, the more the better. A full installation of Linux takes up a little less than 275 megabytes, but you can do quite well in 100 megabytes (40 megabytes if you don't install the X Window System) if you're careful about what you install. In fact, you can get down to 10 megabytes or so if you do a partial installation and run Linux partially from the CD-ROM drive.

The price of hard disks has been falling rapidly, so many people will be able to afford 1-gigabyte drives. This is a good thing, of course; we recently noticed 1.2-gigabyte IDE drives advertised for less than $400. (SCSI hard drives, of course, cost a little more.)

However, if you buy one of these mondo IDE hard drives, you'll need to do a few things before you install Linux on it—or rather, *not* do a few things. MS-DOS can't handle such large drives (in their infinite wisdom, the designers of MS-DOS placed a cylinder limit on DOS, and newer hard drives exceed that 1,023-cylinder limit), so most manufacturers, such as Conner and Western Digital, ship disk-management software (such as Ontrack's *Disk Manager*) that allow MS-DOS to deal with large hard drives. *Don't install this software.* A program like *Disk Manager* is designed to work only with MS-DOS or a variant, not Linux or another operating system.

Instead, change your PC's BIOS per the directions found in the hard-disk documentation. Then, using the steps detailed in Chapter 2, use the DOS FDISK utility to partition the hard drive into two smaller partitions that can be seen both by DOS and Linux.

ON THE

CD-ROM

In theory, your version of Linux should have no problems with larger EIDE hard drives. However, there's a file on the accompanying CD-ROM called **eide.txt** that explains various methods of getting around this should you have problems. Since the current version of Slackware, 2.3, addresses these problems, you probally won't need to address these issues.

SCSI Controllers

In theory, you shouldn't have *any* problems with a SCSI card, since all SCSI cards are written to exacting technical specifications. If you believe that, we have some swampland in Florida for you.

The fact is that SCSI cards are not all alike. You can't assume that since you have a SCSI controller on your PC, you'll be able to use Linux with no sweat. The following SCSI controllers are explicitly supported under Linux: AMI Fast Disk VLB/EISA (works with BusLogic drivers); Adaptec AVA-1505/1515 (ISA; use 152x drivers), AHA-1510/152x (ISA), AHA-154x (ISA; all models), AHA-174x (EISA; in enhanced mode), AHA-274x (EISA), 284x (VLB; AIC-7770); Always IN2000; BusLogic (all models); DPT Smartcache (EATA; ISA/EISA); DTC 329x (EISA; Adaptec 154x compatible); Future Domain TMC-16x0, TMC-3260 (PCI), TMC-8xx, TMC-950; NCR 53c7x0, 53c8x0 (PCI); Pro Audio Spectrum 16 SCSI (ISA); Qlogic/Control Concepts SCSI/IDE (FAS408; ISA/VLB/PCMCIA; does not work with PCI (different chipset); Seagate ST-01/ST-02 (ISA); SoundBlaster 16 SCSI-2 (Adaptec 152x); Trantor T128/T128F/T228 (ISA); UltraStor 14F (ISA), 24F (EISA), 34F (VLB); and Western Digital WD7000 SCSI.

Parallel-port SCSI adapters (popular among laptop users) are not supported by Linux.

The SCSI device must support block sizes of 256, 512, or 1024 bytes.

If you're having trouble with SCSI and Linux, you'll want to read the **SCSI-HOWTO**.

However, be warned that you may need to play around with various SCSI cards, as you'll see from this excerpt from the Slackware FAQ:

Q: Why the $%#@! isn't my UltraStor SCSI detected? It works under DOS!

A: Set the I/O address to 0x340 instead to 0x330.

For any hardware that doesn't work, a good rule is to try playing around with the IRQ and I/O settings on it to see what happens. If your system is up and running and you're having problems with a CD-ROM or tape or something like that, you can always look around for the driver source in **/usr/src/linux/drivers**... really, it won't bite! Often, the source contains important documentation, such as the default IRQ settings for that type of device, and the major number for the entry in **/dev**. Also, try other bootkernels and see if that helps.

A discussion of IRQs and interrupts can be found later in this chapter.

Floppy Drive

The Linux installation process assumes that you'll be creating a bootdisk and a rootdisk for use on a high-density drive. This means that the storage capacity must be 1.44 megabytes (for 3.5-inch diskettes) or 1.2 megabytes (for 5.25-inch diskettes).

Tape Drives

Any tape drive that works from the SCSI connector should be fine under Linux (in other words, if your SCSI card works, so should the tape drive). In addition, Linux works pretty well with other tape drives that are connected via floppy controller, such as the QIC-117, QIC-40/80, and Colorado FC-10 tape drives. (According to the **HARDWARE-HOWTO**, Linux doesn't work with the Emerald and Tecmar QIC-02 tape controller cards, drives that connect via the parallel port, or non-QIC-80 drives.)

 For further information, check out **FTAPE-HOWTO**.

CD-ROM

You can use a SCSI-based CD-ROM for Linux, or else you can use one of the many CD-ROM/sound board combinations from the likes of Creative Labs. If you use a SCSI CD-ROM with a block size of 512 or 2048 bytes, you'll be fine as long as Linux recognizes the SCSI card; Linux works directly with the SCSI card and not necessarily directly with the CD-ROM. In addition, there's explicit support for the following drives: Aztech CDA268; Orchid CDS-3110; Okano/Wearnes CDD-110; EIDE (ATAPI) CD-ROM drives; Matsushita/Panasonic, Kotobuki (both used by Sound Blaster); Mitsumi; and Sony CDU31A/CDU33A.

Linux supports the ISO-9660 filesystem, the Rock Ridge Extensions, and the PhotoCD (XA) format.

Not every Sound Blaster features a proprietary interface, as some versions are based on a SCSI architecture. You'll need to know what specific Sound Blaster board you're using before you sit down for your Linux installation.

Here's another selection from the Slackware FAQ regarding Sound Blaster boards:

Q: I see my Sound Blaster/Panasonic CD-ROM detected at boot, but I can't install from it or mount it. What's going on?

A: Try setting to drive's ID to 0. This is expected by the install disks. There should be a jumper on the back of the drive that selects this—just move it to the leftmost position.

Sound Boards

Though there isn't much occasion for using sound under Linux (unless you want to spend most of your time playing Doom, which wouldn't be an unreasonable pursuit), Linux does support a wide range of sound cards, including: 6850 UART MIDI; ATI Stereo F/X (SB compatible); Adlib; ECHO-PSS (Orchid SW32, Cardinal DSP16, etc); Ensoniq SoundScape; Gravis Ultrasound, Ultrasound 16-bit sampling daughterboard, Ultrasound MAX; Logitech SoundMan Games (SBPro, 44kHz stereo support), SoundMan Wave (SBPro/MPU-401) (OPL4), SoundMan 16 (PAS-16 compatible); Microsoft Sound System (AD1848); MPU-401 MIDI; Media Vision Premium 3D (Jazz16); Media Vision Pro Sonic 16 (Jazz), Pro Audio Spectrum-16; Sound Blaster, Sound Blaster Pro, Sound Blaster 16/ASP/MCD/SCSI-2, Sound Galaxy NX Pro; ThunderBoard; WaveBlaster (and other SB16 daughterboards).

Mouse

We've used various mice with Linux, mostly under the auspices of the X Window System. Basically, if you use a serial mouse with Linux, you'll just be telling the system to look to a specific serial port for the mouse. (You'll learn this in Chapter 2 and the Linux installation.) The same goes for trackballs and joysticks that run off of a serial port. The following mouse models are explicitly supported under Linux: ATI XL

Inport busmouse; C&T 82C710 (QuickPort; used on Toshiba and TI Travelmate laptops); Microsoft serial mouse and busmouse; Mouse Systems serial mouse; Logitech serial mice and busmouse; PS/2 mouse.

Network Cards

If you're planning on using Linux on a network, you'll need a networking card. If you're not planning on using Linux on the network, you won't need a card. Other PC Unices require the presence of a network card to run at all (even on a single-user installation), but Linux is not one of them.

The following network cards are supported by Linux and have been tested: 3Com 3C503, 3C505, 3C507, 3C509 (ISA), 3C579 (EISA); AMD LANCE (79C960), PCnet-ISA/PCI (AT1500, HP J2405A, NE1500/NE2100); Allied Telesis AT1700; Cabletron E21xx; DEC DEPCA and EtherWORKS; HP PCLAN (27245 and 27xxx series), PCLAN PLUS (27247B and 27252A); Intel EtherExpress; NE2000/NE1000; Racal-Interlan NI5210 (i82586 Ethernet chip), Racal-Interlan NI6510 (am7990 lance chip; however, it doesn't work with more than 16 megabytes of RAM); PureData PDUC8028, PDI8023; SMC Ultra; Schneider & Koch G16; and Western Digital WD80x3.

In addition, the following EISA and onboard controllers are supported: Ansel Communications AC3200 EISA; Apricot Xen-II; and Zenith Z-Note/IBM ThinkPad 300 built-in adapter.

The following pocket and portable adapters are supported: AT-Lan-Tec/RealTek parallel-port adapter; D-Link DE600/DE620 parallel-port adapter. The following PCMCIA adapters are supported: 3Com 3C589; Accton EN2212 EtherCard; D-Link DE650; IBM Credit Card Adapter; IC-Card; Kingston KNE-PCM/M; LANEED Ethernet; Linksys EthernetCard; Network General "Sniffer"; Novell NE4100; and Thomas-Conrad Ethernet.

The following line appears in the **HARDWARE-HOWTO** regarding the 3Com 3C501:"Avoid like the plague."

Dealing with a network card is like dealing with any other Linux hardware peripheral: You need to make sure that it's not conflicting with other PC hardware. Note the following from the Slackware FAQ:

Q: I also have an SMC card. I could only get mine to work on IRQ 3 or 4.

A: There might be a way to work around the problem, but I haven't had time to go looking for it. I don't know what happened but when today I rebooted my machine after power shutdown, suddenly the Ethernet card started working. I only changed the base address options in drivers file to look for 0x2a0 address.

Multiport Controllers

Many smaller Linux installations use multiport controllers to allow multiple access to a single UNIX box. As of this writing the following controllers are supported: AST FourPort and clones; Accent Async-4; Bell Technologies HUB6; Boca BB-1004, 1008 (4, 8 port; no DTR, DSR, and CD), BB-2016 (16 port), Boca IO/AT66 (6 port), Boca IO 2by4 (4S/2P; works with modems, but uses 5 IRQs); Cyclades Cyclom-8Y/16Y (8, 16 port); PC-COMM 4-port; STB 4-COM; Twincom ACI/550; and Usenet Serial Board II.

Modems

Again, if a modem works under DOS, it should work under Linux— whether the modem is internal or external. When you install Linux, you'll need to specify the location of the modem (serial port 1, 2, 3, or 4).

 If you, you'll need to want to use ports 3 or 4, or use non-standard IRQ settings for ports 1 and 2, you'll need to make the aapropriate adjustments to your **/etc/rc.d/rc.serial** file. You'll also need to edit **/etc/rc.d/re.s** to run the **rc.serial** setup.

NOTE

Printers

Essentially, any printer connected to a parallel or serial port that works under DOS should work under Linux. During the installation, you'll be asked to specify which port contains the printer.

The issue becomes a little dicier when dealing with XFree86 and Ghostscript, the utility used to create and print PostScript documents. Ghostscript allows you to print PostScript-formatted documents on non-PostScript printers; much of the UNIX documentation that flows down the pike is formatted with PostScript, and this capability is very handy. Ghostscript supports the following printers: Apple Imagewriter; C. Itoh M8510; Canon BubbleJet BJ10e, BJ200, LBP-8II, LIPS III; DEC LA50/70/75/75plus, LN03, LJ250; Epson 9 pin, 24 pin, LQ series, Stylus, AP3250; Hewlett-Packard 2563B, DesignJet 650C, DeskJet/Plus/500, DeskJet 500C/520C/550C color, LaserJet/Plus/II/III/4, PaintJet /XL/XL300/1200C color; IBM Jetprinter color, Proprinter; Imagen ImPress; Mitsubishi CP50 color; NEC P6/P6+/P60; Okidata MicroLine 182; Ricoh 4081; SPARCprinter; StarJet 48 inkjet printer; Tektronix 4693d color 2/4/8 bit, 4695/4696 inkjet plotter; and Xerox XES printers (2700, 3700, 4045, etc.).

Miscellaneous Items

If a device is connected to the SCSI card and Linux has no problems with the SCSI card, then you should have no problems with the device. This would include most CDR, WORM, optical, and floptical drives. Additionally, we've not seen complaints about proprietary drives from the likes of Syquest and Bernoulli.

In addition, there's no explicit support yet for scanners under Linux. There are many alpha (read: not ready for widespread distribution) drivers for some popular scanners out there; check the **HARDWARE-HOWTO** for details.

Linux on Laptops

Generally speaking, Linux should run fine on most laptops. However, you may not be able to get the full functionality of the laptop when running Linux; for example, most laptops feature proprietary power-management and graphics capabilities that Linux simply can't use. In these cases, you'll lose the advanced power management, and you'll need to run Linux and XFree86 in a lower graphics mode (VGA or SuperVGA). However, Linux does support 2.88-megabyte disk drives, as well as a few select PCMCIA drivers (Databook TCIC/2, Intel i82365SL, Cirrus PD67xx, and Vadem VG-468 chipsets).

The **HARDWARE-HOWTO** contains some additional information on laptops and Linux, including a few Web sites that contain information about specific laptop models.

Many laptop users are using parallel-port SCSI adapters. However, these adapters are not yet supported by Linux.

Learning about PC Hardware

You've probably noticed references in this chapter to things like interrupts and IRQ settings. If you're a PC hack, you know what these nasty things mean. If you're not a PC hack, you're in for a rude awakening.

Simply put, the PC architecture assigns addresses to peripheral devices. If these addresses conflict, you have problems. Some peripherals, such as network cards, need to be set to specific addresses, while others don't.

Since our goal here isn't to turn you into a hardware hack (and, quite honestly, discussions of interrupts and IRQ settings really depress us), we'd suggest checking into a more advanced PC hardware book.

Summary

This chapter outlines the hardware requirements for running Linux. Linux actually runs on a wide assortment of PC hardware, which tends to be unusual for a PC UNIX. In the next chapter, we cover a typical Linux installation from beginning to end.

Installing Linux

This chapter covers:

- Preparing your PC for Linux
- Creating new partitions under DOS
- Creating new partitions under Linux
- Creating your bootdisk and rootdisk
- Booting Linux for installation
- Installing from the **setup** command
- Selecting the software to install
- Logging into the virgin Linux system
- Setting up additional users
- Shutting down Linux

Before You Install Linux

Now that you have the perfect PC for running Linux, it's time to prepare for the installation. No, you can't just install Linux from the accompanying CD-ROM; you must first configure your hard drive and create boot floppies. Neither step is particularly difficult. Here, we'll cover how to create boot floppies for booting Linux, followed by a discussion of preparing your hard drive for the Linux installation. The actual installation process is:

- Create boot and root floppies
- Prepare your hard drive for installation
- Boot Linux from boot and root floppies
- Install Linux from the CD-ROM

In the following steps, we're assuming you already have an Intel-based PC up and running with the MS-DOS operating system, with the CD-ROM drive installed correctly, since you'll need to copy some files from the CD-ROM onto your hard drive. (On a PC, you'll need to install special drivers in order to use the CD-ROM drive. These drivers ship with the CD-ROM drive.) This doesn't necessarily need to be the PC on which you plan to install Linux—it just needs to be a PC with a DOS command line and access to the CD-ROM drive.

The procedures in this chapter are closely tied to the installation and configuration routines found on the accompanying CD-ROM. Other distributions of Linux are not exactly the same. If you're using a distribution of Linux other than the Slackware distribution on the accompanying CD-ROM, you can still follow along—keeping in mind that your exact steps will probably be different.

Creating Boot and Root Floppies

Your first steps will be to create two floppy disks used to boot Linux: the *boot* and *root* diskettes. The boot diskette is the diskette used (as the name implies) to boot the PC, while the root diskette contains a set of Linux commands. Creating these diskettes is mandatory.

Your first step should be to create a subdirectory for the various files you'll need to create the floppies. Under DOS, you create a directory with the **MKDIR** command. The name of the subdirectory doesn't matter; in the following, we've arbitrarily chosen **slack** as the name of the subdirectory:

```
C:> MKDIR \SLACK
```

Under DOS, case does not matter (unlike UNIX, where case *always* matters). The DOS commands in this chapter will all be in uppercase, but you don't need to follow this convention.

You'll then want to copy the appropriate files from the CD-ROM to the **slack** subdirectory. From the root directory, you'll need to copy the **RAWRITE.EXE** files:

```
C:> COPY E:\INSTALL\RAWRITE.EXE C:\SLACK
    1 file(s) copied
```

This is assuming that you do indeed want to copy these files from the CD-ROM (which, in our example, has the drive letter E: assigned to it; your drive letter assignment may differ) to the **slack** directory.

Your next step is to determine which bootdisk and rootdisk images you'll be using, and to copy those files into the **slack** directory. Because this can be a relatively large decision, it warrants its own section.

Choosing Bootdisk and Rootdisk Images

Linux needs to know a lot about your PC's hardware, and that knowledge begins the second you boot the system. That's why you need to put some thought into selecting your bootdisk and rootdisk images.

Before we go any further, we should explain what *bootdisk* and *rootdisk images* are. Linux needs to boot from floppies initially, and it needs to know what sort of hardware it's working with. When you boot Linux for the first time, the information is contained on the bootdisk and the rootdisk. To create a bootdisk and a rootdisk, you need to select the proper image and copy it to your hard drive. You'll then use the **RAWRITE.EXE** utility to copy the image byte-for-byte to the diskette.

How do you select the proper image? The first step is to determine the disk size of your drive A:, from which you boot the system. If you're using a 3.5-inch disk drive as A:, you'll need to grab an image from the **bootdsks.144** directory. (This is so labeled because the capacity of a 3.5-inch high-density floppy is 1.44 megabytes.) If you're using a 5.25-inch disk drive to boot from, you'll need to grab an image from the **bootdsks.12** directory. (This is so labeled because the capacity of a 5.25-inch high-density floppy is 1.2 megabytes.)

If you look inside either directory, you'll see a list of filenames. (The filenames are the same in both directories; it doesn't matter from this point which directory you grab the image from.) Each image supports a different set of hardware; a list of the files and the supported hardware is in Table 2.1.

Table 2.1 Linux bootdisks and supported hardware.

Filename	Supported Hardware
AZTCD	IDE, SCSI, and Aztech/Okano/Orchid/Wearnes non-IDE CD support.
BARE	IDE hard–drive drivers only
CDU31A	IDE and SCSI drivers, plus Sony CDU31/33a CD drivers
OLD31a	An old (1.1.59) bootdisk with an autoprobing Sony CDU31/33a CD-ROM driver. The new driver doesn't probe for your drive. If you have problems with it you might want to try this one instead
CDU535	IDE and SCSI drivers, plus Sony CDU531/535 CD drivers
MITSUMI	IDE and SCSI drivers, plus the Mitsumi CD driver
IDECD	IDE, SCSI, and IDE/ATAPI CD-ROM
NET	IDE hard drive and Ethernet drivers
SBPCD	IDE and SCSI drivers, plus SB Pro/Panasonic CD drivers (also for TEAC-55A)
SCSI	IDE hard drive, SCSI hard drive, and SCSI CD-ROM drives
SCSINET1	IDE hard drive, SCSI hard drive, SCSI CD-ROM, and Ethernet drivers. (Supports SCSI cards in list 1 below)
SCSINET2	IDE hard drive, SCSI hard drive, SCSI CD-ROM, and Ethernet drivers. (Supports SCSI cards in list 2 below)
XT	IDE hard drive and XT hard-drive drivers

SCSI Drivers	
List 1:	**List 2:**
Adaptec 152x/1542/1740/274x/284x	Generic NCR5380
Buslogic	NCR 53c7,8xx
ETA-DMA (DPT/NEC/AT&T)	Always IN2000
Seagate ST-02	Pro Audio Spectrum 16
Future Domain TMC-8xx, 16xx	QLogic
	Trantor T128/T128F/T228
	Ultrsator
	7000 FAST

NOTE All of these images support UMSDOS, if you prefer this method of installation. UMSDOS will be covered later in this chapter in the section, "Should You Use UMSDOS?"

You'll need one of these to get Linux started on your system so that you can install it. Because of the possibility of collisions between the various Linux drivers, several bootkernel disk images are provided. You should use the one with the least drivers possible to maximize your chances of success. All of these disks support UMSDOS.

At first glance, Table 2.1 can be a little on the confusing side. To clear things up, Table 2.2 contains a handy little guide where you can match installation medium and hard-disk format to the preferred image and the alternative image.

Table 2.2 A chart for choosing bootdisk images.

Installation Medium	IDE Destination	SCSI Destination	MFM Destination
Floppy	bare	scsi	xt
Hard Drive	bare	scsi	xt
SCSI CD-ROM	scsi	scsi	
Mitsumi CD	mitsumi	mitsumi	

Table 2.2 A chart for choosing bootdisk images. (continued)

Installation Medium	IDE Destination	SCSI Destination	MFM Destination
Aztech, Orchid, Okano, Wearnes CD with Interface card	aztcd	aztcd	
Sony CDU31a or CDU33a CD-ROM	cdu31a old31a	cdu31a old31a	
SoundBlaster, Panasonic, Kotobuki, Matsushita, TEAC CD-55A Lasermate CD-ROM	sbpcd	sbpcd	
Sony 535/531CD-ROM	cdu535	cdu535	
Most IDE/ATAPI CD-ROMs	idecd	idecd	
NFS	net	scsinet1 (see list 1 below) scsinet 2 (see list 2 below)	
Tape	**bare** (for floppy tape) **scsi** (for SCSI tape)	**scsi**	**xt** (for floppy tape)

SCSI Drivers

List 1:	List 2:
Adaptec 152x/1542/1740/274x/284x	Generic NCR5380
Buslogic	NCR 53c7,8xx
ETA-DMA (DPT/NEC/AT&T)	Always IN2000
Seagate ST-02	Pro Audio Spectrum 16
Future Domain TMC-8xx, 16xx	QLogic
	Trantor T128/T128F/T228
	Ultrsator
	7000 FAST

The **scsi** disk and the disks with non-SCSI CD-ROM drivers contain all the SCSI drivers from both lists 1 and 2. The **scsinet1** and **scsinet2** disks should really only be used to install via NFS.

Choosing the Proper Rootdisk Image

After selecting the proper bootdisk, you'll need to select the proper rootdisk. The selections are more limited, so you won't have to put too much work into the selection. Like the bootdisk images, the rootdisk images are stored in directories according to the size of the floppy disk—**rootdsks.144** for 3.5-inch high-density diskettes and **rootdsks.12** for 5.25-inch high-density diskettes.

Your rootdisk image selections are listed in Table 2.3.

Table 2.3 Rootdisk selections.

Filename	Purpose
COLRLITE or **COLOR144**	This image includes a full-screen color install program and should be considered the "default" image. This version of the install system has some known bugs, however—it is, in particular, not forgiving of extra keystrokes entered between screens. It is nice to look at, though. By and large, this is probably the file you'll want to use.
UMSDOS12 or **UMSDS144**	This version of **colrlite** is to install using UMSDOS—a filesystem that allows you to install Linux into a directory on an existing MS-DOS partition. This filesystem is not as fast as a native Linux filesystem but it works, and you don't have to repartition your drive. See README.UMS on the CD-ROM for more information.
TTY12 or **TTY144**	An image that contains versions of the tty-based install scripts from previous Slackware releases.

You'll notice that these filenames are lacking the **.GZ** extension, which indicates that the file was compressed with the **gzip** command. In this particular distribution of Linux, the rootdisk files are not compressed. Other Linux documents will refer to these file as having the **.GZ** extension.

Most users will use the **colrlite** or **color144** rootdisk images.

Should You Use UMSDOS?

The UMSDOS filesystem allows you to install Linux in an MS-DOS directory contained on an existing partition. The advantage of this is that you won't need to reformat or repartition an existing partition.

UMSDOS is now standard in the Linux Kernel, and since they swutched to a 512 byte block mapping it'sbecome nearly as fast as ext2!

Now that you've chosen your bootdisk and rootdisk images, it's time to actually create the bootdisk and rootdisk.

Creating the Diskettes

For this step, you'll need two high-density diskettes. It doesn't matter what's on the diskettes, but they must be formatted—just be warned that this process will completely wipe out anything currently stored on the diskettes.

As you'll recall from an earlier note, the images for the rootdisks are not compressed in the Slackware distribution. There will be no need to uncompress them. In most other Linux distributions, however, you'll need to uncompress the rootdisk images.

In this example, we'll be using the **BARE** and **COLOR144** images. If you're using a different set of images, just use those files instead.

The procedures in this section do not need to be done on the computer you're planning to use as your Linux workstation. You can create the floppies on a different PC, or you can use a UNIX workstation to create the floppies, provided the workstation has a version of **GZIP** (which is not out of the question; although **GZIP** is not a part of most UNIX distributions, it's still a popular piece of freeware), supports the **dd** command, and allows you to write to a floppy drive. When using **dd** to create the boot kernel disk or root disk on Suns and possibly some other UNIX workstations, you must provide an appropriate block size. Here's an example:

```
dd if=scsinet of=/dev/(rdf0, rdf0c, fd0, or whatever) obs=18k
```

To create the diskettes, place the eventual bootdisk diskette in drive A:, and then type the following command:

```
C:\SLACK> RAWRITE
```

RAWRITE is interactive software; it will prompt you for the name of the file you want to write from (in this case, **BARE**) and then the drive to write to. As it writes, **RAWRITE** gives you a status report. After it's completed writing the bootdisk, use the same procedure to write the rootdisk; in this case, you'd tell **RAWRITE** that you want to write the **COLOR144** image. There's really not a lot to the **RAWRITE** command, but things could go wrong if you're not using a high-density diskette or if the diskette is flawed.

Preparing Your Hard Drive for Linux

Now that you've created your boot disks, it's time to prepare your hard drive for Linux. In order to install Linux, you must create a Linux partition on your hard drive. Additionally, you must consider creating a DOS partition on your hard drive in addition to the Linux partition—a step that's not necessary, but one that we follow for many reasons (which we'll explain below).

 If you're a UNIX workstation user, you're not going to be familiar with some of the concepts and operations we describe here. If, after reading this section, you're still a little fuzzy about the IBM PC and its many quirks, you may want to head for your local bookstore and purchase a good guide to the PC.

NOTE

Intel-based PCs have the ability to divide a hard drive into *partitions*. This is why you may have several different drive letters (C:, D:, E:), even though you have only one physical hard drive. (This dates from the early versions of MS-DOS, which lacked the ability to recognize hard-disk partitions larger than 33 megabytes. MS-DOS 4.0 was the first version to do away with this restriction.) The ability to create partitions also yields a bonus (as far as a Linux user is concerned): You can install different operating systems on a hard drive, and these different operating systems won't conflict. As a matter of fact, they can coexist quite nicely; you can configure Linux to give you your choice of operating systems when you boot your PC, and you can access DOS-formatted partitions from within Linux. Linux is relatively good about coexisting with other operating systems—primarily DOS, *Windows*, and OS/2. (It is not good, however, about coexisting with *Windows 95*, based on our rather disastrous attempt to install Linux and a *Windows 95* beta on the same PC.) Linux requires at least one partition for itself.

You must physically create partitions, as Intel-based PCs need to know what type of operating system is residing on a portion of the hard drive. If you've purchased your PC from a clone vendor or superstore and started using it immediately, chances are that you've treated the hard disk as one contiguous drive, without partitioning it into smaller drives. In a perfect world, of course, you're installing Linux on a brand-new system, and there's little of importance currently installed on your hard disk. This is the route we try to follow, since there's little chance to damage anything important.

However, if you've been using your PC for a while, you've probably accumulated software, data files, and configurations that you're loathe to give up. In this case, you'll want to retain as much of the DOS configuration as possible, while making room for Linux. There are two routes you can take:

- Using the **FIPS** utility to partition the hard drive without (theoretically) destroying the existing data.
- Backing up the DOS data, creating the new Linux and DOS partitions, and then reinstalling the backup. (This is our preferred method.) You'll need to make sure that the new partition is large enough to contain all the data from the old DOS partition, of course.

In either case, you'll want to first make a backup of your hard disk, either on floppy disks or some tape-based medium (Bernoulli drive, Syquest tape, or DAT tape). Depending on your system configuration, you'll either want to back up everything or back up those directories that can't easily be reinstalled from floppy or CD-ROM. (We find that a good system cleansing is a good thing every once in a while, so we tend to back up data and irreplaceable configuration files, while reinstalling applications from scratch.) Yes, we know backing up your hard drive is a pain (and we probably don't do it as often as we should), but you should make a backup every time you do something to your hard drive that has the potential to destroy data.

Using FIPS to Divide Your Hard Drive

After you make your backup, you'll need to decide which route to take. The **FIPS** utility described above is stored in the root directory of the accompanying CD-ROM as **FIPS.EXE**; the guide to using **FIPS** is stored in the same location as **FIPS.DOC**. (If you plan on using the **FIPS** utility, we *strongly* advise you to read through this file a couple of times, as it contains far more information and detail than here.)

Basically, **FIPS** works by creating a new partition on the physical end of the hard drive. Before the **FIPS** utility does so, you must first *defragment* your hard drive. A word about how a PC's hard drive stores data is in order here.

When a PC writes to a hard disk, it writes to clusters on disk. Generally speaking, this writing is done sequentially; the first clusters appear at the physical beginning of the disk. As you use the system, you inevitably write more and more to the hard drive, and you probably delete a good amount of data. As you delete the data, the clusters occupied by the data are freed; at the same time, new data is written to the end of the disk. Any hard disk that's been in use for a while will have data scattered throughout the physical drive. (This is why hard drives slow down when they fill with data; the drive head must physically hop around the drive to retrieve scattered data.)

When you defragment your hard drive, you're replacing the freed clusters at the beginning of the drive with data from the end of the drive. While not purely sequential, your data is all crammed at the beginning of the hard drive. This improves disk performance—since your data is physically closer together, the drive head spends less time retrieving data that was scattered in the past.

Newer versions of MS-DOS, PC-DOS, and Novell DOS (that is, versions 6.0 and better) contain a defragmenting utility. (Check your operating-system documentation for specifics, as the utilities differ.) If you're using an older version of MS-DOS, you'll need to use a general-purpose utility package (such as the Norton Utilities or PC Tools Deluxe) to defragment your hard drive.

The **FIPS** utility takes advantage of the fact that the data is crammed at the beginning of the hard drive. It allows you to create a point past the end of DOS data to begin the new Linux partition. (If you use this method, remember to leave room for more data in the DOS partition!)

We're not going to spend a lot of time on **FIPS** here, since the documentation on the accompanying CD-ROM is more than adequate in explaining how **FIPS** works, its limitations, and the exact procedures for dividing a hard drive. The only caveat we offer is that you should know a little about how PCs deal with hard-drive partitions before using **FIPS**; if you're a PC neophyte, we suggest you follow the steps detailed in the next section.

FIPS will not work with OS/2. The details are contained in the **FIPS.DOC** file. In addition, you should run **FIPS** from DOS, rather than a multitasking environment like Windows or DESQview.

Using DOS Utilities to Divide Your Hard Drive

The second method to prepare your hard drive for Linux involves various DOS utilities, which you'll use to create new partitions and configure a floppy diskette you can use to boot your PC with DOS.

The first steps involves creating a DOS boot diskette. (You've already created a Linux boot diskette; the two are different.) This is a rather simple procedure, involving the following command line:

```
C:> format /s A:
```

where *A:* is your boot drive. This command formats a floppy disk and adds the system files (**COMMAND.COM**, as well as hidden files **IO.SYS** and **MSDOS.SYS**) needed to boot DOS from the floppy. If you install a DOS partition, booting from this diskette will give you access to that partition (which will appear as drive C:). It will *not*, however, give you access to the CD-ROM until you install the CD-ROM drivers on the DOS boot diskette.

When you installed OS/2, it should have directed you to create an emergency boot floppy. You may need this diskette if something goes wrong in the installation.

After doing this, you'll need to copy some additional utilities to the floppy. You'll need to be fairly selective about what files you copy to the floppy, since the sum of all DOS .EXE and .COM files (essentially, the utility files) in a typical DOS installation won't fit on a floppy disk. You'll need to copy the FDISK.EXE and FORMAT.COM files to the floppy drive with the following command lines:

```
C:> copy \DOS\FDISK.EXE A:
        1 file(s) copied

C:> copy \DOS\FORMAT.COM A:
        1 file(s) copied
```

You may also want to copy onto floppy the files that restore your system backup, if you used operating-system utilities to create the backup. Check your documentation for the specific files, since they differ between operating systems.

What are FDISK and FORMAT?

Since we've told you to copy **FDISK.EXE** and **FORMAT.COM** onto the floppy for future use, we should take some time to explain what they do.

FDISK.EXE is the program that creates MS-DOS partitions. Every operating system has a program that does something similarly (you'll use the Linux **fdisk** command later in this process). You'll need to use the partitioning software specific to the operating system—for example, you can't use **FDISK** to create Linux or OS/2 partitions. **FDISK.EXE** works very simply: You delete an existing partition or partitions, and create new partitions in their place.

Creating a partition merely leaves a portion of your hard disk devoted to the particular operating system. After you've used **FDISK.EXE** to create a new DOS partition, you'll use the **FORMAT.COM** program to format that partition for use under MS-DOS. If you don't format the MS-DOS partition, the operating system won't be able to recognize it.

Using the DOS FDISK Utility

Now that you've created the system backup and a boot diskette, it's time to destroy the data on your hard drive with the **FDISK** utility. Destroy? Yup. The act of creating new partitions is by definition a destructive act. You must destroy the existing partitions and the records of the data contained therein in order to create the new partitions.

 You can use **FDISK** if your system has more than one hard drive. In this case, you'll want to make sure that you're working on the correct hard drive. **FDISK** does not use the normal DOS drive representations (C:, D:, E:, etc.); rather, **FDISK** uses numerals, such as *1* or *2*.

Begin by booting your PC from the floppy drive you created in the previous section. This vanilla boot will ask you for today's date and time (ignore both; they don't matter) and then give you the following command line:

        A>

You're now ready to run the DOS **FDISK** utility:

        A> fdisk

There are no command-line parameters to **FDISK**. The program loads and displays something like the screen shown in Figure 2.1.

```
                    MS-DOS Version 5.00
                  Fixed Disk Setup Program
              (C) Copyright Microsoft 1983 - 1991


                       FDISK OPTIONS


Current fixed disk drive: 1


Choose one of the following:


1. Create DOS partition or Logical DOS Drive
2. Set active partition
3. Delete partition or Logical DOS Drive
4. Display partition information


Enter choice: [1]


Press Esc to exit FDISK
```

Figure 2.1 The opening screen to the **FDISK** utility.

NOTE The figures in this section are for a specific version of MS-DOS. However, most versions of MS-DOS follow the conventions shown and explained here. If the choices on your system aren't exactly like the choices here, read through them carefully and use the similar choice. Remember: You are essentially deleting a partition and creating a new one in this procedure.

At this point you'll need to delete the existing partition, so you'll choose *3*. If you're not sure about the existing partitions on your disk, or whether you're even working on the correct disk (should you have more than one) select *4*.

When using the **FDISK** utility, you'll see references to primary and extended partitions, as well as logical drives. Here is an explanation:

- The **primary** partition is the partition containing the files (**IO.SYS, MSDOS.SYS**, and **COMMAND.COM**) needed to boot MS-DOS. In essence, this is your C: drive. The partition cannot be divided into other logical drives.

- The **extended** partition or partitions do not contain these boot files. An extended partition can exist as its own logical drive (such as D: or E:), or be divided into additional logical drives.

- The **logical drive** is the portion of a partition assigned a DOS drive letter. For instance, an extended partition can be divided up into up to 23 logical drives (A: and B: are reserved for floppies, and C: is reserved for the primary partition, leaving 23 letters).

Additionally, the non-DOS partition is for another operating system, such as Linux. Chances are that you won't need to deal with more than a primary partition or an extended partition.

After selecting 3, you'll see the screen shown in Figure 2.2.

What you do at this point depends on how your hard drive has been configured. If you have primary and extended partitions, delete them. If you have only a primary drive, delete it. **FDISK** will confirm that you do indeed want to delete a partition. This is your last chance to chicken out and check the DOS partition one more time before actually wiping it out.

After deleting a partition, you'll need to create a new DOS partition—a choice that's listed in Figure 2.1 as option 1. After choosing 1, you'll be shown a screen like that in Figure 2.3.

```
              Delete DOS Partition or Logical DOS Drive


Current fixed disk drive: 1


Choose one of the following:


1. Delete Primary DOS Partition

2. Delete Extended DOS Partition

3. Delete Logical DOS Drive(s) in the Extended DOS Partition

4. Delete Non-DOS Partition


Enter choice: [ ]


Press Esc to return to FDISK Options
```

Figure 2.2 The delete screen for **FDISK.**

Of course, you'll want to create a new primary partition; this is the partition that will be used for DOS.

The next thing you'll need to decide is how much of the hard drive to devote to DOS. There are no hard-and-fast rules concerning partition sizes. Obviously, you'll first need to think about how much of a priority Linux is—if you plan on running Linux a lot, then you should give it a lot of hard-disk space. If you plan on using it as much as DOS, you should equalize the two installations somewhat, keeping in mind that Linux will require far more hard-disk space than DOS. And if you plan on using Microsoft *Windows* along with DOS and Linux, you should assume that *Windows* will suck up as much hard-disk space as it can get.

```
                Create DOS Partition or Logical DOS Drive


Current fixed disk drive: 1


Choose one of the following:


1. Create Primary DOS Partition
2. Create Extended DOS Partition
3. Create Logical DOS Drive(s) in the Extended DOS Partition


Enter choice: [1]


Press Esc to return to FDISK Options
```

Figure 2.3 Creating a new partition with **FDISK**.

Our only advice: Don't be stingy when it comes to Linux hard-disk allocation, and remember that Linux applications tend to eat up a *lot* of disk real estate. It's not unusual to run across freely available binaries on the Internet that are more than a megabyte (such as the popular Web browser NCSA Mosaic for X Window), and in time these applications add up. If you're really careful during installation and install only the applications you need, you can keep a Linux installation down to 100 megabytes or so. Realistically, however, by the time you include everything worth having, you'll be up to 275 megabytes or so. If you only have a 325-megabyte hard disk, you'll obviously want to keep the DOS partition to 10 or so megabytes.

Don't bother with any other partitions—at least none for Linux usage. You won't want to create a logical DOS drive, more than likely; if you do, you can't use it for a Linux installation, as all Linux partitions must be created through Linux later in the installation process.

After deciding how much hard-disk space to give to DOS, you'll want to exit FDISK. Go ahead and make the DOS partition active (this means that you can boot from it later, which you'll want to do; you can have multiple partitions able to boot).

After quitting **FDISK**, you'll reboot the system, leaving the DOS diskette in drive A:. You'll now want to format drive C:—or at least the DOS portion of it—with the DOS **FORMAT** command:

```
A> FORMAT /S C:
```

This command formats the DOS partition with the core of the operating system (the **COMMAND.COM**, **IO.SYS**, and **MSDOS.SYS** files). The **FORMAT** command makes sure that you want to go ahead with the format (this is to make sure that DOS neophytes don't accidentally format and thus delete a partition containing valuable information); you'll answer in the affirmative when asked whether you want to proceed with the format.

You can use any version of DOS for these steps, as long as it's DOS 4.0 or better. DOS doesn't care if you format the hard drive with one version of DOS and install another version later.

Now that you've prepared the DOS side of your hard disk (and after looking back, realize that it's a lot easier than extended verbiage in previous sections would make it seem), it's time to boot Linux.

FDISK and OS/2

When preparing a PC for use with OS/2 and Linux, you'll need to use a slightly different route for preparing your hard drive.

OS/2 has trouble with partitions not originally created with *its* **FDISK** utility. Therefore, you must start by partitioning your hard disk with the OS/2 **FDISK** utility (keeping in mind that OS/2 needs more than 35 megabytes of hard-disk space to run at all). Then you must create the Linux partition with the OS/2 **FDISK** utility—marked as another OS/2 partition—and make that a potential boot partition using OS/2's Boot Manager. (OS/2 gives you the ability to select a boot partition every time you boot the PC.)

You'll then boot your PC with the instructions given below. However, later in the process you'll do something a little different when it comes to the Linux **fdisk** command (which we'll cover at that point in the installation process).

Obviously, you boot Linux with the bootdisk you've previously prepared. Put it in your boot drive and restart your PC with either a cold or warm boot (it doesn't matter).

Installing from Microsoft Windows

The accompanying CD-ROM contains a program that allows you to create bootdisks and view online documentation from within Microsoft *Windows*. To install it directly from the CD-ROM, pull down the **File** menu and select **Run**. When the dialog box appears, enter the following command:

```
e:\spl\setup
```

assuming, of course, that your CD-ROM drive letter is e:. If not, you'll need to insert the proper drive letter.

After the program installs itself into a new group, you just click on the icon and it'll will ask you which drive is your CD-ROM. An opening screen will provide you a number of options in buttons. Select **Install**, and you'll be guided through the installation process, beginning with the creation of boot floppies, as shown in Figure 2.4.

The instructions that you've already covered in this chapter should aid you through the *Windows*-based installation.

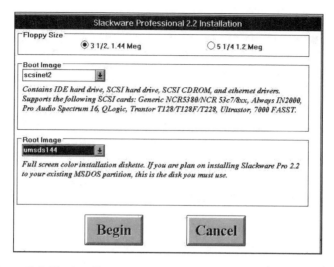

Figure 2.4 The Installation procedure from within Microsoft Windows.

Booting Linux with the Bootdisk

Obviously, you boot Linux with the bootdisk you've previously prepared. Put it in your boot drive and restart your PC with either a cold or warm boot. (It doesn't matter.)

Initially, your PC will do the things that it normally does when it boots, such as checking the memory and running through the BIOS. However, soon the word *LILO* will appear on your screen, followed by a full screen that begins with the line:

```
Welcome to the Slackware Linux 2.3.0 bootkernel disk!
```

You'll also see some verbiage about passing parameters along to the kernel. Most users won't need to pass along any additional parameters.

NOTE

There are some cases where LILO appears on the screen and the system hangs, or else rows of 0s and 1s cascade down the screen. In these cases, you probably are using the wrong bootdisk for your PC. The first thing to do is to create a few alternate bootdisks and try them; if the problem persists, you'll want to scan the Usenet newsgroups and the FTP archives (see Appendix A for details) to make sure that your PC and its peripherals are indeed supported by Linux.

The bootdisk runs through your system hardware, noting which hard drives and peripherals are present, as well as scouting out other salient details about your PC. It's at this point that Linux discovers any problems with your PC, and if you have problems installing or using Linux, it's a place you'll want to check. (The same information is displayed and gathered every time you boot.)

If there are no problems, you can put in your rootdisk and press **Enter**. A core of the Linux operating system is then copied to the RAM disk, which then gives you access to some Linux commands, including the important **fdisk** command. The installation process instructs you to login the Linux system as *root*:

```
slackware login : root
```

There will be no password required.

If you're asked for a password, it means you don't have enough memory to install.

Before you proceed, carefully look through the instructions on the screen. There are a few notes that may apply to your specific computing situation.

Linux and Hard-Disk Names

After logging in, you'll want to directly run the **fdisk** command (ignoring what the screen instructions say about the **setup** command). The **fdisk** command assumes that the first IDE drive is the default drive. If you plan on installing Linux on another drive, you'll need to specify that on the command line. Table 2.4 lists some of the hard-disk device names.

Table 2.4 Linux hard-disk device names.

Name	Meaning
/dev/hda	First IDE hard drive
/dev/hdb	Second IDE hard drive
/dev/sda	First SCSI hard drive
/dev/sdb	Second SCSI hard drive
/dev/fd0	First floppy drive (A:)
/dev/fd1	Second floppy drive (B:)

Note the pattern in Table 2.4? Additionally, Linux allows you to specify the partitions in the device names. For example, the first primary partition on the first IDE drive would be known as **/dev/hda1**, the second primary partition on the first IDE drive would be known as **/dev/hda2**, and so on. If you're installing logical partitions, the first logical partition would appear as **/dev/hda5**, the second logical partition would appear as **/dev/hda6**, and so on.

The files representing these devices will end up in the directory **/dev**.

To run **fdisk** on the second SCSI hard drive, you'd use the following command line:

```
# fdisk /dev/sdb
```

Most of you (since most PCs are sold with IDE drives), will be told that Linux is using the first hard drive as the default. When you press *m* for a list of options, you'll see the following listing:

```
Command action
   a   toggle a bootable flag
   c   toggle the dos compatibility flag
   d   delete a partition
   l   list known partition types
   m   print this menu
   n   add a new partition
   p   print the partition table
   q   quit without saving changes
   t   change a partition's system id
   u   change display/entry units
   v   verify the partition table
   w   write table to disk and exit
   x   extra functionality (experts only)
```

There are really only three options you'll ever use, unless you run into some esoteric configurations:

- *d*, which deletes a current partition. This will work on non-Linux partitions.
- *n*, which creates a new partition.
- *p*, which prints a rundown of the current partition table. This will list non-Linux partitions as well.

WARNING

Linux allows you to make your hard-disk configuration (as well as any configuration) as complex as you want it to be. Our philosophy is to keep it as simple as possible; unless you have a real need for multiple partitions and the like, just keep to the basics—a DOS partition, a Linux partition, and perhaps a partition for an additional operating system (like OS/2) if you like.

Some argue that by creating multiple Linux partitions, you'll be able to recover more easily if something happens to the boot partition. (Damage to one partition doesn't automatically mean that all the partitions are damaged.) However, if you're making frequent backups of important files (mostly data and configuration files), you'll have a more reliable setup. Additionally, if there's damage to the PC's File Allocation Table (FAT), you'll have problems with *all* your partitions.

If you select *p*, you'll see the following:

```
   Device Boot  Begin   Start   End  Blocks   Id  System
  /dev/hda1   *      1       1    63  20762+    4  DOS 16-bit (32M)
```

This is the DOS partition created in previous sections.

Before you actually create the Linux partition, you should decide if you want to install a swap partition.

Linux and a Swap Disk

If you are using a PC with four megabytes of RAM, you may want to set up a *swap partition*. This partition is treated by the system as extended RAM; if you run low on memory (and with four megabytes of RAM, you're guaranteed to), Linux can treat this hard-disk section as RAM, or *virtual memory*. You'll take a performance hit, as a hard disk will always be slower than real RAM, and you'll have the joy of watching your hard disk churn furiously when you try and use a few applications. However, a swap partition can be used *only* for swap space by Linux; it can't be used for any other storage. Therefore, you need to weigh your RAM needs versus your hard-disk storage needs, keeping in mind that Linux should have as much hard-disk territory for storage as possible.

Additionally, you may want to consider a swap partition if you have more than four megabytes of RAM. We've found that XFree86 is a little tight when running under only eight megabytes of RAM, and some swap space can't hurt—especially if you have a very large hard disk. (XFree86 won't tell you that it's low on RAM. It simply refuses to do anything, such as failing to load an application.) Some recommend that you have 16 megabytes of virtual memory. If you have only 8 MB of RAM, this would mean that you'd want to set up at least an 8 MB swap partition.

A swap partition can be no larger than 128 megabytes in size. However, You can create up to eight swap partitions.

If you do want to create a swap partition, read on. If you don't, you can skip to the end of this section and on to the next section, "Creating the Main Linux Partition."

Your first move is to create a swap partition with the **fdisk** command. You'll need to decide how large to make this partition. That will depend on how much free space you think you can give up on your hard drive. For the purposes of this chapter, we'll devote 10 megabytes to swap space.

Run the **fdisk** command and then choose the n option, for creating a new partition. You'll see the following:

```
Command action
   e   extended
   p   primary partition (1-4)
```

Type *p,* and enter the partition number. If you've already installed a DOS or OS/2 partition, you'll need to select the number 2, as partition number 1 is already is use:

```
Partition number (1-4): 2
```

You'll then be asked about where to place the partition and how large to make it. Generally speaking, you'll want to place the partition immediately after the previous partition:

```
First cylinder (64-1010): 64
```

Your numbers will undoubtedly be different. The point here is that **fdisk** automatically lists the first unassigned cylinder here (in this case, it was cylinder *64*), and you should go with that number.

You'll then be asked how large you want to make the partition:

```
Last cylinder or +size or +sizeM or +sizeK (64-1010): +10M
```

Since we're not into figuring out how many cylinders or how many kilobytes it would take to make up 10 megabytes, we take the easy way out and specify 10 megabytes directly as *+10M.*

This won't apply to most users, but Linux doesn't do very well if it's installed as a boot partition on cylinder 1023 or above. (This occurs with very large hard drives—I gigabyte or larger.) This has nothing to do with Linux, but rather with the limitations in the PC's BIOS. Subsequently, you should avoid installing the Linux boot partition on a partition containing this cylinder or better.

Fdisk then creates the partition. To make sure that everything went correctly, type *p* to see a list of the current partitions:

```
   Device Boot  Begin   Start    End  Blocks   Id  System
/dev/hda1    *     1       1      63  20762+    4   DOS 16-bit (32M)
/dev/hda2          63      64     95  10560     83  Linux native
```

The number of blocks listed here will be handy when you actually make this partition a swap partition. Jot it down.

Fdisk then gives you its command prompt; type *w* and exit.

You may notice that the hard disk is pretty quiet when you're making all of these changes to the partition. The **fdisk** command doesn't make its changes until you type the w command to exit. You can make all the changes you want and change your mind many times, but until you type w, it won't matter.

You'll then want to use the **mkswap** command to make the partition a swap partition. The command line is quite simple: You list the partition you want to make a swap partition (remembering that Linux lists partitions as **/dev/hda1**, **/dev/hda2**, and so on), along with the size of the partition *in blocks*. The command line would look like the following:

```
# mkswap -c /dev/hda2 10560
```

Remember when we told you the number of blocks would come in handy?

The -*c* option checks for bad blocks on the partition. If **mkswap** returns any errors, you can ignore them, as Linux already knows of their existence and will ignore them.

After creating the swap partition, you'll need to activate the swap partition, with a command line like:

```
#  swapon /dev/hda2
```

Finally, you'll need to tell the filesystem that **/dev/hda2** is indeed a swap partition, again using the **fdisk** command. In this instance, you'll need to change the *type* of the partition. When you created this partition, it was set up as a Linux native partition. However, Linux needs to explicitly know that this is a swap partition, so you need to change the type with the *t* command:

```
Partition number (1-4): 2
Hex code (type L to list codes): 82
```

Linux supports a wide range of partition types, as you'd see if you typed *L*. However, you can take our word for it regarding 82 as the proper hex code. (You don't need to know every single hex code; there's little reason for you to know that 8 is the hex code for AIX or that 75 is the hex code for PC/IX.)

Quit **fdisk** using *w*, making sure that your changes are written to disk. It will take a few seconds for this to happen.

You're now ready to create your main Linux partition.

Creating the Main Linux Partition

Most of you will want to designate the remainder of the hard drive as the Linux partition, so that's the assumption made in the remainder of this chapter. With *Command (m for help)*: on your screen, select *n* for new partition. You'll see the following:

```
Command action
   e   extended
   p   primary partition (1-4)
```

Type *p*, and enter the partition number. If you've already installed a DOS or OS/2 partition, you'll need to select the number 2, as partition number 1 is already is use:

```
Partition number (1-4): 2
```

If you've already installed a swap partition, you'll need to designate this partition as 3.

You'll then be asked about where to place the partition and how large to make it. Generally speaking, you'll want to place the partition immediately after the previous partition:

```
First cylinder (64-1010): 64
```

Your numbers will undoubtedly be different. The point here is that **fdisk** automatically lists the first unassigned cylinder here (in this case, it was cylinder *64*), and you should go with that number.

You'll then be asked how large you want to make the partition:

```
Last cylinder or +size or +sizeM or +sizeK (64-1010): 1010
```

Since Linux gives us the number of the last cylinder (*1010*), we'll go with that. There are no advantages to creating more than one Linux partition, unless you're using a *very* large hard drive (larger than four gigabytes).

NOTE This won't apply to most users, but Linux doesn't do very well if it's installed as a boot partition on cylinder 1023 or above. (This occurs with very large hard drives—1 gigabyte or larger.) This has nothing to do with Linux, but rather with the limitations in the PC's BIOS. Subsequently, you should avoid installing the Linux boot partition on a partition containing this cylinder or better.

Finally, you'll want to make sure that this is a Linux boot partition, so you can boot from the hard disk in the future via LILO. The *a* command toggles whether or not you want to use a partition as a boot partition. Type **a**, and then specify this partition (2) as the partition you want to boot from.

Fdisk will then ask you for a command. You'll need to make sure your changes are recorded, so select w, which writes the partition table to disk and exits **fdisk**. After this is done, Linux gives you a command prompt (#) again. It's now time to run the **setup** program.

OS/2 Partitions and the Linux Fdisk Command

If you've used the OS/2 **FDISK** command to create your Linux partitions, now is when you'll change the partition from an OS/2 partition to a Linux partition.

With the Linux **fdisk** command, you can change the current status of partitions, by changing the tag. Using the Linux **fdisk**, you'll change the tag of the OS/2 partition to a Linux native partition. In this instance, you'll need to change the type of the partition. When you created this partition, it was set up as a OS/2 partition. However, Linux needs to know that this is a Linux partition, so you need to change the type with the *t* command:

```
Partition number (1-4): 2
Hex code (type L to list codes): 83
```

Linux supports a wide range of partition types, as you'd see if you typed *L*. However, you can our word for it regarding 83 as the proper hex code for a Linux native partition.

Quit **fdisk** using *w*, making sure that your changes are written to disk. It will take a few seconds for this to happen.

Installing Linux From the Setup Program

Now comes the fun part—Actually installing Linux. For this, you'll run the **setup** command from a command line:

```
# setup
```

You'll then be presented a menu with the following choices:

```
HELP        Read the Slackware Setup Help file
KEYMAP      Remap your keyboard if you're not using a US one
QUICK       Choose quick or verbose install mode [now: VERBOSE]
MAKE TAGS   Experts may customize tagfiles to preselect files
ADDSWAP     Set up your swap partition(s)
TARGET      Set up your target partition
SOURCE      Select source media
DISK SETS   Decide which disk sets you wish to install
INSTALL     Install selected disk sets
CONFIGURE   Reconfigure your Linux system
EXIT        Exit Slackware Linux Setup
```

By all means you should first look through the help file, listed first. Some of the steps presented therein may assist you in your own Linux installation process.

To move through the selections in this menu, you use the cursor (arrow) keys, or else type the first letter in each line (such as **H** for help).

Basically, the installation from CD-ROM is pretty simple and follows these steps:

- Set up swap space for Linux
- Tell Linux where you want it to be installed
- Select the source for the files needed to install Linux (in most cases, this will be the CD-ROM
- Select the software you want to install
- Actually install the software
- Configure the installed software

Each of these steps will be covered in its own section.

Before you get started on the above steps, you should know that the Slackware distribution of Linux supports many different keymaps for different languages and setups. If you want access to another language—say, German—or another keyboard layout, such as the Dvorak keyboard, you should select **Keymap** from the Setup menu.

Setting up the Swap Space

As you've probably guessed by now, a lot of Linux installation involves an actual installation and then additional steps, telling Linux about the installation. This is certainly true if you've installed a swap partition. (If you have not, you can skip this step.) You've already installed the partition, made it active, and change the partition type to a Linux swap partition. Now you again need to tell Linux about this partition. However, you don't need to format this partition, as you've already done so with the **mkswap** command.

Selecting the Target for Linux

This selection should be rather simple: You'll want to install to the Linux partition you set up earlier in this chapter. When you select **Target** from the Setup menu, you'll automatically be presented with this partition. This section covers the choices you'll make; for the most part, you'll want to go with the default choices.

Formatting the Linux partition is the next step. You'll want to format the Linux partition for a new installation; however, if you're using the Setup program to upgrade from a previous installation, you won't want to format the Linux partition.

Choosing inode density is next. Again, you'll want to go with the default, unless you have Linux experience and know that the default won't help you.

After the hard disk chugs and formats the Linux partition, you'll be asked if you want to make a DOS or OS/2 partition visible (or, more technically speaking, mounted) from Linux—assuming that you've created such a partition. Making this partition visible won't affect Linux performance, nor will it eat away at the size of the Linux partition. Since you may find it handy to move files via the DOS or OS/2 partition, you'll probably want to make this partition visible. You'll also be asked to provide a name for the drive; the name doesn't really matter, so we use **dos** or **dosc**. When you run the **ls** command later in your Linux usage, you'll see **dos** or **dosc** listed as just another directory, and the files within will appear as Linux files.

Selecting the Source for Linux

You have five choices for where you want to install Linux from:

- hard-drive partition
- floppy disks
- NFS
- premounted directory
- CD-ROM

Since you've bought this book, we'll assume you want to use the accompanying CD-ROM for installation. However, other installation methods will be discussed later in this chapter.

There may be cases where DOS sees a CD-ROM drive with no problems, but Linux cannot. In these cases you won't necessarily know about this problem until you install Linux from the CD-ROM and being told that the CD-ROM drive does not exist. In this case, there are two ways to go: Search for a Linux bootkernel that supports your CD-ROM, or else use DOS to copy the installation files to a hard-drive partition. The first option was discussed earlier in this chapter; the second option will be discussed later in this chapter.

The **Setup** program then gives you a set of choices about the CD-ROM you're installing from. The choices are straightforward; if you're using a Sony or SoundBlaster CD-ROM interface, you certainly would have known about it before now (you would have needed the proper bootdisk to get to this point), so there are no surprises on this menu.

Should You Keep Some Stuff on the CD-ROM?

For those of you with smaller hard drives, Slackware gives you the option of doing a partial install, leaving some of the program files on the CD-ROM and running it from there. The advantage, of course, is that you keep hard-disk space free that normally would be devoted to Linux. The disadvantages come in the form of speed—accessing your CD-ROM drive is slower than accessing your hard drive—and in tying up your CD-ROM drive with Slackware.

ON THE CD-ROM

Our recommendation, of course, is to install everything to hard drive; this offers the best performance overall, and it's the easiest system to maintain.

However, Slackware does offer three alternatives that make use of the CD-ROM called **slacktest**. It uses 8.5 megabytes of a DOS partition, or 3.5 megabytes of a ext2 partition. You can use X, C, Ctt, and more just fine from the CD-ROM—including DOOM.

If it sounds like we're a little negative about the idea of running Linux off of the CD-ROM, it's because we are. If you're careful about installation, you can easily install only the parts of Linux you're really going to use. And by running partially from the CD-ROM, you're sacrificing both speed and flexibility.

If you're doing a normal install, choose that menu selection.

Choosing the Disk Sets to Install

Now comes the fun part—choosing the software you want to install. True to its roots as a diskette-based operating system, Linux divides software into *disk sets*. Each disk set is uniquely named and corresponds to a specific part of the operating system. For instance, the *A* series contains the core of Linux, and its installation is mandatory.

The *ram* program divides disk sets and the software within into mandatory and optional installations. Some of the elements of Linux, such as the aforementioned *A* series, are mandatory. Other installations, such as terminal packages, are optional. During the installation process, Linux will automatically install the mandatory packages, while prompting you before installing the optional packages.

There is a way to override this, as will be explained later in this section.

During the initial menu entitled *Series Selection*, you'll be presented with a list of the disk sets, as well as a short explanation of what is contained on the disk sets. Generally speaking, you won't want to install *all* of the disk sets, as there are some disk sets that overlap, and their coexistence on the hard drive is not a wise thing (particularly when it comes to development tools). In addition, you don't want to waste the hard-disk space needed for a full installation—will you really need three or four text editors, as well as multiple text-formatting packages and a slew of fonts you will never use? Accordingly, choose the software you think you're likely to use. You can always run the **setup** program again and install additional disk sets again in the future.

Technically speaking, all that's needed for a minimal installation of Linux is the *A* disk set.

The full set of disk sets is listed in Table 2.5.

Table 2.5 A full listing of the Linux disk sets.

Series	Purpose
./a1-./a4	The base system. If you install only this disk set, you'll have enough to get up and running and have **elvis** and comm programs available. Based around the 1.2.8 Linux kernel, and concepts from the Linux filesystem standard.
	These disks are known to fit on on 1.2MB disks although the rest of slackware won't. If you have only a 1.2MB floppy, you can still install the base system, download other disks you want and install them from your hard drive.
./ap1-./ap5	Various applications and add-ons, such as the manual pages, **groff**, **ispell**, **term** (and many TCP/IP programs ported to **term**), **joe**, **jed**, **jove**, **ghostscript**, **sc**, **bc**, **ftape** support, and the **quota** patches.

Table 2.5 A full listing of the Linux disk sets. (continued)

Series	Purpose
./d1-./d9	Program development. GCC/G++/Objective C 2.6.3, **make** (GNU and BSD), **byacc** and GNU **bison, flex**, the 4.6.27 C libraries, **gdb**, kernel source for Linux 1.2.8, **SVGAlib**, ncurses, clisp, **f2c, p2c, m4, perl, rcs**, and **dll** tools.
./e1-./e5	GNU **Emacs** 19.28.
./f1-./f2	A collection of FAQs and other documentation.
./i1-./i3	Info pages for GNU software, readable by **info, jed,** or **emacs.**
./n1-./n4	Networking. TCP/IP, UUCP, **mailx, dip,** PPP, **deliver, elm, pine,** BSD **sendmail, cnews, nn, tin, trn, inn.**
./oop1	Object-oriented programming. GNU Smalltalk 11.1 and the Smalltalk Interface to X (STIX).
./q1-./q9	This series contains extra kernels. Most people will want to use a kernel from this series. These kernels contain drivers such as UMSDOS, PPP, drivers for SCSI, networking cards, and the following non-SCSI CD-ROMs: Mitsumi, Sony cdu31/33a, Sound Blaster Pro /Lasermate/Panasonic, Aztech, Okano, Wearnes, Orchid, Sony 535/531, and many IDE/ATAPI CD-ROM drives.
	With the exception of the PS/2 mouse driver (and the similar C&T 82C710 mouse, as on TI Travelmate) driver, there is *no* busmouse support in any of the precompiled kernels. The drivers interact when you compile them all in. If you need these drivers, be sure to recompile your kernel. Some people take the menu that sets the **/dev/mouse** link to be an indication that their busmouse will work right out of the box. It's not, and it won't.
./t1-./t10	NTeX Release 1.2.1. NTeX is a very complete TeX distribution for Linux. Thanks to Frank Langbein for contributing this!
./tcl1-./tcl2	Tcl, Tk, TclX, **blt, itcl**. David Engel's port of the major Tcl packages to Linux, including shared library support.
./y1-./y3	Games. The BSD games collection, **Tetris** for terminals, **Sasteroids,** and ID software's **DOOM** for Linux (console and X versions).
./contrib	This is a new one, and probably long overdue. Now that the new Slackware release contains scripts capable of creating packages (**installpkg/makepkg/explodepkg**), there is a directory for user–contributed packages. The contents of this directory can basically be considered "as is", and subject to change without notice. There aren't any fancy install menus here either. Just raw packages to install with **pkgtool** or **installpkg.**

Table 2.5 A full listing of the Linux disk sets. (continued)

Series	Purpose
./xl-./xl4	The base XFree86 3.1.1 system, with **libXpm**, **fvwm** 1.23b, and **xlock** added. Also includes a beta version of an XF86 Config-writing program–just tell it your video card, mouse and monitor, and it will create your XF86 config file for you.
./xapl-./xap3	X applications: XII **ghostscript**, **libgr13** (newly compiled with working shared stubs), **seyon**, **workman**, **xfilemanager**, **xv** 3.01, GNU **chess** and **xboard**, xfm 1.3, **ghostview**, **gnuplot**, **xpaint**, **xfractint**, and various X games.
./xdl-./xd3	XII server link kit, static libraries, and PEX support.
./xvl-./xv3	Xview 3.2p1-XIIR6. XView libraries, and the Open Look virtual and nonvirtual window managers for XFree86 3.1.1.
./ivl-./iv2	Interviews libraries, **doc**, **idraw**, and other applications and utilities from the Interviews 3.1 distribution.

Mark the disk sets you want to install by pressing the space bar. You'll then be asked whether you want to use the default tagfiles or create your own. When a piece of software is installed, it's said to be *tagged*. By using the default tagfiles, you are installing software deemed to be mandatory, while the system prompts you before installing packages that aren't mandatory. Again, your best move is to go with the default, unless you've had experience with custom tagfiles and know exactly what you want to install.

WARNING

At this point there's an option to install *everything*. Don't do this, unless you've designated a small group of disk sets to be installed and know that you do indeed want to install everything.

Linux will begin on the installation. It will tell you what's being installed, even mandatory packages. When it comes to a nonmandatory piece of software, it will stop and ask you if you do indeed want to install the software. (It also further differentiates between software, noting whether the installation is recommended—which means you really should install it—or merely optional.) An added bonus during this process is that Setup will tell you how much disk space the nonmandatory software will use (alas, there's no overall reckoning of how much space the entire installation will use). Use the cursor keys to move between the **Yes** and **No** choices, and use **Enter** to move on.

We're not going to list every piece of software that can be installed. You are an adult, and you can make most of these decisions on your own. However, there are some things to note as the disk sets are installed:

- Linux will install a kernel best suited for your PC configuration; by and large, most of the precompiled kernels should meet the needs of most users. However, during the installation process, you'll be asked about installing various kernels that are not applicable to your PC configuration. In fact, one of the first disk sets includes support for a Linux kernel lacking SCSI support. Since the Setup program doesn't know anything about your hardware, it will ask you if you want to install this kernel. (It also will warn you about waiting for the Q series of disk sets if this particular kernel doesn't meet your needs.)

- During the installation process you'll be asked whether you want to install a package called **gpm**, which manages the mouse for Linux running in character mode. This package can cause conflicts with the X Window System and its mouse control if your using PS/2 a bus mouse, so if you planning on using X with the mice, you shouldn't install this software. (However, if you don't plan on using X with these mice, you should install **gpm**, since it allows you to make better use of the Midnight Commander, a useful text-based disk utility.)

- There are many text editors available in the Linux disk sets, including **emacs** and a **vi** clone called **vim**. These should meet your needs. If you're tight on space, you can avoid the other text editors, such as **jove** and **joe**. (Not that we're saying anything pejorative about **jove** or **joe**, mind you.)

- You'll be asked about alternate shells, including **zsh**, **ash**, and **tcsh**. The default Linux shell is **bash** (*Bourne Again SHell*), and most users—especially beginners—will find that it works well.

However, you may find that one of the alternate shells better fits your needs or works most like a shell you've used in the past. Since the shells don't take up much disk space, you should go ahead and install them all.

- If you install the GNU C compiler, you need to also install **binutils, include, libc,** and the third part of the kernel source. (Some of these packages are tagged as mandatory by he Linux Setup program; the warning applies if you use your own tagfiles.)

- The version of **emacs** that's initially installed from the CD-ROM was compiled with the assumption that it would be running under the X Window System. If you don't plan on using X, skip this version and wait to be prompted for the **emac_nox** package, which doesn't contain the X Window support and can be run in character mode.

- If you install the **x** series of disk sets, you'll be asked about the chipset used in your graphics card, as there are some X Window servers tailors to specific chipsets. If you're not sure about what chipset you have, don't respond to any specific chipsets and install the SuperVGA or VGA X server, as you can always change this when you install XFree86 (as described in Chapters 3 and 4).

- Some of the older applications require some older libraries to run, and at some point you'll be asked about including those libraries. You should install the older libraries.

- Generally speaking, you should install as many fonts as possible if you plan on heavy X Window or text usage. If not, you should skip most of the font packages.

Being a Good Linux Citizen

As you install the disk sets, you'll occasionally see a message pointing out that Linux is installing unregistered software. This means that the UNIX freeware is being included as a service, and it's up to you to pay a registration fee. (The best example of this is **xv**, an outstanding graphics program from John Bradley.) As a good Linux citizen, you'll want to check through the online-manual pages or **README** documents associated with these programs and register the software.

NOTE Though this is a very infrequent occurrence, you may experience an error message or two when installing Linux from the disk sets. One of the errors may be *Device Full*, which means that you've filled your hard drive. Slackware, however, will continue to attempt to install software, even if the disk is full.

To end the installation program, you can either hit the **Esc** key a few times or type **Ctrl-C**.

Configuring the Installed Software

There are two main tasks involved after the Linux disk sets are installed: configuring XFree86 and setting up boot options. Because setting up XFree86 is such an involved task, we've devoted two chapters to it (Chapters 3 and 4). Here, we'll discuss boot options.

Creating a Boot Floppy

Linux will boot from either a floppy drive or hard drive. However, it's recommended that you set up the means to boot either way. Hence, the request from the Setup program to create a boot floppy. This floppy can be used to boot Linux at any point. This will be handy should you experience some hard-disk problems or you screw up your hard disk so severely that the system won't load.

Configuring the Modem

If you're planning on using a modem for connecting to online systems or to a TCP/IP network via SLIP or PPP, you need to configure the modem. Essentially, this merely involves telling Linux exactly what serial port the modem is connected to. The first serial port on a PC is called **com1**, and in Linux parlance this becomes **cua0**; the second serial port on a PC is called **com2**, and in Linux parlance this becomes **cua1**; and so on. (Note the numbering difference: UNIX likes to start things at 0, and PCs prefer to start things at 1.)

After you set up the modem, you'll be asked to set the speed for the modem. The choices (38400, 19200, *et al*) are pretty clear.

If you're using a modem and the speed isn't represented on the menu, use the next-fastest speed. For instance, to properly configure a 28800-bps modem, you'd choose 38400.

Configuring the Mouse

You'll want to use a mouse if you're using the X Window System, and this menu allows you to set up the proper mouse. For newer PCs, setting up a mouse isn't a hassle at all, since they usually contain a serial port for that purpose. All you need to do is tell Linux what kind of mouse you're using, its location (if using a serial mouse, specify where the mouse is connected), and move on from there.

Configuring LILO

LILO is the LInux LOader, and it's used to boot Linux from the hard disk. Additionally, it can be used to boot additional operating systems (like OS/2 and MS-DOS) from the hard disk.

   LILO's actually a pretty simple beast, and the configuration process here makes it even simpler. LILO works with a configuration file that's generated automatically through this Setup program. Your first move will be to start the process, then mark any operating systems you want to appear in this configuration file. Since you want Linux to be able to boot, you'll want to begin by specifying Linux. After that, you can designate another operating system (MS-DOS or OS/2) as a possible boot option. You'll want to specify Linux first, however, so it appears first in the configuration file. When you're done running through these queries, you'll end up with a file that looks like this:

```
# LILO configuration file
# generated by 'liloconfig'
#
# Start LILO global section
boot = /dev/hda
#compact        # faster, but won't work on all systems.
delay = 50
vga = normal    # force sane state
```

```
ramdisk = 0       # paranoia setting
# End LILO global section
# Linux bootable partition config begins
image = /vmlinuz
  root = /dev/hda2
  label = Linux
  read-only # Non-UMSDOS filesystems should be mounted read-only
for checking
# Linux bootable partition config ends
# DOS bootable partition config begins
other = /dev/hda1
  label = DOS
  table = /dev/hda
# DOS bootable partition config ends
```

This file is stored as /**etc/lilo.conf**.

You'll also be asked about how long to wait before loading Linux. LILO is pretty handy in that it lets you specify a period of time (five seconds or 30 seconds) between when LILO loads and the first operating system is loaded. (In the **/etc/lilo.conf** file, this appears as the numeral *50* if you chose five seconds, and *300* if you chose 30 seconds.) This gives you time to specify another operating system to boot, should you want to boot DOS or OS/2 instead of Linux. This is done by pressing the left **Shift** key after LILO loads, which then gives you the prompt:

```
boot:
```

If you specify DOS, then DOS will boot from the DOS partition (provided, of course, that you've marked this partition as a boot partition). Pressing the **Tab** key gives you a list of options.

 If you're using OS/2's Boot Manager, you may want to use that for the primary boot loader, and use LILO to boot Linux.

Miscellaneous Installation Notes

At this time you can configure your Linux box for use on the network. However, since this is an advanced subject, we'll skip it for now and revisit it in Chapter 9.

There might be other configuration options presented to you, depending on what you installed (for instance, if you installed **sendmail**, there will be a query regarding its installation). Again, these tend to be advanced topics, so we'll revisit them through the course of this book.

Now that the installation is finished, it's time to actually run Linux. Before we get to that point, however, we'll discuss some alternate installation methods.

Other Installation Methods

You may run into situations where you are able to access a CD-ROM drive from DOS, but not from Linux's installation process. (This will happen if a SCSI card is not supported by Linux, but there are drivers available for DOS or OS/2.) If this occurs, you can still use the accompanying CD-ROM for installation; but you'll need to copy the files to your hard drive, floppy disks, or a tape drive. All three types of installation are explained here.

Installing from Hard Drive

This installation method involves moving installation files from the CD-ROM to a DOS hard-disk partition and installing from there. This must be a straight DOS partition and not altered via a disk-doubling technology, such as the disk doubler in MS-DOS 6.x or *Stacker*.

You'll need to replicate the file structure from the CD-ROM on the DOS partition, keeping intact the many subdirectories (*A1, A2*, and so on).

When you run the Setup program and specify the source of the installation files, you'll choose a hard-disk partition instead of a CD-ROM.

Installing from 3.5-Inch Floppy Disk

The disk sets contained on the CD-ROM can be copied directly to a DOS-formatted diskette. (You'll end up with a slew of diskettes, of course.) For each disk, make an MS-DOS format disk and copy the proper files to it. Then, when you run the Setup program, you can specify that you're installing from diskettes and not from another source.

The **00index.txt** files are added by the FTP server. You don't need those.

Installing from 5.25-Inch Floppy Drive

Linux prefers to be installed from a 3.5-inch disk drive. However, it is possible to install on a machine that has only a 5.25-inch drive. This isn't as easy as installing from a 3.5-inch drive, but if you install off of your hard drive it may actually be easier.

The first three disks of Slackware Linux, the A disks, should all fit within a 1.2-megabyte diskette. To install them, you'll need a boot kernel and a rootdisk. To make the boot-kernel disk, copy the boot kernel of your choice to a floppy using the UNIX command **dd** or **RAWWRITE.EXE**. To make the root disk, write **colrlite, tty12, umsdos12** to a floppy in the same way. (These are in **./rootdsks.12**.)

Use the boot kernel disk to boot the rootdisk, and install from there. This will load the ramdisk. Once you have the *slackware:* prompt you may remove the disk from your machine and continue with the installation.

Once you've got the base system installed, you can install the rest of the disks by downloading them on to your hard drive and installing them from there. Disk series other than A won't fit onto 1.2-megabyte disks.

Installing from Tape

The **TAPE144** rootdisk files can be used to install Slackware from tape. This has been tested on a Colorado Jumbo 250, but it should work for most floppy tape and SCSI tape drives. To do this, you'll need to know a little about UNIX and its filesystem.

Any of the 2.0.0 bootkernel disks will work for floppy tape support. If you're installing from a SCSI drive, make sure you use a bootkernel with SCSI support.

You need to have a blank MS-DOS formatted disk ready to store the install scripts and installation defaults. The installation uses two tape passes—one to read these files from the tape, and the second to do the actual installation. Once you've written the files from the first tape pass to your floppy, you won't need to scan those files again if you install from the same tape in the future.

The tape must be written in GNU **tar** format (or a compatible block size with some other **tar**). This is the command that would write out the tape, assuming you're sitting in a directory set up like **/pub/linux/slackware** on **ftp.cdrom.com**:

```
tar cv
{a?,ap?,d?,e?,f?,i?,iv?,n?,oop?,t?,t10,tcl?,x?,xi,xap?,xd?,xv?,y?}/*
```

This insures that the files are written to the tape in the proper order. You must set your TAPE variable first, like these lines in the **.profile** file under BASH:

```
TAPE=/dev/ftape
export TAPE
```

Unlike installing from floppy disks, you don't need to install all the ***.tgz** files, or even all the directories. The only requirement is that **base.tgz** must be the first package (***tgz** file) written to the tape.

This method isn't fully guaranteed to work.

Installing When RAM is Very Tight

Installation can be tricky on a machine with four megabytes of RAM or less. Here are a few tricks that can be helpful if you run into problems. (Symptoms might include: system hangs while booting the bootdisk; root password required on the rootdisk; inability to run **fdisk** or **mkswap**; and so on.)

If you have DOS and a 5.25-inch floppy drive, you can save 240K by using **Loadlin** in conjunction with a 5.25-inch rootdisk. Here's how:

1. Make the rootdisk using **RAWRITE.EXE**.
2. Unzip **lodlin15.zip** (look in /**kernels**) in a directory on your DOS partition.
3. Select an appropriate kernel from a subdirectory under /**kernels**. The /**bootdsks.12/WHICH.ONE** document might be helpful in selecting the proper one for your hardware. Copy it into the directory where you put **loadlin**.
4. Put the rootdisk into the floppy drive, and use this command to load it:

```
loadlinx scsi root=b: ramdisk=1200
```

where *b*: is the drive you put the disk in, and *scsi* is the name of the kernel you selected. Then, install as usual.

You can get the same effect this way (now that LILO works correctly) from a bootdisk's LILO prompt: `mount root=/dev/fd1 ramdisk =1200`

There will be times when even these methods save enough memory to allow installation. Here's another method that may possibly even allow installation to a machine with two megabytes:

1. If you have a second floppy drive, use that for the rootdisk. If not, you'll have to make due with the rootdisk in your boot drive. With the rootdisk in the boot drive you won't be able to install from floppy disks or make a bootdisk at the end of the installation process, since the disk will be "mounted" in the boot drive and cannot be removed (no matter what the screen tells you) until the machine is rebooted. Make a rootdisk using **RAWRITE.EXE** for the floppy drive you selected.
2. Unzip **lodlin15.zip** (look in /**kernels**) in a directory on your DOS partition.
3. Select an appropriate kernel from a subdirectory under /**kernels**. The /**bootdsks.12/WHICH.ONE** document might be helpful in

selecting the proper one for your hardware. Copy it into the directory where you put **loadlin**.

4. Put the rootdisk (*not* write protected) into the floppy drive, and use this command to boot it:

```
loadlinx scsi root=b: ramdisk=0
```

where *b*: is the drive you put the disk in, and *scsi* is the name of the kernel you selected. Then, install Linux. If you're using the boot floppy drive for the rootdisk, you will not be able to install from floppy disks. *Don't* take the rootdisk out of the floppy drive for any reason during the installation! Also, since scratch files may be written to the rootdisk, you'll want to start with a fresh copy if you need to start over for some reason. Again this will work from a bootdisk's LILO prompt type:

```
mount root=\dev\fd1 ramdisk=0
```

(the randisk is optional).

Once installed, you'll need to have a way to start your new system. If you were lucky enough to have a second floppy drive to use for your rootdisk, then you'll be able to make a bootdisk at the end of the installation process. This is highly recommended. If your boot drive is occupied by the rootdisk, then you've got two options: **loadlin** (a method of booting from DOS) or LILO. If you're using the UMSDOS filesystem, then **loadlin** is your only choice.

To boot the system with **loadlin**, you'll use a command similar to the one you used to start the rootdisk, but you'll replace A: or B: with the name of the device you're using for your root Linux partition, like this:

```
loadlinx scsi root=/dev/hda2 ramdisk=0
```

Alternately, at a bootdisk's LILO prompt type:

```
mount root= \dev\hda2
```

Once your machine is up and running, you'll probably want to switch to a different kernel, such as one of the ones on the A or Q series. The kernels in the /**kernels** directory are designed for installation and aren't as full-featured as some of the other ones. Or, you could compile a custom kernel especially for your machine from the source code in /**usr/src/linux**. This will provide optimal performance, since it won't contain any unnecessary drivers.

Recompiling a Kernel

Most Linux users will find that the precompiled kernels that come on the accompanying CD-ROM should work for them; PC hardware is becoming reasonable homogenized, and if you paid any attention at all to Chapter 1, you'll have a hardware configuration that optimizes Linux installation and usage.

However, on the remote chance that you'll need to recompile your kernel (whether directed to in a Linux HOW-TO or through the advice from an expert on the Usenet, this will happen if you're using a nonsupported SCSI CD-ROM, bus mouse, or sound card), here's how to do so.

1. If you haven't installed the C compiler and kernel source, do that.
2. Use the bootkernel disk you installed with to start your machine. At the LILO prompt, enter:

   ```
   LILO: mount root=/dev/hda1
   ```

   assuming that /**dev/hda1** is your Linux partition. (This is the assumption made through the rest of this section.) If not, enter your Linux partition instead. After this, ignore any error messages as the system starts up.
3. Log in as root, and recompile the kernel with these steps:

   ```
   cd /usr/src/linux
   make config
   ```

At this point you'll choose your drivers. Repeat this step until you are satisfied with your choices.

If you are using LILO, this will build and install the new kernel:

```
make dep ; make clean ; make zlilo
rdev -R /vmlinuz 1
```

If you are using a bootdisk, these commands will build the kernel and create a new bootdisk for your machine:

```
make dep ; make clean ; make zImage
rdev -R zImage 1
rdev -v zImage -1
rdev zImage /dev/hda1
fdformat /dev/fd0H1440
cat zImage > /dev/fd0
```

You'll need to place a clean floppy disk into your drive before the **fdformat** command.

You should now have a Linux kernel that can make full use of all supported hardware installed in your machine. Reboot and try it out.

Upgrading from a Previous Version of Linux

The new versions of **pkgtool** (a package maintenance tool developed for the Slackware distribution) should provide a clean upgrade path from earlier versions of Slackware. Since it can now remove packages from your hard drive while running on a self-contained Linux filesystem loaded into a ram disk, it can remove *any* files from your system, including ones that were difficult or impossible to remove while running on the hard drive, such as the shell, shared libraries, **init**, and other crucial system files.

If you're using an older version of Slackware and want to upgrade to the version on the accompanying CD-ROM, you can do so without going through the agony of a full installation.

Upgrading through this method is probably more trouble than it's worth. For instance, several commonly reported bugs are caused by improper upgrading—mixing disks from different versions of the distribution and/or failing to remove old packages first. We need to face the fact that things haven't quite settled down yet, and that it's not always possible to foresee differences in filesystem structure, daemons, utilities, etc, that can lead to problems with the system.

The *correct* and best way to upgrade to a new distribution version is to back up everything you want saved and then reinstall from scratch. This is especially true for the A and N series disks. If you do upgrade packages from one of those disk sets, you should seriously consider which packages from the other one might be related somehow and install those too. Again, it can be tricky to know just which packages are related, given the overall complexity of the Linux system. That's why unless you really know what you're doing there is a substantial risk of screwing up a system while attempting to upgrade it.

Here's how you'd upgrade to a newer version of Slackware from any previous version that supports package information files in **/var/adm/packages**. (If your system puts these files elsewhere, you might still be able to do this by creating a symbolic link from the package information directory to **/var/adm/packages**.) The steps are as follows:

1. Back up important files, or take your chances. Odds are you'll come through OK. However, there are two important exceptions to this rule. The first (and most obvious) is when a package overwrites a file you meant to keep with a new one. The second, and possibly more serious situation is when the system needs to replace an existing file with a symbolic link. It will replace the file, whether it's a simple file, a file with a file permission of 444, or a directory filled with other subdirectories, each containing part of your doctoral dissertation. Be careful.

2. Make a list of the packages you plan to replace.

3. Use a bootkernel disk to boot one of the root/install disks. Log in as root.

4. Mount your root Linux partitions under /**mnt** while logged into the install disk. The method used here differs depending on what filesystem you're using for Linux. Here are some examples: How to mount an *ext2fs* partition:

```
mount /dev/hda1 /mnt -t ext2
```

Replace /**dev/hda1** this with the name of your root partition.

Similarly, if the partition was of type *xiafs*, you would use this command:

```
mount /dev/hda1 /mnt -t xiafs
```

If you're using UMSDOS (the system that allows you to install onto an existing MS-DOS filesystem), this is the command you would use:

```
mount /dev/hda1 /mnt -t umsdos
```

If you've got other partitions that are part of your Linux filesystem, mount them after you've mounted that root partition. The method is the same—for example, here's how you'd mount an *ext2fs* /**usr** partition:

```
mount /dev/hda2 /mnt/usr -t ext2
```

5. Once the partition has been mounted, we need to activate swap space if the system has less than eight megabytes of RAM. (If you have eight or more megabytes of RAM, you may go on to step 6.)

You may use either a swap partition or a swapfile. To get a quick listing of your partition information, you can always type **fdisk -l**. Doing this on a typical machine provides the following information:

```
Disk /dev/hda: 15 heads, 17 sectors, 1001 cylinders
Units = cylinders of 255 * 512 bytes
    Device Boot  Begin   Start   End   Blocks   Id  System
   /dev/hda1            10      10    90   10327+   1  DOS 12-  bit FAT
   /dev/hda2            91      91  1000  116025    5  Extended
```

```
/dev/hda3   *     1     1     9   1139    a  OPUS
/dev/hda5   *    91    91  1000 116016+   6  DOS 16-bit >=32M


Disk /dev/hdb: 16 heads, 31 sectors, 967 cylinders
Units = cylinders of 496 * 512 bytes


  Device Boot  Begin  Start   End  Blocks   Id  System
/dev/hdb1   *     1     1   921 228392+   6  DOS 16-bit >=32M
/dev/hdb2       922   922   966  11160   82  Linux swap
```

From this display, you can see that **/dev/hdb2** has been designated as the Linux swap partition. If the partition has not been previously prepared with **mkswap**, here's how that would be done:

```
mkswap /dev/hdb2 11160
```

To activate the swap partition, you would type:

```
swapon /dev/hdb2
```

6. Remove the packages. To do this, type **pkgtool** and select the option *remove installed packages*. You'll be given a list of packages that you've installed—just select the list of packages that you plan to replace.

   If you're using one of the full-color versions of **pkgtool**, you select the packages to remove by moving up and down through the list with + and -, and toggling packages to remove with the spacebar. Once you've toggled all the packages you want to remove, hit **Enter** to remove them.

   If you're using one of the tty-based versions of **pkgtool**, you'll have to type in the names of the packages you with to remove. Separate each name with a space. Don't worry about how long the line ends up—just keep typing in the names until you've entered them all, and then hit **Enter** to remove them.

That's it! Now you've cleaned up the old packages and you're ready to install the new ones. Type **setup** at a command line and proceed to install the new packages as normal.

Although it never hurts to play it safe and remove all packages from the bootdisk, almost all of them can be removed using **pkgtool** from your hard drive. The A series is the important exception here.

Booting the System

After Linux has been installed, you can go ahead and reboot. If you've installed LILO, you'll see it appear after the PC runs through its BIOS check. As Linux boots, you'll see a long Linux-related diagnostic, as Linux checks the system and makes sure everything is where it's supposed to be. For the most part, you can ignore any errors messages you see here (such as a proclamation that the name of the machine **darkstar** does not appear to be supported). After all of the diagnostics, you'll finally be presented with a command prompt:

```
Welcome to Linux 1.2.8.
darkstar login:
```

Since there are no users on the system, you'll login as the *root user*, so go ahead and type in **root** as the login. There will be no prompting for a password.

NOTE   A *root user* is the supreme being on a UNIX system. Most of the traditional security tools within the UNIX operating system don't apply to the root user—when logged in as root, you can do just about anything. It's generally not a good idea to use the UNIX system as the root user, however; the proscribed practice is to set up your own account and then save the root login only for those times when you're performing system administration.

After you're logged in, you'll see the following *command prompt*:

```
darkstar:~#
```

A command prompt is where you enter commands into the UNIX system. Your first commands will be to change your machine name and to set up a user account for yourself.

Adding Users

Your first action as the Linux supreme being is to set up an account for your daily usage. To do this, type the following at the command prompt:

```
darkstar:~# adduser

Adding a new user. The username should not exceed 8 character
in length, or you may run into problems later.

Enter login name for new account (^C to quit): kevinr
```

The **adduser** command does exactly what it says: adds a new user to the system. In the previous example, the user *kevinr* has been added to the system. After specifying the username, you'll be asked additional information about the preferences of user *kevinr*. Unless you're familiar with Linux, you'll want to stick with the defaults for now. (The defaults will be listed in brackets. Wherever there's a default, you can go ahead and hit the **Enter** key instead of typing in the default selection. In our example, we'll type in the defaults.) The entire sequence will look something like this:

```
Editing information for new user [kevinr]:

Full name: Kevin Reichard
GID[100]:100

Checking for an available UID after 500

First unused uid is 501

UID [501]: 501
```

```
Home Directory [/home/kevinr]: /home/kevinr

Shell [/bin/bash]: /bin/bash

Password [kevinr]: newpassword1

Information for newuser [kevinr]:
Home Directory: [/home/kevinr] Shell: [/bin/bash]
Password: [newpassword1] gid: [100] uid: [501]
Is this correct? [y/n]:

Adding login [kevinr] and making directory [/home/kevinr]

Adding the files from the /etc/skel directory:
././.kermrc -> /home/kevin/././.kermrc
././.less -> /home/kevin/././.less
././.lessrc -> /home/kevin/././.lessrc
././.term -> /home/kevin/././.term
././.term/termrc -> /home/kevin/././.term/termrc
././.emacs -> /home/kevin/././.emacs
```

If you're not planning on using Linux for anything but a single-user operating system, you don't need to worry about things like GID (which is short for group ID) and UID (which is short for user ID). And even if you do plan on using Linux on a network, you can change these parameters later.

Additionally, you probably noticed that the name *darkstar* appears as the name of your machine. Since you probably don't want to leave this as the name of your machine, you should change it right off the bat. This name is contained in the file **/etc/HOSTNAME**, and the default is **darkstar.frop.org**. To change it, you'll use a text editor (in the example, we'll use **vi**) and edit this file. To load the **vi** text editor and the **/etc/HOSTNAME** file, use the following command line:

```
darkstar:~# vi /etc/HOSTNAME
```

You'll see a screen like the one in Figure 2.5.

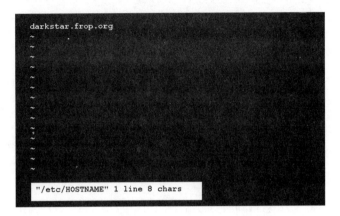

```
darkstar.frop.org
~
~
~
~
~
~
~
~
~
~
~
~
~
~
"/etc/HOSTNAME" 1 line 8 chars
```

Figure 2.5 Editing the /etc/HOSTNAME file.

You may have to make further changes if you're on a TCP/IP network. For now, you can change the name to anything you'd like.

You'll want to edit this file, changing *darkstar.frop.org* to whatever you'd like. If you've never used the **vi** text editor, skip ahead to Chapter 7 for short tutorial.

If your system is configured properly, you should have the following directories in your root directory:

```
bin/     dev/    home/           mnt/     sbin/    var/
boot/    dos/    lib/            proc/    tmp/
cdrom/   etc/    lost+found/     root/    usr/
```

If you've installed Slackware from the CD-ROM and then the system refuses to see the drive when you boot, you'll need to install a new kernel. The problem is probably that you used a bootkernel disk with support for your CD-ROM drive, but didn't install a kernel with support. If you have a non-SCSI CD-ROM drive, or a SCSI CD-ROM drive on a controller with alpha (experimental) support, then you may need to use a kernel from the Q disk series that contains the proper support.

You can use the same bootkernel disk you installed the system with to get into your machine. Use a command like this on the LILO prompt, but replace the root device name with the one you used on your machine:

```
mount root=/dev/hda
```

Once you're logged in, you need to install a new kernel. Use **pkgtool** or **installpkg** to install it:

```
cd /cdrom/slakware/q4 (or possibly another directory with kernel
```
packages)
```
installpkg mitsumi.tgz (this one has Mitsumi CD support)
```

You'll need to install LILO, build a bootdisk or have **loadlin** boot the new kernel before it will work. For the best possible results, you need to compile a kernel that contains only drivers for the hardware you have.

Looking for Help

Most UNIX systems have an online-manual-page system, and Linux is no exception. You can use the **man** command to summon information about specific commands:

```
darkstar:~# man vi
```

Online-manual pages aren't organized by topic; they're organized by specific command.

There are other informational sources included with the Linux operating system. They'll be discussed in Chapter 7.

Shutting Linux Down

Like any good UNIX, Linux responds to the **shutdown** command. You'll need to provide it with a command-like parameter, as well as an amount of time to wait before actually shutting the system down. This may seem odd if you're used to working alone on a PC, but the **shutdown** command is usually saved for serious shutdowns, as most UNIX installations support many users and rarely shut down. Use the following command line:

```
$ shutdown -r now
```

This shuts down the system immediately.

 Don't just turn off the power to turn off a Linux system. This can cause damage to important files.

An alternative method of shutting down Linux is the old tried-and-true PC **Ctrl-Alt-Del** sequence, which is used to reboot a system. When running Linux, this sequence performs the same functions as **shutdown -r now**. When the PC cycles to reboot, simply turn it off. Despite what others may claim, this is a perfectly acceptable way to shut down a Linux system.

What to Do If Things Go Wrong

For the most part, installation of Linux from the accompanying CD-ROM is a pretty straightforward proposition, and you shouldn't have many problems in the installation. However, there may be some cases when you run into problems when you reboot the Linux system after installation. For example: you're told that the system is out of memory. You'll probably run into this problem if you're operating with four megabytes of RAM or less.

Summary

This chapter covers Linux installation and configuration. Basically, the process is:

- Creating boot and root floppies
- Preparing your hard drive for installation with DOS utilities
- Boot Linux from boot and root floppies
- Prepare your hard drive for installation with Linux utilities
- Install Linux from the CD-ROM

None of the above steps is exceptionally complicated; if you're attentive at all to detail, you'll have no problems following the steps detailed here.

The chapter ends with a few of the basic commands you'll need after installing Linux, such as **adduser** and **shutdown**.

The next chapter introduces XFree86, a version of the X Window System optimized for PCs and compatibles.

Installing XFree86

This chapter covers:

- An overview of the X Window System
- X Window on the network
- An overview of X on Linux
- XFree86 and Linux
- X and window managers
- Supported chipsets
- How XFree86 works
- Installing XFree86
- Setting up the proper X server executable
- Some initial configuration details

The X Window System

Simply put, the *X Window System*, or just X, provides graphics on UNIX. (It's never called X Windows; to call it X Windows is a sign of ignorance.) Although X runs on many more operating systems than UNIX, such as Windows NT, Windows, MacOS, and DOS, X is by far the *de facto* graphics system on UNIX. As such, X tends to be confusing for anyone with more experience in the personal-computer world.

Since X tends to confuse, this chapter provides an overview of both the X Window System and X on Linux. If you're experienced with X in general, then jump ahead to the section covering X on Linux for a rundown of how X differs on Linux.

The X Window System began life as an academic exercise at the Massachusetts Institute of Technology's Project Athena. The goal was to link a motley crew of disparate workstations from various vendors. Instead of providing the link at the operating-system level, the decision was made to create a C-based graphical windowing layer that could exist with any operating system. And so the X Window System was born.

Now under the supervision of the not-for-profit X Consortium Inc., the X Window System is made available to the computing public at large, which has engendered its widespread adoption in the UNIX world. Virtually every UNIX vendor supports X on some level. The popular interfaces OSF/Motif and OpenWindows, as well as the upcoming Common Desktop Environment (CDE), are based directly on X Window.

X on the Network

True to its UNIX roots, the X Window System runs graphics with multiple processes. The main process, simply called **X**, is the X server itself. The server deals with local requests (thus its usage on a single-user Linux workstation) and TCP/IP-based network requests. Because of this networking capability, it's possible to run an X application on one workstation and display the results of the application on another workstation. You could, for example, save your local computing resources for something important while running *DOOM* on your boss's workstation and displaying the game on yours.

The X server controls the monitor, keyboard, and mouse and allows graphics applications—called *X clients*—to create windows and draw into them. On the face of it, this seems so basic that it shouldn't require any explanation. But, as is true of most of UNIX, X takes a simple concept and makes it difficult. You do benefit a lot from the complexity of X, but it sure can make things tough getting going.

The X server process is the only process allowed to draw dots on the screen or track the mouse. X application programs then connect to the X server via an interprocess communication link, usually some form of TCP/IP network socket (see Chapter 9 for more on networking). Because it uses a network link, programs running on other machines connected by a network can display on your workstation.

Many programs can connect to the same X server at the same time, allowing you to run multiple applications on the same screen—again, a basic fact you've probably taken for granted. One thing you cannot take for granted is that one of these X applications you run must be a window manager. (Technically, you don't have to run a window manager, but it makes things a lot more difficult if you don't.)

The Window Manager

Unlike the Macintosh and *Windows* environments, X makes the window manager a separate process. In fact, a window manager is merely an X application program, although it's a special application. By separating the windowing system from the window manager, you are free to run any of a variety of window managers, whichever suits your needs best.

Linux comes with a number of window managers, including those listed in Table 3.1.

Table 3.1 Linux window managers.

Window Manager	Description
fvwm	The most common window manager, presenting a Motif-like look
twm	Tab Window Manager, bare bones, comes with X
olwm	Open Look Window Manager, from Sun Microsystems
olvwm	A virtual-screen version of **olwm**

NOTE

Linux doesn't ship with the Motif window manager, **mwm**. Technically, **mwm** is commercial software. However, if you purchase a version of OSF/Motif for Linux (see Appendix A for details), you'll have a version of **mwm** for Linux.

The key concept if you're new to X is that the window manager—not the application— owns the window's titlebar. This is really odd if you come from the *Windows* or Macintosh worlds. To show this, we'll run the same X application, **xman** (which displays UNIX **man** pages—a useful program), under different window managers.

The **fvwm** window manager provides a vaguely Motif-like look for the window titlebars, as we show in Figure 3.1.

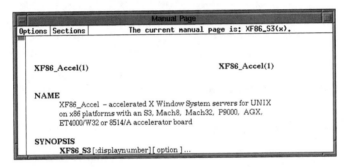

Figure 3.1 Xman running under the fvwm window manager.

If we switch to **olwm**, we see an Open Look visual display, as shown in Figure 3.2.

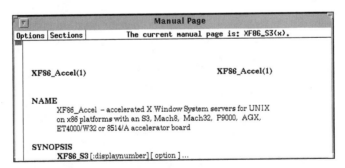

Figure 3.2 Xman running under the olwm window manager.

If we switch yet again, to **twm**, we see yet another look for the titlebar of the application, as shown in Figure 3.3.

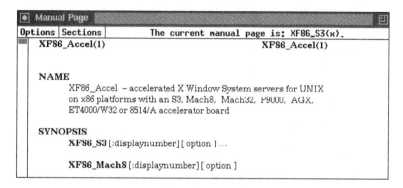

Figure 3.3 Xman running under the twm window manager.

With all three window managers, the **xman** program itself looks the same—it's only the window-manager-controlled titlebar that's different.

X Resource Files

Another topic under X that is different from the *Windows* and Macintosh environments is resource files. You'll find that X resource files are either the savior or bane of your existence. Like the Windows and Macintosh systems, resource files on X allow you to customize fonts, colors, and even text messages, all without access to the application's source code.

This concept is just great. You can tell an application to use a more readable font, you can get rid of those garish colors, you can even write Finnish messages in place of all the English ones, or you can fix up the English messages to something more to your liking.

Unlike in other platforms, in X, resource files are simple text files. Each line of the resource file specifies a resource to set and its value.

For example, the following X resource file, called **XTerm** and pertaining to the **xterm** application (yes, the capitalization is purposely different) sets two resources in the application: *font* and *scrollBar*, as shown below:

```
*font: -*-courier-medium-r-normal—14-140-75-75-m-90-*
*scrollBar: True
```

This part is usually easy. The hard part comes because there are a number of places where resource files can be found (see Chapter 6 for more on resource files). For now name thid file: **XTerm** and put it in your home directory.

X on Linux

X is very hardware-dependent. In the UNIX workstation world, you don't see many problems with this, since the UNIX vendors maintain a tight control over the hardware and do the hard work of supporting X for that hardware.

The PC realm, though, is different. You have zillions of vendors and a huge number of combinations of various graphics cards, monitors, buses, and even lowly mice. So, as we'll repeat again and again, you need to know the intimate details of your hardware in order to get the X Window System up and running. If you're used to the UNIX workstation world, this will come as a rude surprise.

X on Linux is actually in the form of XFree86, a public project devoted to bringing X Window to PC-based Unices. While there are some changes between a straight X Window System installation on a workstation and XFree86, you probably won't ever notice these differences.

How XFree86 Works

Remember that X is both the X server (also named **X**) and a number of X application programs (also called clients). To get X going, you must first start the X server and then start a number of X applications. Almost always, one of these X applications will be a window manager.

To start X, you must first login your Linux system, such as in the following:

```
Welcome to Linux 1.2.8
yonsen login:
Password:
```

Once you login and get the Linux shell prompt, you can start X with the
startx script:

```
younsen~#: startx
```

This assumes that XFree86 has been configured correctly for your Linux
installation. This configuration process is covered in Chapter 4.

The **startx** script runs a program called **xinit**, which starts up the X
server, **/usr/bin/X,** and looks for a file named **.xinitrc** (note the leading
dot) in your home directory. The **.xinitrc** is a shell script that launches
all the X applications you want. For example, our **.xinitrc** file launches a
number of instances of the **xterm** program, which provides a shell
window, and the rounded clock called **oclock**, as shown in Figure 3.4.

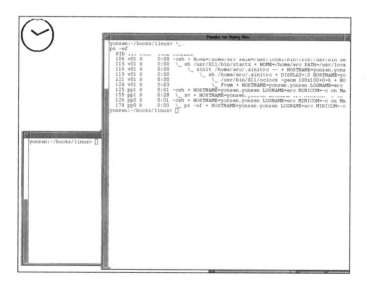

Figure 3.4 A typical X environment started from the .xinitrc file.

Before any of these programs get launched, though, the X server must be started, a task also handled by **xinit**.

The X server looks for the XFree86 configuration file—the most critical file for X on your system. This file, usually named **XF86Config** and stored in **/usr/lib/X11**, is a specially formatted file that tells XFree86 about your system's hardware.

The hardest part about installing XFree86 on your system will be in fleshing out this file. There are tools that help, but the process is still dangerous and fraught with error.

The **XF86Config** file contains six sections, each of which describes some part of your system to the X server. We list these sections in Table 3.2.

Table 3.2 Sections in the XF86Config file.

Section	Usage
Files	Tells where font and RGB files are located
ServerFlags	Special X server flags like *DontZap*, which turns off the **Ctrl-Alt-BackSpace** sequence that aborts the X server
Keyboard	What kind of keyboard you have
Pointer	Information on your mouse
Monitor	Excruciating details about your monitor
Device	Graphics card
Screen	Combined card and monitor

Once you get the X server up and running, the next step is to launch some X applications. Usually, you'll automate this and launch the X clients you want from your **.xinitrc** file in your home directory. The **.xinitrc** file will look something like the following:

```
#!/bin/sh
# Modified by Eric F. Johnson, for Linux.
#
userresources=$HOME/.Xresources
usermodmap=$HOME/.Xmodmap
```

```
if [ x"$XWINHOME" != x ]; then
    XINIT_DIR=$XWINHOME/lib/X11/xinit
else
    XINIT_DIR=/usr/X11R6/lib/X11/xinit
fi
sysresources=$XINIT_DIR/.Xresources
sysmodmap=$XINIT_DIR/.Xmodmap

# merge in defaults and keymaps

if [ -f $sysresources ]; then
    xrdb -merge $sysresources
fi

if [ -f $sysmodmap ]; then
    xmodmap $sysmodmap
fi

if [ -f $userresources ]; then
    xrdb -merge $userresources
fi

if [ -f $usermodmap ]; then
    xmodmap $usermodmap
fi

# Start X applications
xsetroot -solid bisque3
/usr/bin/X11/oclock -geom 100x100+0+6    &
/usr/bin/X11/xterm -ls -geom 80x24+3+372 &
/usr/bin/X11/xterm -ls -geom 80x48+264+13 &
fvwm
```

Most of the **.xinitrc** file comes from the standard XFree86 installation for
Linux; it looks for certain files, few of which will actually exist, and it

executes programs using those files it finds. The section at the end is where you'll set up the X applications you want started when X starts.

In our case, we use **xsetroot** to change the screen's background color and then launch **oclock**, a rounded clock, the **fvwm** window manager, and two **xterms**.

Installing XFree86

To install and properly set up XFree86, you need to go through the following steps:

- Determine your system configuration.
- Set up the proper X server for your graphics card.
- Fill out the infamous **XF86Config** file.
- Test that you can run X at all.
- Tune your **XF86Config** file.

We'll cover the first two steps in the rest of this chapter, and the last three steps in the next chapter.

Virtually all of XFree86 installs into the **/usr/X11R6** directory. Note that many other directories, such as **/usr/bin/X11** and **/usr/lib/X11**, will be symbolic links into locations in **/usr/X11R6**.

If you installed Linux and XFree86 from the accompanying CD-ROM, all the files are in the right place.

If you picked up an update to XFree86 from the Internet, then you'll likely need to unpack the collected files. Check the **README** file that was in the same directory as the XFree86 files you grabbed. Most likely, the files are compressed tar archives. For example, if you see a file like **X311bin.tar.gz**, you know that this file was compressed with GNU zip (**.gz**) from a tar file (**.tar**). To extract this file, use the following commands:

```
mv X311bin.tar.gz /usr/X11R6
cd /usr/X11R6
gunzip X311bin.tar.gz
tar xvof X311bin.tar
```

The first two commands move the XFree86 file (and your current working directory) to the **/usr/X11R6** directory, where Linux expects X files to be located.

Especially if you acquired XFree86 over the Internet, you must untar any XFree86 archives as the root user. Otherwise, you'll find that XFree86 does not install properly.

If you load XFree86 from the Slackware CD-ROM and use Slackware's installation program, you shouldn't have any problems.

Setting Up XFree86

Because there's so much variety in PC graphics hardware, and because doing something wrong can actually destroy your hardware, XFree86 ships in a mode that prevents you from running X. This fact still strikes us as bizarre, but setting up X is probably the hardest thing you have to do to get Linux up and running.

Before you start setting up XFree86, track down every piece of documentation that came with your monitor and graphics card. You'll need to know some obscure values about your monitor, such as the horizontal and vertical frequency ranges.

We'll cover more on this in the next chapter. If your graphics card can support standard Super VGA, then you should be able to use the example **XF86Config** file that comes with XFree86.

We list the graphics cards supported by XFree86 in Tables 3.3 and 3.4. Table 3.3 lists the accelerated chipsets and Table 3.4 the Super VGA chipsets.

Table 3.3 Accelerated cards and chipsets supported by XFree86.

Type	Chips and Cards
8514/A	8514/A and true clones
ATI	Mach8, Mach32, Mach64
Cirrus	CLGD5420, CLGD5422, CLGD5424, CLGD5426, CLGD5428, CLGD5429, CLGD5430, CLGD5434
IIT	AGX-014, AGX-015, AGX-016
S3	86C911, 86C924, 86C801, 86C805, 86C805i, 86C928, 86C864, 86C964, 86C732, 86C764
Tseng	ET4000/W32, ET4000/W32i, ET4000/W32p
Weitek	P9000
Western Digital	WD90C31, WD90C33

The Cirrus and Western Digital cards are supported in the Super VGA server, **XF86_SVGA**. The other types each have their own X server.

The Super VGA server, **XF86_SVGA**, supports a whole range of graphics cards and chipsets, which we list in Table 3.4.

Table 3.4 Super VGA chipsets supported by the **XF86_SVGA** server.

Vendor	Chipsets
ATI	18800, 18800-1, 28800-2, 28800-4, 28800-5, 28800-6, 68800-3, 68800-6, 68800AX, 68800LX, 88800
Advance Logic	ALG2101, ALG2228, ALG2301, ALG2302, ALG2308, ALG2401
Chips & Technology	65520, 65530, 65540, 65545
Cirrus Logic	CLGD5420, CLGD5422, CLGD5424, CLGD5426, CLGD5428, CLGD5429, CLGD5430, CLGD5434, CLGD6205, CLGD6215, CLGD6225, CLGD6235, CLGD6410, CLGD6412, CLGD6420, CLGD6440
Compaq	AVGA
Genoa	GVGA
MX	MX68000, MX680010

Table 3.4 Super VGA chipsets supported by the **XF86_ SVGA** server (continued)

Vendor	Chipsets
NCR	77C22, 77C22E, 77C22E+
Oak	OTI067, OTI077, OTI087
Tseng	ET3000, ET4000AX, ET4000/W32
Western Digital/Paradise	PVGA1
Western Digital	WD90C00, WD90C10, WD90C11, WD90C24, WD90C30,]WD90C31, WD90C33
Trident	TVGA8800CS, TVGA8900B, TVGA8900C, TVGA8900CL, TVGA9000, TVGA9000i, TVGA9100B, TVGA9200CX, TVGA9320, TVGA9400CX, TVGA9420
Video 7/Headland Technologies	HT216-32

Note that each release of XFree86 supports more cards. If your card or chipset isn't listed here, don't give up hope. You may need to get a new release of XFree86, though. (When this book was written, the most recent release of XFree86 was 3.1.1, and that's the version on the accompanying CD-ROM.) To see which chipset your graphics card uses, you'll need to look in the documentation that came with your graphics card.

You'll need about 42 megabytes of disk space for XFree86, and you should have 16MB of RAM to run X effectively. You can launch X and perform some basic functions with 8MB of RAM, but you'll soon run into some performance problems with limited RAM. To compound matters, you won't be told that you're running low on RAM; your chosen X window manager will simply fail to respond to your commands.

Once you've determined your system configuration, the next step is to set up the proper X server for your graphics card. XFree86 ships with a number of X servers, each compiled with drivers for a certain type of graphics card or chipset. Each of these X server executables usually starts with **XF86_** and ends with the type of cards supported. For example, the **XF86_SVGA** X server is built with support for standard Super VGA chipsets. **XF86_S3** is the X server for S3-based graphics cards.

You'll need to know which chipset your graphics card has and then figure out which X server to use. We list the X servers in Table 3.5.

Table 3.5 XFree86 X servers.

File Name	For Chipsets
XF86_8514	8514/A and true clones
XF86_AGX	IIT AGX-014, AGX-015, AGX-016
XF86_Mach8	ATI Mach8
XF86_Mach32	ATI Mach32
XF86_Mach64	ATI Mach64
XF86_Mono	Monochrome VGA, also Hercules, Hyundai HGC1280, Sigma LaserView, Visa and Apollo monochrome cards
XF86_P9000	Weitek P9000
XF86_S3	S3-based cards
XF86_SVGA	SuperVGA
XF86_VGA16	16-color VGA server
XF86_W32	Tseng ET4000/W32, ET4000/W32i, ET4000/W32p

The reason you have to know which X server to use is that the wrong server at best—won't work and at worst it may damage your system.

XFree86 is set up to run only one X server, the program named **X** and stored in **/usr/bin/X11**. Because of this, you need to link the X server you chose above to the file named **X**. The following command, when run as root user, links the S3 X server we use to the standard named **X**:

```
ln -sf /usr/X11R6/bin/XF86_S3 /udr/X11R6/bin/X
```

ON THE CD-ROM

All the XFree86 files are stored in **/usr/X11R6**, but there are many links to other parts of the file system. For example, **/usr/bin/X1** is linked to **/usr/X11R6/bin**, where the X binaries really reside. The Slackware installation should have taken care of these links for you.

Now you have the proper X server set up to run when you start X. The next step is to tell XFree86 about your hardware in even more detail by filling out the infamous **XF86Config** file.

Setting Up the XF86Config File

The **XF86Config** file, located in **/usr/lib/X11** (really a link to **/usr/X11R6/lib/X11**), is read when the X server starts up; it describes your graphics hardware and other configuration options for XFree86.

When you've gotten to this step, there are two routes you can take. You can set up a generic **XF86Config** file, for Super VGA graphics, or you can tune the **XF86Config** file for your particular card. We'll cover both routes in the next chapter.

Summary

The X Window System is a graphical interface used by Linux, and it comes in the form of XFree86, a version of X optimized for the PC architecture. X has become the leading interface in the UNIX world, and this chapter covered the X Window System and a beginning of the installation of XFree86.

The next chapter finishes the XFree86 installation and configuration.

Configuring XFree86

This chapter covers:

- Setting up an **XF86Config** file, the most daunting task under Linux
- More than you ever wanted to know about your PC video hardware
- Configuring X for your monitor and graphics card
- Setting up your mouse
- Defaults versus customized settings
- Programs to help automate the configuration
- Testing your X configuration
- How to fall back to a generic SuperVGA configuration if all else fails
- Troubleshooting your X configuration
- Stopping X

The Most Daunting Task Under Linux

Now that you've installed XFree86, we'll cover how to configure XFree86 for your Linux system. This has proven (in our experience) to be the most daunting task under Linux. Nothing else has been this difficult. So be warned—dangerous waters lie ahead.

The main reason that this is a difficult task is because virtually all graphics-card vendors write device drivers for DOS and Microsoft *Windows*, but virtually none write drivers for Linux. Because of this, you're left with the task of setting up your system to run with the graphics card.

Hardware, Hardware, Hardware

We keep repeating the mantra that you need to know your system's hardware inside and out. If you know your hardware, you can get the most out of X. If you don't, you run the danger of destroying your system. Yes, we'll repeat that: Making a mistake in your X configuration can result in damaged hardware.

Unless you're independently wealthy, that should cause you to pause for a moment. Take advantage of the time and go dig up all the documentation on your mouse, monitor and graphics card. This can be hard. On a system that's a few years old, you may not be able to find everything. On a new system, your computer case may be full of no-name, off-brand hardware and the documentation may simply tell you nothing of value.

We've found that some newer systems just tell you the amount of video RAM and how to run DOS Terminate-and-Stay-Resident (TSR) programs to configure the card, which is not very useful for a non-DOS operating system like Linux. Let's face it: the vast majority of PC users run DOS and Microsoft *Windows*, not Linux. As one of the few pioneers, your task is harder. One hint that served us well is to examine the original boxes that the system came in. On at least one of our pre-packaged systems, we found more technical information about the graphics card (especially the chipset) than we did in all of the printed manuals that came with the system.

Some of the key bits of information you want to discover about your system are listed in Table 4.1.

Table 4.1 Information you need to know about your system.

Aspect	What You Need to Know
Card	Vendor and model, of course
Card	Chipset, such as S3
Card	Amount of video RAM, such as 1 or 2 MB
Card	RAMDAC, if one is used, such as ATT20C490
Monitor	Bandwidth in MegaHertz (MHz), such as 25.2
Monitor	Horizontal Sync range, such as 31.5-64.3 kiloHertz (kHz)
Monitor	Vertical refresh range, such as 55-120 Hertz (Hz)
Mouse	Serial or parallel? If serial, which serial port it's connected to
Mouse	Vendor and model, such as Logitech Firstmouse

Note that some of the more obscure details, such as the RAMDAC, may be described for you in the XFree86 documentation. XFree86 comes with a description of a number of graphics cards and monitors. If you're lucky, you can pull some of these values directly from the XFree86 documentation and into your **XF86Config** file, the master file that describes your hardware to X.

Normally located in **/usr/X11R6/lib/X11**, the **XF86Config** file is an ASCII text file, formatted in a special way that the XFree86 X server understands. By default, XFree86 searches for this file in a number of directories, in order:

```
/etc/XF86Config
<Xroot>/lib/X11/XF86Config.hostname
<Xroot>/lib/X11/XF86Config
```

ON THE

CD-ROM

The *<Xroot>* is shorthand for the top-level X directory. In Slackware Linux, this is **/usr/X11R6**. Previous to Release 6 of X11 (hence the X11R6), XFree86's top directory was **/usr/X386**.

You can create the **XF86Config** file with a text editor such as **vi** or **emacs**. In most cases, though, you'll want to copy an example file to avoid entering the whole thing. Under Slackware, this example file is named **XF86Config.eg**. While this example is not ready to go, you can get a lot of useful information out of it. (See the section on SuperVGA, below.)

The **XF86Config** file contains six sections, as shown in Table 4.2.

Table 4.2. Sections in the XF86Config file.

Section	Usage
Files	Tells where font and RGB files are located
ServerFlags	Special X server flags like *DontZap*, which turns off the **Crtl-Alt-BackSpace** sequence that aborts the X server
Keyboard	What kind of keyboard you have
Pointer	Information on your mouse
Monitor	Excruciating details about your monitor
Device	Graphics card
Screen	Combined card and monitor

In the **XF86Config** file, each section follows the same basic pattern:

```
Section "SectionName"
  data entry...
  ...
EndSection
```

The # acts as a comment character, which is very useful in documenting the odd syntax in the **XF86Config** file.

In the next sections of this chapter, we'll cover these six sections in depth, and also show how you can automate part of the process by using a program called **xf86config**.

Never, ever use someone else's **XF86Config** file. And, don't use the examples we provide verbatim. Always configure X for your hardware. Wrong data in the file may cause X to damage your hardware.

Automating the Configuration Process

For a number of years, various programs have attempted to automate the difficult creation of **XF86Config** files. So far, though, all have failed miserably for us—that is, until XFree86 3.1.1 and a program called **xf86config**. For the first time, though, **xf86config** seems to create a workable **XF86Config** file—and we don't even have any odd hardware.

Before running **xf86config**, read over each of the sections below that describe the various parts of the **XF86Config** file that the **xf86config** program will be filling in. By having a greater understanding of the **XF86Config** file, your success rate with the **xf86config** program will be much greater.

Because of this, we'll discuss each of the six sections, and then cover using **xf86config**.

Setting Up Paths in the Configuration File

The **Files** section is by far the easiest to set up in your **XF86Config** file. That's because just about everybody has the same paths. In the **Files** section, you need to tell X where the RGB (Red-Green-Blue) color database file is kept and also where the fonts are located. Since both should go in standard locations, you can simply use the following section in your **XF86Config** file (in fact, the sample version already comes this way):

```
Section "Files"
    RgbPath      "/usr/X11R6/lib/X11/rgb"
    FontPath     "/usr/X11R6/lib/X11/fonts/misc/"
    FontPath     "/usr/X11R6/lib/X11/fonts/Type1/"
    FontPath     "/usr/X11R6/lib/X11/fonts/Speedo/"
    FontPath     "/usr/X11R6/lib/X11/fonts/75dpi/"
    FontPath     "/usr/X11R6/lib/X11/fonts/100dpi/"
EndSection
```

The above **Files** section tells XFree86 that your RGB database is located in **/usr/X11R6/lib/X11/** and that the fonts are located in **/usr/X11R6/lib/X11/fonts/**. These are the standard locations for both. One tricky part to note, though, is that you may not have loaded all the above font directories (we recommend you do, though). Because of this, you should check the **/usr/X11R6/lib/X11/fonts/** directory:

```
$ ls /usr/X11R6/lib/X11/fonts/
100dpi/  75dpi/   PEX/     Speedo/ Type1/  misc/
```

On our system, we have all the above directories and a **PEX** directory for PEX fonts (you can ignore this for now; see Appendix B for more on PEX). What you should do is delete any entries in the **XF86Config** file if you *don't* have the corresponding font directory. For example, if you did not load the 100 dots-per-inch fonts (the **100dpi**) directory, then your **Files** section should look like:

```
Section "Files"
    RgbPath      "/usr/X11R6/lib/X11/rgb"
    FontPath     "/usr/X11R6/lib/X11/fonts/misc/"
    FontPath     "/usr/X11R6/lib/X11/fonts/Type1/"
    FontPath     "/usr/X11R6/lib/X11/fonts/Speedo/"
    FontPath     "/usr/X11R6/lib/X11/fonts/75dpi/"
EndSection
```

We removed the entry for 100dpi fonts.

When running **xf86config**, you should say you do not intend to use the X font server, even if you'd like to. If the font server isn't running before you start X, then your system may lock up. We found it's much easier to split the problem. First, get X up and running. Then, configure the X font server (which provides scaled fonts). You may have to go back and edit the **XF86Config** file, but that's a lot easier than having your system lock up. See Chapter 6 for more on the X font server.

Configuring the Server Flags Section

After the **Files** section comes the **Server Flags** section. Again, you rarely have to do much with this. In fact, we normally have everything commented out in this section. The main options you can set here are listed in Table 4.3.

Table 4.3 Server flags options.

Option	Meaning
NoTrapSignals	Core dumps X when a signal arrives; useful For debugging
DontZap	Disables **Crtl-Alt-BackSpace**
DontZoom	Disables switching between graphics modes

Mots of these flags work backwards. If you uncomment the entry, then it turns the feature off. By default, we comment out (leaving on) the two *don't* features. We also comment out (leaving *off*) the **NoTrapSignals** option.

We like being able to kill an errant X server by simply holding down **Crtl-Alt-BackSpace**, so we always comment out **DontZap**. If you turn on **DontZap**, then you are disabling this feature.

DontZoom disables the keyboard sequences that allow you to switch between graphics modes. We find this switching to be essential in testing our **XF86Config** files, so we always leave this feature on by commenting it *out* in the **XF86Config** file.

Our **ServerFlags** section, with everything commented out, looks like:

```
Section "ServerFlags"
#    NoTrapSignals
#    DontZap
#    DontZoom
EndSection
```

Just like in shell scripts, the # character marks a comment line in the **XF86Config** file.

Configuring the Keyboard Section

The **Keyboard** section allows you to set up a number of options about your keyboard, which we list in Table 4.4.

Table 4.4 Options in the Keyboard section.

Option	Usage
Protocol	Standard (the default) or Xqueue
AutoRepeat *delay rate*	Sets up the keyboard auto-repeat delay and rate
ServerNumLock	Asks X server to handle **NumLock** internally
LeftAlt *key*	Overrides default for left **Alt** key (**Meta**)
RightAlt *key*	Overrides default for right **Alt** key (**Meta**)
ScrollLock *key*	Overrides default for **scrolllock** key (**Compose**)
RightCtl *key*	Overrides default for right control key (**Control**)
XLeds	Allows programs to use LEDs, rather than keyboard
VTSysReq	Uses **Alt-SysRq-***Fn* to switch to virtual terminals
VTInit *command*	Runs *command* passed to **/bin/sh -c**, when X server starts up and has opened its virtual terminal

You almost never want to run the **Xqueue** protocol, which uses an UNIX SVR3 or SVR4 event queue driver. With Linux, skip this option.

With X11 Release 6, X finally handles the **NumLock** key properly. You probably don't need to worry about the **ServerNumLock** protocol unless you have older applications that prove to be a problem.

For the key-mapping overrides, you can set each to one of the following values:

- **Compose**
- **Control**
- **Meta**
- **ModeShift**
- **ModeLock**
- **ScrollLock**

This is probably more than you want to know about your keyboard. See the online-manual page for **XF86Config** for more information on this.

Virtual Terminals

Linux supports *virtual terminals*. A virtual terminal is a pseudo-tty UNIX terminal connected to your screen. X uses up one virtual terminal, but you may often have a good number more.

Each virtual terminal takes over your entire display and presents a traditional UNIX textual terminal, much like what you see when you login. A special key sequence allows you to change between virtual terminals. When you do this, the screen gets cleared and you see the next virtual terminal.

The magic key sequence to change to a virtual terminal is **Alt-Fn**, where F*n* is one of your keyboard's function keys, such as **F1**. But, watch out. In X, the magic key sequence to change to a virtual terminal is not **Alt-Fn**, but **Ctrl-Alt-Fn**. The discrepancy is because most window managers capture all **Alt-Fn** keys.

A virtual terminal is not very worthwhile when you have a whole screen with multiple **xterm** terminal windows. The X environment allows you to use the font of your choice, provides a great many lines, supports a scrollbar, and copies and pastes—none of which the virtual terminals do. So, we only rarely use a virtual terminal.

But there's one place where a virtual terminal comes in handy: if your X display gets locked up, you can often switch to another virtual terminal and kill off all the X processes (see Chapter 6 for more on this).

The **VTSysReq** option in Table 4.4, above, allows you to use **Alt-SysReq-F***n* instead of the default **Ctrl-Alt-F***n*.

Putting this all together, our **Keyboard** section follows:

```
Section "Keyboard"
      Protocol     "Standard"
#     Protocol     "Xqueue"
      AutoRepeat   500 5
#     ServerNumLock
#     Xleds        1 2 3
      LeftAlt      Meta
      RightAlt     ModeShift
#     RightCtl     Compose
#     ScrollLock   ModeLock
EndSection
```

Note that we comment out most of it.

Configuring the Mouse Section

The mouse—called *pointer* in X terminology—is rather easy to set up, but you must watch out for some tricks. The main reason for this is that many vendors' mice (e.g., Logitech) are set up to emulate other vendors' mice, most notably Microsoft mice. Because of this, you may have to lie about your mouse.

For example, one of our test systems uses a serial Logitech Firstmouse. This mouse, though, was designed by Logitech to emulate the Microsoft serial mouse. What's odd is that the Logitech mouse has three buttons (a very good thing for X, as most X programs expect three-button mice), while the Microsoft serial mouse sports only two buttons.

When we configure the **XF86Config** file, we claim our Logitech mouse is really a Microsoft mouse (the other common choice for Logitech mice is to claim they are Mouseman mice).

The two key things you must specify for your **Pointer** section is what kind of mouse, e.g., Microsoft, and what port, if a serial mouse.

With this, our **Pointer** section is rather short:

```
Section "Pointer"
    Protocol    "Microsoft"
    Device      "/dev/ttyS0"
EndSection
```

Be sure to put in the type of mouse you have, and the device it is connected to, rather than merely filling in our configuration.

The protocol must be one of the options listed in Table 4.5.

Table 4.5 Pointer protocols.

Protocol
BusMouse
Logitech
Microsoft
MMSeries
Mouseman
MouseSystems
PS/2
MMHitTab
Xqueue
OSMouse

For Logitech mice, you'll most likely use BusMouse (if a bus mouse) or for serial mice, the Microsoft or Mouseman protocols, rather than the more obvious Logitech protocol. If your mouse is connected to a PS/2 port, use the PS/2 protocol.

The Xqueue protocol is only used if you set that up for the keyboard, too. We don't advise using this. The OSMouse is only for SCO UNIX, not for Linux.

In our case, the mouse is connected to serial port number one, often called **com1** in the DOS lexicon. In true UNIX tradition, though, Linux starts counting serial ports with 0. To specify our mouse is connected to **com1**, we use a device name of **/dev/ttyS0**, the Linux device file for this port. We list commonly used ports in Table 4.6.

Table 4.6 Commonly used serial ports in Linux.

Port	Device file name in Linux
com1	/dev/ttyS0
com2	/dev/ttyS1
com3	/dev/ttyS2
com4	/dev/ttyS3

Your system may also have the **/dev/mouse** device file set up for the mouse port. No matter what device file you choose, the device must exist beforehand. (On our system, **/dev/mouse** is a link to **/dev/ttyS0**.)

The bus mouse device files are listed in Table 4.7.

Table 4.7 Bus mouse device names.

Device	Usage
/dev/atibm	ATI bus mouse
/dev/logibm	Logitech bus mouse
/dev/inportbm	Microsoft bus mouse
/dev/psaux	PS/2 or Quickport mice

Note that except for the **/dev/psaux** PS/2 mice, all the bus mice should use a protocol of **busmouse**.

There are a few more options for the **Pointer** section, but you're normally better off leaving them alone. (We know; we were curious and we managed to mess things up.)

We list the other **Pointer** options in Table 4.8.

Table 4.8. Other Pointer section options.

Option	Usage
BaudRate *rate*	Specifies the baud rate for the serial mouse
Emulate3Buttons	Allows a two-button mouse to act like it has three; the third is emulated by pressing both at once
ChordMiddle	Fixes a problem with some Logitech Mouseman mice
SampleRate *rate*	Fixes a problem with some Logitech mice
ClearDTR	May be required by dual-protocol mice in MouseSystems protocol mode
ClearRTS	May be required by dual-protocol mice in MouseSystems protocol mode

We generally don't set the baud rate. When we tried to, we generally made it so the mouse didn't work. If you, do this, it is one time where the **Ctrl-Alt-BackSpace** zapping sequence comes in handy.

For best results in X, you want to have a three-button mouse. Many X programs assume such a mouse.

Configuring the Monitor Section

The **Monitor** section describes your monitor to X. You can define a number of monitors in the **XF86Config** file, as each monitor section is named. The screen section (see below) then connects a monitor to a video card. For example, the following abbreviated entry defines our NEC MultiSync XE17 monitor:

```
Section "Monitor"
Identifier  "NEC MultiSync XE17"
VendorName  "NEC"
ModelName   "MultiSync 4FGe"
HorizSync   31.5 - 64.3
VertRefresh 55-120
```

```
# Modes from the NEC MultiSync 4FGe monitor, a close monitor.
ModeLine "640x480"  31  640  680  704  832 480 489 492 520
ModeLine "800x600"  50  800  864  976 1040 600 637 643 666
ModeLine "1024x768" 81 1024 1068 1204 1324 768 776 782 807
EndSection
```

For each monitor, you need to define the following items, as listed in Table 4.9.

Table 4.9 Monitor data.

Item	Usage
Identifier *string*	Used to identify the monitor later
VendorName *string*	Used for your reference
ModelName *string*	Used for your reference
Bandwidth *bandwidth*	The bandwidth for the monitor, in MHz
HorizSync *range*	Horizontal sync frequencies, in kHz
VertRefresh *range*	Vertical refresh range, in Hz
Gamma *value*	Gamma correction value for your monitor
Modeline *values*	A single resolution mode

The identifier is a string used to refer to the monitor later. You can indeed define more than one monitor in the **XF86Config** file.

The **HorizSync** range describes the horizontal sync frequencies for your monitor. It can be a set of comma-separated values or a range separated by a dash, such as 42-65, for multisync monitors. You should get this value from your monitor documentation (where you'll find most of the key information needed here).

The format for a **Modeline** is:

```
Modeline "name" horizontal-values vertical values
```

For example, the following sets up a standard VGA mode:

```
# 640x400 @ 70 Hz, 31.5 kHz hsync
Modeline "640x400"  25.175 640  664  760  800   400 409 411 450
```

There can be a whole set of **Modeline** values. You can get this from the **probeonly** mode of X (see below) or from documentation that comes with XFree86. Some of the relevant documentation is listed in Table 4.10.

Table 4.10 Video-mode documentation with XFree86.

File	Usage
VideoModes.doc	Explains—in excruciating detail—how to calculate modes
modeDB.txt	Database of modelines for monitors
Monitors	Database of modelines for monitors

All of these files are located in **/usr/X11R6/lib/X11/doc**. An example entry from the **Monitors** file follows:

```
#Date: Sat, 17 Sep 1994 00:50:57 -0400
#From: Erik Nygren <nygren@mit.edu>
Section "Monitor"
   Identifier "NEC MultiSync 4FGe"
   VendorName "NEC"
   ModelName "MultiSync 4FGe"
   BandWidth 80Mhz        #\
   HorizSync 27-62KHz       #> from monitor documentation
   VertRefresh 55-90Hz    #/
   ModeLine "640x480"  31  640  680  704  832 480 489 492 520
   ModeLine "800x600"  50  800  864  976 1040 600 637 643 666
   ModeLine "1024x768" 81 1024 1068 1204 1324 768 776 782 807
EndSection
```

NOTE

One of the monitors we have, an NEC MultiSync XE17, was not in either the **modeDB.txt** or **Monitors** file. We found the closest monitor in the listing, for a NEC MultiSync 4FGe, and experimented with those **Modelines**. Calculating the **ModeLines** yourself is a real pain, so you want to find a monitor or a close facsimile in the **Monitors** or **modeDB.txt** files.

WARNING

Having said that, be careful about using **Modelines** for other monitors. You can destroy your monitor if you're not careful.

Configuring the Graphics-Card Section

The **Device** section describes your graphics card to X. For example, a standard SuperVGA device appears as the following:

```
# Standard VGA Device:
Device
     Identifier   "Generic VGA"
     VendorName   "Unknown"
     BoardName    "Unknown"
     Chipset      "generic"
#    VideoRam     256
#    Clocks       25.2 28.3
EndSection
```

A more detailed device section, for an Actix S3 accelerated card, follows:

```
# Device configured by xf86config:
Section "Device"
Identifier   "Actix GE32+ 2MB"
VendorName   "Actix"
BoardName    "GraphicsENGINE Ultra"
#VideoRam     1024
```

```
#Option "dac_8_bit"
Ramdac      "att20c490"
Clocks      25 28 40 72 50 77 36 45 90 120 80 32 110 65 75 95
EndSection
```

Of the above options, the clocks are the hardest things to fill in. One option is to try X in **probeonly** mode (see below) to fill in the details. You can also look in a file called **AccelCards** in **/usr/X11R6/lib/X11/doc** for more information on accelerated chipsets and cards. An entry from the **AccelCards** file follows:

```
Card Vendor             : Actix
Card Model              : GraphicsEngine32 Plus
Card Bus (ISA/EISA/VLB) : ISA
Chipset                 : S3 86C801
Video Memory            : 2048k
Memory Type (DRAM/VRAM) : DRAM
Memory Speed            : 45ns
Clock Chip              : Avasem AV9194-11
Programmable? (Y/N)     : No
Number of clocks        : 16
Clocks                  : 25.175 28.322 40.0 0.0 50.0 77.0 36.0
44.9
Clocks (cont)           : 130.0 120.0 80.0 31.5 110.0 65.0 75.0
95.0
Option Flags            :
RAMDAC                  : AT&T 20C490-11
Submitter               : David E. Wexelblat <dwex@xfree86.org>
Last Edit Date          : Sept 25, 1993
```

You can convert the above Clocks lines into the proper syntax for the **XF86Config** file by placing the same values in order in a line (or lines) starting with Clocks in the **Device** section:

```
Clocks 25.175 28.322 40.0 0.0 50.0 77.0 36.0 44.9
Clocks 130.0 120.0 80.0 31.5 110.0 65.0 75.0 95.0
```

Be sure to put all the clock values in the original order.

Combining the Graphics Card With the Monitor to Make a Working X Setup

The **Screen** section connects a monitor with a graphics card. Your **XF86Config** file may have multiple **Devices** and **Monitors** defined. It is the **Screen** section that connects the two.

A complicated **Screen** section can look something like:

```
Section "Screen"
   Driver      "accel"
   Device      "Actix GE32+ 2MB"
   Monitor     "NEC MultiSync XE17"
   Subsection "Display"
      Depth      8
      Modes      "1024x768" "800x600" "640x480"
      ViewPort   0 0
      Virtual    1024 768
   EndSubsection
   Subsection "Display"
      Depth      16
      Modes      "640x480" "800x600"
      ViewPort   0 0
      Virtual    800 600
   EndSubsection
   Subsection "Display"
      Depth      32
      Modes      "640x400"
      ViewPort   0 0
      Virtual    640 400
   EndSubsection
EndSection
```

Note that the **Screen** section uses the monitor and device identifiers we entered above. This is essential to connect the screen to the proper monitor and card.

The **Driver** tells what kind of X server you're using. The choices are **Accel**, **SVGA**, **VGA16**, **VGA2**, or **Mono**. In almost all cases, you'll use **SVGA** for SuperVGA cards (and the **XF86_SVGA** X server) or **Accel** for any accelerated chipset and X server, such as the **XF86_S3** server we mentioned in the last chapter.

Each **Display** subsection covers the modes available at a particular depth. (A depth of eight specifies eight planes for color, or 256 maximum colors.) The **Modes** used refer back to the **Modelines** for the monitor that we defined above.

Virtual Screens

The **Virtual** line allows you to define a virtual screen that is larger than the number of pixels supported by your monitor. The X server will automatically scroll the display when the mouse hits the end. If you like this effect (we don't), then set the **Virtual** resolution to something larger than your monitor allows, such as:

```
Virtual 1152 900
```

The above virtual setting creates a traditional Sun Microsystems resolution. This is useful if you need to run older programs that were designed with Sun systems in mind and want to grab more than the default 1024-by-768 screen areas available on most PCs.

The **ViewPort** line tells where the X server should start up. For example, a **ViewPort** of 0,0 tells X that when it starts up, it should display position 0,0 in the upper left-hand corner (which is what you'd expect on X). If you'd rather start in the middle (an unlikely option), you can change this.

Running the Xf86config Program

Now that we've gone over the contents of the **XF86Config** file, we can now run the **xf86config** program, or, if you'd prefer, fill in the file by hand. We recommend using **xf86config** and then checking the **XF86Config** file it builds by hand. The **xf86config** program isn't flawless and needs careful supervision.

When you run **xf86config**, you should *not* be in the **/usr/X11R6/lib/X11** directory. Instead, put an **XF86Config** file in a directory in your user account, and then try copying it to **/usr/X11R6/lib/X11**.

As the program starts up, it will start asking you a lot of questions. The **xf86config** program will prompt you for a lot of the values necessary for the **XF86Config** file, such as type of mouse, questions about your desires for the keyboard, monitor frequencies and the like. When you're done, **xf86config** will write out the data into a file named **XF86Config** in the current directory. (For this reason, you don't want to be in **/usr/lib/X11**, which is a symbolic link to **/usr/X11R6/lib/X11**, when you run this program.)

Once the **xf86config** program finishes, you should carefully examine the **XF86Config** file it generates. This file will still be incomplete, since you haven't probed for the clocks yet. Edit the **XF86Config** file. If it looks OK, then, as the root user, copy the file to **/usr/X11R6/lib/X11**. Be sure to backup any existing **XF86Config** file first.

Now you're ready to try X in **probeonly** mode.

Probing for Dot Clocks

The XFree86 X server has a special **probeonly** mode that outputs values from the **XF86Config** file and values it detects. You need to run X in this mode to see if things are going to work, and also to see if there are any problems it detects.

Run the command line:

```
X -probeonly
```

when your system has no extra load on it. Stop any unneeded programs before running this, as any extra system load may influence the timings X obtains.

The following command runs X in **probeonly** mode and sends the output to the file named **/tmp/x.values**:

```
X -probeonly > /tmp/x.values 2>&1
```

Be sure to run X from the console. Don't try to run X if you're already running X.

 If you have some dot clocks in the **XF86Config** file, then **X -probeonly** won't try to detect new ones. Because of this, the first time you run X this way, you should comment out the clocks in your **XF86Config** file. After you run X in **NOTE** probeonly mode, you can then add in the clocks to the **XF86Config** file and try it again, seeing if things still seem to work.

You can then look at the file **/tmp/x.values**, which should contain something like the following:

```
XFree86 Version 3.1.1 / X Window System
(protocol Version 11, revision 0, vendor release 6000)
Operating System: Linux
Configured drivers:
  S3: accelerated server for S3 graphics adapters (Patchlevel 0)
      mmio_928, s3_generic
(using VT number 7)


XF86Config: /usr/X11R6/lib/X11/XF86Config
(**) stands for supplied, (-) stands for probed/default values
(**) Mouse: type: Microsoft, device: /dev/ttyS0, baudrate: 1200
(**) S3: Graphics device ID: "Actix GE32+ 2MB"
(**) S3: Monitor ID: "NEC MultiSync XE17"
(**) FontPath set to
"/usr/X11R6/lib/X11/fonts/misc/,/usr/X11R6/lib/X11/fonts/Type1/,/us
r/X11R6/lib/X11/fonts/Speedo/,/usr/X11R6/lib/X11/fonts/75dpi/,/usr/
X11R6/lib/X11/fonts/100dpi/"
(-) S3: card type: ISA
```

```
(-) S3: chipset:    928, rev E or above
(-) S3: chipset driver: mmio_928
(**) S3: videoram:  1024k
(**) S3: Ramdac type: att20c490
(-) S3: Ramdac speed: 110
(-) S3: clocks:  25.24  28.32  39.99   0.00  50.13  77.02  37.35
44.89
(-) S3: clocks:  90.11 119.98  80.30  31.50 110.16  65.08  75.17
94.68
(-) S3: Maximum allowed dot-clock: 110.000 MHz
(**) S3: Mode "1024x768": mode clock =  81.000, clock used =
80.300
(**) S3: Mode "800x600": mode clock =  50.000, clock used =  50.130
(**) S3: Mode "640x480": mode clock =  31.000, clock used =  31.500
(-) S3: Using 6 bits per RGB value
(**) S3: Virtual resolution set to 1024x768
```

Note that many of these values come from our **XF86Config** file.

Now, add in the clocks to the **Device** section of your **XF86Config** file. Note that each time we ran **X -probeonly**, it returned slightly different clock values. For example, in this run, we got the following clock values (formatted for the **XF86Config** file):

```
Clocks  25.24  28.32  39.99   0.00  50.13  77.02  37.35  44.89
Clocks  90.11 119.98  80.30  31.50 110.16  65.08  75.17  94.68
```

From the **AccelCards** file, we found these clocks—close, but not exact:

```
Clocks 25 28 40 72 50 77 36 45
Clocks 90 120 80 32 110 65 75 95
```

Testing Your Configuration

So now, you're ready to start X and see if things work. Type in the following command and see if things start up:

```
startx
```

The **startx** shell script is the official way to start X from a user account.

Starting X

The **startx** script runs the **xinit** program, which does two things: **xinit** runs the X server (the program named X) and then runs the commands in the **.xinitrc** file in your home directory. If there's no **.xinitrc** file in your home directory, then **xinit** runs a default script. The system default .xinitrc file is **/usr/lib/X11/xinit/xinitrc** (no dot). This file launches the following X programs:

```
twm &
xclock -geometry 50x50-1+1 &
xterm -geometry 80x50+494+51 &
xterm -geometry 80x20+494-0 &
exec xterm -geometry 80x66+0+0 -name login
```

NOTE

X quits when the last program in the **.xinitrc** (system or local) stops. Usually, this last program is preceded by an **exec** statement. When you quit this program, X stops and you're back at the   console. Unfortunately, in this odd case, the **xterm** program started in the top left of the screen is the last program (normally this would be the window manager, **twm**.) Because of this, you must exit this **xterm** shell window to quit X in the default case.

Chances are you'll want to change this, as it's much easier selecting **Quit** from a window-manager menu than it is remembering which of the many **xterms** is the key program that stops X.

If all goes well, you should see a screen something like the picture in Figure 4.1.

See Chapter 6 for a description of the **.xinitrc** file and how to customize it to start up the applications you want.

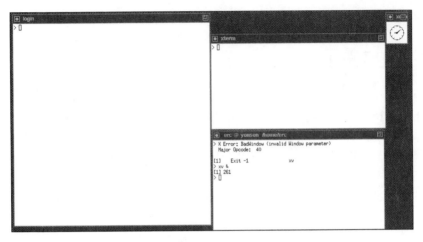

Figure 4.1 The default X display.

Stopping X

To stop X in the default configuration, you need to find the **xterm** window that started out in the upper left corner (you might have moved this window) and exit it. You'll soon be out of X and back to the boring old terminal mode. Also, the **fvwm** and **tvm** window managers have menu options for quitting X.

Tuning Your Modes

It's likely that the default mode in the **XF86Config** file will specify a 640-by-480 resolution. Chances are, your hardware supports much higher resolutions. While running X, you can press the **Ctrl–Alt–Keypad–+** keys simultaneously to switch to the next mode in the **XF86Config** file.

This is very useful, because the way X comes up may not look like a normal screen (see Figure 4.1). If this is the case, try switching modes to see if things get better.

You can also change the **XF86Config** file to start up in the best mode. Look for the "Screen" section in your **XF86Config** file. You'll want to change the modes line from something like:

```
Modes "640x480" "800x600" "1024x768"
```

to:

```
Modes "1024x768" "800x600" "640x480"
```

Note that we merely put the best mode first. This makes XFree86 start up in 1024-by-768-pixel-resolution mode, a much nicer display mode, especially for X. Before doing this, though, make sure that all graphics modes work, using **Ctrl-Alt-Keypad-+** while X is running. Ensure that each change results in a valid display.

SuperVGA to the Rescue

If all the above methods have failed, you may want to fall back on SuperVGA, just to get X up and running. This is presuming, of course, that you don't have a plain old SuperVGA card, for which the SuperVGA modes would be most appropriate. Instead, the theory is that if you can't get your super-duper card to run X in its super-duper accelerated mode, maybe you can get it running in plain old SuperVGA. Most PC graphics boards support the SuperVGA modes, so this method, while it won't take advantage of the power of your graphics card, may at least allow you to run X, presuming you can't so far.

In the next section, we show how to get a generic SuperVGA file built. This is because this step is usually a lot quicker than getting the file properly built for your graphics hardware.

WARNING

Setting up XFree86 incorrectly can harm your system hardware, so watch out. In this section, we discuss using the sample SuperVGA **XF86Config** file that comes with XFree86. You should always set up the **XF86Config** file set up for your exact hardware configuration. We only mention this technique because setting up X can prove to be nearly impossible. It is always best to set up X for your hardware. Remember, you were warned.

The first thing to do is to find the example **XF86Config** file that comes with XFree86. This file, usually named **XF86Config.eg** and stored in **/usr/X11R6/lib/X11**, has the default mode for a 640-by-480-pixel

SuperVGA device. Since most PC graphics boards support this mode, you might be in luck.

Copy the **XF86Config.eg** and edit it. You'll need to add the data about your mouse and monitor. In fact, the more you can fill in, the better. When you're done, you can copy this file to **XF86Config** and start up X. If you do use the SuperVGA example file, you must use this X server. (Unless you have an **Accel** screen section set up, none of the accelerated X servers will work.)

Remember that running X this way may damage your hardware (don't say we didn't warn you). The only reason you want to run in a lower-resolution mode is if all else fails.

Again, it's best to configure X for your hardware. Only try the SuperVGA mode if you have a card for which all else fails (unless, of course, your graphics card *is* a SuperVGA card and the **XF86_SVGA** program is the appropriate X server.)

Summary

This chapter deals with one of the most tedious, nonintuitive, and uninspiring aspects of Linux installation and configuration—messing around with XFree86. You learned about all the mundane details that go into a typical XFree86 configuration process, including mucking around with various files and settings.

The next chapter shifts gears and moves to a (we hope) more inspiring topic: actually using Linux.

Section II

Using Linux

Now that you have Linux installed and configured on your PC, it's time for the fun part—actually using it:

Chapter 5 covers basic Linux tools that you'll probably use every day in some fashion. The coverage here focuses on tools that are unique to Linux, whether they be features not found in other UNIX implementations or features found in the UNIX world that have been slightly changed for use under Linux. A good example of this is the **elvis** text editor, which is a clone of the ubiquitous **vi** editor.

Chapter 6 covers X Window-based tools, including **xterm** and the windows managers that ship with Linux.

Chapter 7 covers additional Linux tools that you probably won't use every day, but will still come in handy. This would include the **emacs** text editor, as well as the Mtools, which are specific to Linux and allow Linux to interoperate easier with PC architecture.

Basic Linux Tools

This chapter covers:

- Linux tools
- The Linux filesystem
- File types
- File permissions
- Basic Linux commands
- Wildcards
- Other ways of viewing files
- Linux and passwords
- Linux shells
- Using the **elvis** text editor

Linux Tools

As a UNIX workalike, you'd expect Linux to toe the line when it comes to UNIX design philosophy and user tools. Design philosophy? Yes. As an operating system, UNIX can be seen as a collection of tools, some more important than others. Since UNIX (and Linux, for that matter) originally evolved through the contributions of a widespread computing community, UNIX tools tended to spring up in response to specific situations: When a problem needed to be solved, either a new command was added, or new options were added to old commands.

This tool-based approach is what gives UNIX a lot of its perceived complexity. Compared to Microsoft *Windows* and the Macintosh operating system, the use of UNIX tools like **vi** and **ls** may seem to be fairly archaic and nonintuitive. For the outsider, they are.

But once you spend some time with UNIX and its command structure, you'll see that there's a great deal of logic underlying the UNIX operating system—and by extension, the Linux operating system. Once you've mastered a few UNIX commands, you can move on to more complex command lines, as well as more complex computing chores. We'll begin this chapter with a discussion of basic UNIX/Linux commands, followed by a rundown of more advanced Linux tools. In the next chapter, we'll discuss additional Linux tools used in conjunction with the X Window System. The tools in this chapter can be run from a command line or under the X Window System in an **xterm** window.

If you're a computing neophyte, you may want to check out a basic UNIX text (such as *Teach Yourself UNIX*) for a more detailed explanation of UNIX file, directories, files, commands, command lines, pipes, and standard input/output. See Appendix A for details.

The Linux Filesystem

Linux organizes your information in *files*. Files can contain text, programming information, shell scripts, or virtually any other kind of information.

We're not going to spend a lot of time on this basic concept here, or the different types of files under the UNIX operating system; if you're not sure what a file is, you should check out one of the basic UNIX texts listed in Appendix A. However, there are some things you should know about how Linux treats files:

- **Linux has no practical limit on the length of filenames.** While there are some internal limits on filename size (namely, 256 characters), you're probably not going to run into these limits. If you're frustrated by DOS's eight-dot-three filename limitation, you'll be pleased with this aspect of Linux. However, if you're using Linux on a network with other forms of UNIX, you'll probably want to limit your filenames to a 14-character limit, since this is the general limit in the UNIX world.

- **Linux has few limitations on what characters can be used in filenames.** Generally speaking, you shouldn't use the following characters in filenames:

  ! @ # $ % ^ & ( ) [ ] { } ' " ? | ; < > ` + - \ / . ..

  These characters have a tendency to conflict with shell. In addition, you can't use spaces in the middle of a filename.

- **With Linux, case always counts, and that includes filenames.** Under Linux, **report**, **Report**, and **REPORT** would be three different files.

A file can be looked at in a few different ways when it comes to the name. When we refer to files throughout this chapter, we're mainly speaking about the filename itself (like **test**) and not the *absolute* pathname. Under Linux, an absolute filename is the name of the file as measured from the root directory. Therefore, a file that's stored in a subdirectory (which you'll learn about later in this chapter) named **/home/kevinr** would have an absolute pathname of **/home/kevinr/test**. When we refer to **test** without a reference to the subdirectory containing it, we're referring to its *relative* pathname.

There's a lot more rigmarole to do with relative pathnames, but you probably won't deal with it all that often.

One difference from DOS that you'll notice: With Linux, there's no such thing as drive names. With Linux, there's a single filesystem, and any differences in physical media are pretty much abstracted away. This is why the CD-ROM drive actually appears as part of the filesystem as **/cdrom**. Similarly, the floppy drive is represented by a device driver, not a physical drive letter. (There are ways that Linux deals with floppy drives; some of them will be covered in Chapter 7.)

File Types

Under Linux, a file can be one of several types:

- Ordinary file
- Directory
- Link
- Special device file

We're not going to spend a lot of time discussing each of these file types; you should be able to see the difference between them in the short explanations here. If you want more information about UNIX file types, check out one of the UNIX texts listed in Appendix A.

Ordinary Files

Ordinary files win the UNIX prize for truth in advertising, since they tend to be rather ordinary. Generally speaking, you'll spend most of your time working with ordinary files of some sort:

- *Text files* are made up of ASCII text. For example, when you create a file in **emacs**, you're creating a text file. In addition, if you create source-code files for use in programming, you're creating text files.
- *Data files* may contain special characters not contained in the ASCII set. For example, the **xv** graphics editor creates and edits

files in various graphics formats. Since these files contains non-ASCII characters, they are data files. The same goes for files created by a database manager or a spreadsheet manager.

- *Command text files*, also known as *shell scripts*, are ASCII characters, but are marked differently than other Linux files.
- *Executable files* are binary program files, created when source-code files are compiled.

Directories

Directories are, well, directories. Under Linux, a directory is also a file that contains information about the directory. (Talk about the ultimate in self-referential logic....) You'll learn more about directories below, but the important thing to know is that directories can have the same sort of limitations—i.e., permissions—as can files.

Links

A *link* is a reference to another file within the filesystem. This allows a file to be two (or more) places at the same time—in its original file location as well as at the reference elsewhere in the filesystem. You'll learn more about links later in this chapter.

Special Device Files

In a sense, you've already covered these files in Chapter 2, when you learned how Linux refers to various portions of the PC architecture, such as **/dev/hda** for the hard drive. These references are called *device files*, and they are used by Linux to represent physical portions of the PC. Under Linux—and under UNIX, for that matter—everything is a file, whether it is a collection of data, a device file representing a physical piece of hardware (such as a printer, disk drive, etc.), or the kernel of the operating system itself. Similarly, even if you've installed Linux on a PC with multiple hard drives, you'll never see a difference in the way Linux treats the separate drives—there will be only one large filesystem.

How Linux Organizes Files and Directories

Most important Linux commands deal with the management of files and directories. Therefore, it's important that we take a moment and explain exactly how Linux treats these files and directories.

Like DOS, *Windows*, the Macintosh OS, and other versions of UNIX, Linux stores files in a hierarchical fashion: files are stored in directories, and directories (or subdirectories) are stored in other directories. The only directory that's not a subdirectory of another directory is the *root* directory. This directory doesn't have a name (like **bin**, as seen in Table 5.1). Instead, the root directory is indicated by a slash (/). This is the opposite of MS-DOS, which uses the backslash (\) to indicate the root directory. The directory above the current directory in the hierarchy is called the *parent* directory.

The Linux installation process creates quite a few directories, including the main subdirectories of the root directory. It's handy to know what's contained in these directories, since they'll be the first place to look for specific files. Table 5.1 lists the main directories found in the root directory.

Table 5.1 The main subdirectories of the root directory.

Directory	Contents
bin	Binary files
boot	Information needed to boot the system
cdrom	CD-ROM drive, if Linux supports your CD-ROM drive
dev	Device drivers
etc	Miscellaneous files, mostly used in system administration
home	The home directory for users
lib	Programming libraries
tmp	Temporary storage of temporary files
usr	Commands
var	System definitions

Case counts in Linux across the board, as you'll learn time and time again. (This is different from DOS, where case doesn't matter.) If you tell Linux to look for a directory named **BIN**, the system won't find this directory. However, if you tell Linux to look for **bin**, the system will find this directory.

The same goes for Linux commands—when we tell you use the **cd** command, we mean **cd**, not **Cd**, **CD**, or **cD**. Again, this is different from DOS.

Depending on how you installed Linux, you may also have a directory called **dos**, **dosc**, or something similar, which contains the DOS partition on your hard drive.

Your Home Directory

When you set up a user account in Chapter 2, you also created a *home* directory for the user (in this case, you). You can think of your home directory as a base for operations. When you log in the system, you're automatically placed in this directory, and default files for important applications (such as **emacs**) have been automatically been copied to this directory. Generally, it's a good idea to name the directory the same as the login name of the user; in Chapter 2, for example, the home directory was named **kevinr**. The absolute filename of this home directory is **/home/kevinr**.

You should keep all your files in your home directory. In fact, the default Linux installation gives you no choice other than to store your files in this directory, as file permissions don't allow you to write to any other directories. (The root user, on the other hand, can do anything to any directory.) You can create subdirectories, however, to better help you organize the many files that you'll inevitably create as a result of your Linux usage.

You can *always* use the tilde character (~) as a shortcut for the home directory, as you'll see in the following commands.

Moving between Directories with Cd

At any one given time, you can be placed in only one directory, which is your *current* or *working* directory. If you visualize the directory scheme as a hierarchy, you can also visualize moving between various parts of that hierarchy. The Linux command that allows you to move between directories is **cd**. You can use the **cd** command to point to a specific directory:

```
gilbert:/$ cd /usr
gilbert:/usr$
```

The Bourne Again SHell, or **bash**, is set up by default on Linux systems. **Bash** is designed to show the name of the machine on a prompt (in this instance, *gilbert*), as well as the current directory. (The semicolon is used to separate the machine name and the current directory.) As you can see in the previous example, the first line shows that the current directory is /, or the root directory. In the second line—after running the **cd** command—the current directory is **/usr**.

We're getting ahead of ourselves here a tad, diving into UNIX commands without every really describing them. For now, suffice it to say that a command is a direct instruction to the Linux system.

The **cd** command can be used in many different ways. You can use it to make the root directory your current directory:

```
gilbert:/usr$ cd /
gilbert:/$
```

You can also use it to move up a single directory in the hierarchy. In the next example, your current directory is **/usr/doc**, and you want to make the **/usr** directory your current directory. To do this, you'll need to know that Linux always represents the current directory with a period (.) and the parent directory with two periods (..). The following command line, then, would move your current directory to the parent directory:

```
gilbert:/usr/doc$ cd ..
gilbert:/usr$
```

The explanation probably made this example seem more complex than it is.

You can also use **cd** to make a subdirectory your current directory. The trick here is knowing that you'll want to move to a directory relative to your current directory. Knowing that **doc** is a subdirectory of the current directory **/usr**, you would move to the **doc** directory with the following command line:

```
gilbert:/usr$ cd doc
gilbert:/usr/doc$
```

However, if you used the following command line, you'd experience failure:

```
gilbert:/usr$ cd /doc
bash: /doc: No such file or directory
```

You're generating this error message because **doc** and **/doc** would be two different directories—**doc** exists as a subdirectory of the current directory, while **/doc** would need to be a subdirectory of the root directory (hence the leading slash). Beginners sometimes are confused by this point.

Another command line that would generate a failure is:

```
gilbert:~$ cd..
bash: cd..: not found
```

Without the space between the **cd** command and the notation for the higher-level command, the shell doesn't understand your request.

You can also move to your home directory at all times, no matter what the current directory is, with the following:

```
gilbert:/usr$ cd ~
gilbert:~$
```

The tilde (~) symbol can be used at all times and in other commands as shorthand for your home directory. In addition, using **cd** without a new directory specification will automatically lead you to your home directory:

```
gilbert:/usr$ cd
gilbert:~$
```

 There's really only one restriction to the **cd** command: You must have execute permission for the directory to which you're switching.

If you decide to go with another Linux shell that *doesn't* list the current directory (see "Linux Shells," later in this chapter) at the beginning of the prompt, you'll need to use the **pwd** (short for *print working directory*) command to print the name of the current working directory:

```
gilbert:/usr$ pwd
/usr
```

File Permissions and Linux

When you first use your Linux system and are not logged in as the root user, you might be in for some rude surprises when you try to write to a directory that's not your own home directory. Essentially, Linux will tell you that you cannot write to the directory.

Because UNIX is a creature centered around security, Linux allows *permissions* to be designated for files and directories. If you lack the proper permissions, you can't change files or directories. The root user, of course, has the proper permissions to access every file in the Linux filesystem (which means that you shouldn't expect absolute security if you're working on a larger system). Under Linux, there are three different levels of permissions: *owner*, *group*, and *world*.

Permissions are an extremely frustrating part of Linux if you're a new user. While there are permissions under DOS, they are not frequently used.

To find what permissions are applied to files, use the following command line:

```
gilbert:/$ ls -l
-rwxrwxrwx  1 kevinr  group1    512 Apr  3 19:12 test
-rwxrwxrwx  1 kevinr  group1    512 Apr  3 19:27 test.bk
drwxrwxrwx  1 kevinr  group1   2146 Apr  1 04:41 memos
-rwx------  1 kevinr  group1    854 Apr  2 19:12 data
```

There's actually a rhyme and reason to the mess of numbers and letters presented here, but it's best explained going right to left in columns (and focusing on the first line of the listings):

- The eighth column (**test**) lists the filename.
- The seventh column (**19:12**) lists the time the file was created.
- The sixth column (**Apr 3**) lists the date the file was created.
- The fifth column (512) lists the size of the file, in bytes.
- The fourth column (**group1**) lists the group the file belongs to. (Yes, we'll explain this later.)
- The third column (**kevinr**) lists the owner of the file.
- The second column (**1**) shows the number of links to the file.
- The first column (**-rwxrwxrwx**) lists the permissions associated with the file, as well as the type of the file.

The leading hyphen (**-**) tells us that the file is an ordinary file, which was covered earlier in this section. When you do a **ls -l**, you'll see various file-type listings, which are listed in Table 5.2.

Table 5.2 File types listed with the ls -l command line.

Listing	File Type
-	Ordinary file
d	Directory
l	Link

There are other file types listed with this command, but you won't usually get into them with Linux.

Permission Lines

The remainder of the first column, covering specific permissions, commands most of our attention in this discussion. Basically, the permissions are broken down into three groups. Remember that permissions are applied to the owner of the file (in this case, **kevinr**), the group of the file (in this case, **group1**), and the world at large. Applying this trinity to a permission line of **rwxrwxrwx**, we can see that the owner has the ability to read the file (as indicated by *r*), write the file (as indicated by *w*), and execute the file (as indicated by *x*). Moving on, the group has the ability to read the file (as indicated by *r*), write the file (as indicated by *w*), and execute the file (as indicated by *x*). Finally, the world has the ability to read the file (as indicated by *r*), write the file (as indicated by *w*), and execute the file (as indicated by *x*). In other words, this file is fair game for anyone with access to your Linux filesystem.

Things are a little different with the following listing:

```
-rwx—   1 kevinr  group1    854 Apr  2 19:12 data
```

When there are no letters indicating a permission—as in the case with the hyphen—the permissions are restricted. With this file, the owner has the ability to read the file (as indicated by *r*), write the file (as indicated by *w*), and execute the file (as indicated by *x*). However, no one else has *any* permissions with this file.

With most of the Linux operating system, you'll see a permission like **rwxr-xr-x**, with **root** being the owner of the file. In this instance, an average user (that is, someone not logged in as root) has the ability to execute files (an important capability to have) and to read the files, but lacks the ability to write (that is, change) the file. This protection exists for many reasons, but mainly it exists to prevent users from wreaking unanticipated havoc.

When you install and configure new software on your Linux system and want to install it in one of the standard file locations, you'll need to login as **root**.

Changing Permissions

The Linux command **chmod** changes file permissions. You may want to change permissions for some popular directories in order to avoid logging in as **root** in order to install or configure software.

Unless you have write permission for a file or directory, you can't change the permissions. Of course, this means that you may need to be logged in as **root** in order to change permissions.

Permissions can be changed in *numeric* or *symbolic* form. Neither method is what could be called intuitive, so we'll spend some time explaining each of them.

The Numeric Method

The numeric method uses numbers to track permissions. Like the permissions listings earlier in this section, the numeric method divides permissions into threes, albeit in a different manner.

The numeric method forces you to add three different sets of numbers in determining who has what permissions. The actual types of permissions (owner, group, world) hasn't changed—only the method of listing them.

You'll use *modes* to track permissions, as seen in Table 5.3.

Table 5.3 Modes and their meanings.

Mode	Meaning
400	Owner has read permission
200	Owner has write permission
100	Owner has execute permission
040	Group has read permission
020	Group has write permission

Table 5.3 Modes and their meanings. (continued)

Mode	Meaning
010	Group has execute permission
004	World has read permission
002	World has write permission
001	World has execute permission

You must now translate these numbers into the numeric form by adding them together. For example, using the following directory listing:

```
-rwx–x–x  1 kevinr  group1    854 Apr  2 19:12 test
```

we arrive at a numeric permission of 711:

400	Owner has read permission
200	Owner has write permission
100	Owner has execute permission
010	Group has execute permission
001	World has execute permission
───	
711	

A file or directory that's totally open to the world would have a permission of *777*; a file or directory inaccessible to anyone would have a permission of *000*.

Changing the permissions entails combining the desired permissions with the **chmod** command. For example, to change the file permissions of the **test** command to make it totally accessible to all users, you'd use the following command line:

```
gilbert:/$ chmod 777 test
```

To change the permissions so that only the owner of the file has the ability to totally access the file, but permission to every other user is denied, you'd use the following command line:

```
gilbert:/$ chmod 700 test
```

To change the permissions so that the owner of the file has the ability to totally access the file, but other users and the group have the ability to read and execute (but not change) the file, you'd use the following command line:

```
gilbert:/$ chmod 744 test
```

The Symbolic Method

When using the numeric method, you don't need to know the existing permissions of the file, which means that you need enter only the desired permissions. The other main method of setting permissions, called the *symbolic* method, requires that you know the existing permissions, as you're setting new permissions relative to the existing permissions.

The symbolic method eschews numerals, using letters instead. And it's very precise in adding or subtracting permissions relative to existing permissions. For instance, the following command line gives execute permissions to the world (all users):

```
gilbert:/$ chmod o+x data
```

Here, *o* refers to others (in **chmod** parlance, the world), *x* refers to execute permission, and the plus sign (+) adds the execute permission to others. If a minus sign (-) were used, this command line would remove execute permission for others.

The symbolic method uses some quirky language, as you've already seen with the reference to others. The owner of the file is referred to as the user, and setting permissions for the owner means using *u*:

```
gilbert:/$ chmod u+x data
```

Setting the permission for the group is a matter of using *g*:

```
gilbert:/$ chmod g+x data
```

The above statements, of course, would be meaningless if the users already had the ability to execute the file.

Table 5.4 lists the various symbols used with the **chmod** command.

Table 5.4 Symbols used with the symbolic method.

Symbol	Meaning
u	User (owner of the file)
g	Group
o	Other (the world)
a	Everyone (the owner, the group, and the world)
+	Adds permission
-	Removes permission
r	Read permission
w	Write permission
x	Execute permission
t	Sets the "sticky bit" on a directory

NOTE

If you create your own shell scripts or use the **perl** language, you'll need to set permissions to make your scripts usable.

Changing Ownerships and Permissions

In the act of creating a file or directory, you automatically assign permissions to the file or directory. To see what permissions are the default, use the **umask** command:

```
$ umask
744
```

This means that the owner of the file has full privileges, while your group and the world have the ability to read the file. To change this permission, you'll again use the **umask** command, listing a new permission on the command line:

```
$ umask 007
```

This may look odd—and it is indeed odd. The **umask** command changes permissions relative to a baseline of 777. The input to the **umask** command is therefore subtracted from the baseline 777, leaving you with the total of 770, meaning that the owner of the file and the group have full permissions to the file, while the rest of the world has no permissions at all.

In the same way, you're automatically the owner of a file when you create it, but there may be times when you want to transfer this ownership to another user. You can do so with the **chown** command, provided you're logged in to the system as the root user. (You didn't think you could change the ownership logged in as an ordinary user, did you? If anyone could change the ownership of a file, security in the UNIX operating system would be nonexistent.) When using the **chown** (short for *ch*ange *own*ership, by the way) command, you list the new owner of the command and the file in question:

```
gilbert:~$ chown pat report
```

You can also transfer ownership of an entire directory by adding the **-R** option to the **chown** command:

```
gilbert:~$ chown -R pat reports_1995
```

Similarly, the **chgrp** command changes group ownership of a file, listing the new group membership and the file in question:

```
gilbert:~$ chgrp linux_book chap5
```

The Sticky Bit

In our continuing obsession with security, we present you information about the sticky bit. In the past, UNIX hackers used to get around file permissions by messing with entire directories, as most system administrators would forget to set restrictive permissions for the directory itself.

The sticky bit is a response to this security problem. Linux allows you to set the sticky bit, which makes a directory impregnable to everyone but the owner of a directory and the root user. To set the sticky bit, you'd use the **chmod** command in the following manner:

```
gilbert:/$ chmod +t directoryname
```

Once the sticky bit is set, no one (except the root user and the owner of the directory) has the ability to move or delete files in a directory, no matter what permissions are associated with a file.

Dealing with Files and Directories

We've thrown around the term *command* a great deal without ever really defining it (our copy editor is probably gnawing her red pen by this point), but we're assuming you know what a command is and how you give a command to the computer. And you also know that the combination of a command and any options is called a *command line*.

NOTE   Under Linux, commands can be run at a command line or run under the X Window System in an **xterm** window (which you'll learn more about in Chapter 6). However, there are some cases when there's an X Window version of the UNIX command; for example, there's a version of **man** for the X Window System, called **xman**, that you should use instead. In this chapter we'll also note the X Window versions, even though you'll be dealing more with XFree86 in the following chapter.

If you've used MS-DOS for any extended period, you'll instantly recognize the Linux counterparts presented here. If you've used Microsoft *Windows* for an extended period and hidden from the command line, you may be somewhat confused initially when you run through this series of Linux commands. And if you're a UNIX workstation user, you'll find that there may be slight differences between the commands/options and the version of UNIX you're used to working with. (If you're a Cray supercomputer user, you're *really* slumming.)

You've already learned about the **cd** and **pwd** commands, used to move between directories and print the working directory, respectively. There are many more Linux commands used to deal with directories and files.

Listing Files and Directories with ls and Dir

You'll use the **ls** command, short for *list*, quite often—probably every time you use Linux, as a matter of fact. You've already used **ls** in a discussion of permissions. This command lists the contents of the current directory or a specified directory:

```
gilbert:/$ ls
bin/      dev/      home/        mnt/     sbin/    var/
boot/     dos/      lib/         proc/    tmp/     vmlinuz
cdrom/    etc/      lost+found   root/    usr/
```

If you're a UNIX user, this is probably not the version of **ls** you're used to, especially if you try this command on your own Linux box. The **ls** version contained with Linux is actually the GNU version of **ls**. As such, it makes several improvements to the basic **ls** command found on other versions of UNIX. One improvement—which we can't show you within the confines of a black-and-white text—is the addition of color to indicate directories (which will appear on your color monitor as blue) and special types of files. (Later in this section we'll explain how to change these colors and what the colors mean.) Linux also uses slashes after the name to indicate directories.

In addition, **ls** (by default) sorts files and directories in ASCII order, in columns. That's why the first column contains the directories beginning with *b* and *c*, followed by the rest of the alphabet. If there were directories that began with any capital letter, they'd be listed first—the directory **X/** would appear before **bin/**, because under ASCII, uppercase letters precede lowercase letters.

 The Bourne Again SHell, **bash**, also supports the **dir** command, in a limited sense. The **dir** command does the same thing as the **ls -l** command, which will be explained later in this section. DOS users will be relieved to know that their familiar **dir** command can also be used under Linux.

You can use one of the many command-line options to the **ls** command. For example, if you use the **ls** command in your home directory, you'll discover that there are no apparent files to be found:

```
gilbert:~$ ls
gilbert:~$
```

However, if you run the command with the *-a* option, you'll see the following:

```
gilbert:~$ ls -a
./       .bash_history  .kermrc .lessrc
../      .emacs         .less   .term/
```

The files beginning with the period (.) are called *hidden* files. Actually, they're not so hidden as to be mysterious; they're merely hidden when you use the **ls** command to search for files. The *-a* option tells the **ls** command to look for *all* files.

There are also two other listings, . and .., that may be unfamiliar if you're not a UNIX user. The single period (.) is merely another way to display the current directory, while the double periods (..) are used to display the parent directory.

The *-l* (ell, not one) option to **ls** prints a "long" listing of the directory's contents:

```
gilbert:~$ ls -l
```

The **ls** command can also be used to determine the existence of a single file in short form:

```
gilbert:~$ ls data
data
```

or in long form:

```
gilbert:~$ ls -l data
-rwx——  1 kevinr  group1    854 Apr  2 19:12 data
```

Table 5.5 summarizes the **ls** command's important options.

Table 5.5 A summary of the ls command options.

Option	Result
-a	Lists *all* files, including hidden files
-A	Lists *all* files, except for the . and .. listings
-c	Sorts files by the time they were last changed, not by the default ASCII order, beginning with the oldest file
-d	Lists only the name of a directory, not its contents
-l	Lists files and directories in long format
-r	Lists the contents in reverse order
-t	Sorts files by the time they were last changed, beginning with the newest file
-x	Lists files and sorts them across the page, instead of by columns

NOTE The **ls** command isn't the only tool for viewing files and directories on a Linux system. If you've installed XFree86, there's a file manager that can be used to graphically display the contents of your Linux system (see Chapter 6 for details).

Changing the ls Colors

Although we can't show you, **ls** does indeed display different types of files in different colors. While you probably don't want to change these colors, Linux gives you the ability to do so. (Indeed, Linux gives you the ability to do a great many things you'll probably never bother to do, but that's to the credit of the people who put Linux together.) The settings for these colors are stored in the file **/etc/DIR_COLORS**, and this file is used by all users. If you want to change these settings, you need to copy this file to your home directory, rename the file to **.dir_colors** (making it a hidden file), and edit the listings in the file. As with many of the configuration files used with Linux, there are enough comments in the default **/etc/DIR_COLORS** to guide you through any editing session.

Wildcards

Like UNIX (and DOS, for that matter), Linux supports *wildcards* in command lines and shells scripts. A wildcard is merely shorthand for a character or a string of characters. Wildcards can come in handy if you're looking for a file and you've forgotten the specific filename (geez, I *know* the file ends in *1995*), or else you want to see a listing of files that fall within specific parameters (such as ending with *.c*, useful if you plan on using Linux for software development).

There are three types of Linux wildcards: *, ?, and [...]. Each will be explained.

Technically, wildcards are the province of the shell, and in theory a discussion of wildcards should take place with a discussion of shells. For our purposes, however, we're going to discuss wildcards at this point in your Linux discussion, since what we're saying here applies to all shells.

In the previous section covering the **ls** command, we covered the command's use when applied to single files. However, there may be times when you want to list a set of files that share a common characteristic, such as ending with *.c*. In this instance, you can tell **ls** to look for every file that ends with *.c*, using the following command line:

```
gilbert:~$ ls *.c
aardvark.c      stuff.c titles.c        xylophone.c
```

In this instance, **ls** is told to substitute * for any portion of a filename preceding an ending of .c. And, as you can see from the listing of files, the command was successful. The **ls** is used to match any number of characters in a string, including zero characters:

```
gilbert:~$ ls titles*
titles  titles.c
```

In the case of **titles**, the wildcard matched zero characters.

The asterisk (*) can be used at the beginning or the end of a wildcard expression. You can also use more than one asterisk in an expression:

```
gilbert:~$ ls t*.*
titles.c
```

If you wanted to list the files with the string *titles* anywhere in the filename, you could use the following command line:

```
gilbert:~$ ls *titles*
subtitles       titles titles.c
```

The asterisk wildcard is the most expansive wildcard available. On the other end of the spectrum is the question-mark wildcard, which is used to match a single character:

```
gilbert:~$ ls title?
titles
```

In this instance, **ls** did not match **titles.c**, which contains *two* characters after the search string of *title*. **Titles**, meanwhile, contained only one character after the search string of *title*—which matched the parameters of the **ls** command.

The final wildcard is used to return specific characters, as defined by brackets ([]). For example, you're looking through a directory filled with memos from the last 12 months. Since you've been a good Linux user, you've been placing a number at the end of every file, signifying the month it was written. (Yes, we know you're not likely to have too many files if you've just installed Linux. Think of this advice as something you'll need in the future.) You want to track down a memo you wrote sometime in the summer, but you can't remember the name of the file, and a reading through the directory listings don't spark a memory. In this instance, you'll want to narrow down the directory listings to files ending in *6*, *7*, or *8* (corresponding to June, July, and August). To do this with the **ls** command, you'd enter *6*, *7*, and *8* in brackets:

```
gilbert:~/memos$ ls *[6-8]
golf.8          golfanne.8     golfpat.6      golfjim.6
golftod.6       golftom.7
```

This narrows down the list of files returned by **ls**. It also means you probably play too much golf.

In the above example, we asked **ls** to return files that ended with a range of characters—i.e, in *6*, *7*, or *8*. You can also use this wildcard to return a single character:

```
gilbert:~/memos$ ls *[6]
golfpat.6       golfjim.6      golftod.6
```

If you're searching for a character (remembering, of course, that Linux distinguishes between uppercase and lowercase letters at all times) or range of characters, you can list them in the brackets:

```
gilbert:~/memos$ ls report.[Ee]rc
report.Erc      report.erc
```

Wildcards can be used with any Linux command.

Creating Directories with Mkdir

The **mkdir** command is used to create directories. If you plan on using Linux for most of your day-to-day stuff, we advise creating directories to help organize the many files Linux (and any other version of UNIX, for that matter) creates. Using **mkdir** is simple:

```
gilbert:~$ mkdir directory
```

where *directory* is the name of the directory you want to create. To create a directory named **letters** in your home directory, you'd use the following command:

```
gilbert:~$ mkdir letters
```

To see if the directory was really created, you can use the **ls** command:

```
gilbert:~$ ls
letters/        text
```

You can also use it to create a new directory elsewhere in the directory hierarchy:

```
gilbert:~$ mkdir /users/kevin/letters
gilbert:~$ ls /users/kevin
letters/
```

Mkdir can create more than one directory on a command line:

```
gilbert:~$ mkdir letters data
gilbert:~$ ls
data/           letters/        text
```

Mkdir can also create a directory and a subdirectory in a single command line:

```
gilbert:~$ mkdir -p /letters/eric
```

Other options to **mkdir** are listed in Table 5.6.

Table 5.6 The option to the mkdir command.

Option	Result
-m *mode*	Sets the mode for the new directory

Using Cat

The **cat** command does so many things under the UNIX and Linux operating systems, it's a wonder you just don't use it for everything. On a very basic level, **cat** can be used to view the contents of a file:

```
gilbert:~$ cat filename
```

where *filename* is the name of the file you want to view. For example, to view the contents of a file named **test**, you'd use the following command line:

```
gilbert:~$ cat test
This is our Linux test file. Big whoop.
```

Cat, by default, displays its output to the screen. However, **cat** can be told to send its output elsewhere, which brings us to another of its many uses: It can also be used to store a file under a different filename, much in the manner of the **cp** command (which will be covered later in this chapter). For instance, to create another copy of the **test** file (which we'll then call **cat.kr**), you'd use the following command line:

```
gilbert:~$ cat test > cat.kr
gilbert:~$ ls
test    test.kr
```

In the above example, **cat** uses the output from the **test** file as the input for the **cat.kr** file.

Cat can also be used to create simple ASCII files; we say simple because **cat** sends your keyboard input directly to a file, rather than giving you the chance to edit the file. (The full-screen editors **elvis** and

emacs can be used to edit files.) To create a simple file named **memo**, you'd use the following command line:

```
gilbert:~$ cat > memo
```

Anything you type would then go directly into the **memo** file one line at a time. When creating a file like this, there are a few things to remember:

- Hit the **Enter** key at the end of every line. Otherwise, part of your typing will end up in the ether.
- You can move within the line using the Backspace key (well, partially, anyway, since **Backspace** will merely delete the preceding character). You can't move to a previous line, however.
- Type **Ctrl-D** when you're finished typing.

 The **Ctrl-D** sequence can be used whenever you run a Linux command that requires keyboard input.

Finally, **cat** can be used to combine files. For example, you can add to the aforementioned **memo** file with the following command line:

```
gilbert:~$ cat >> memo
```

Whatever you type will be added to the **memo** file. The previous rules apply. In addition, you redirect two existing files as input to a new third file:

```
gilbert:~$ memo1 memo2 > memo3
```

The order of the files on the command line determines the order of the data in the new file.

There are a host of options to the **cat** command, as listed in Table 5.7.

Table 5.7 Options to the cat command.

Option	Result
-b	Numbers all lines, except for those not containing characters
-n	Numbers all lines
-s	Replaces a series of blank lines with a single blank line
-v	Prints nonprinting (i.e., control) characters

Other Ways to View a File

Linux contains two handy tools for viewing a file: **more** and **less**. The **more** command is pretty simple—the following command line launches **more** with the file **test**:

```
gilbert:~$ more test
```

The **more** command presents one page of text at a time, with the percentage of text displayed at the bottom of the screen. Use the **Enter** key to move forward one line in the document, or press the space bar to move ahead one entire page. Unfortunately, you can't move back to the beginning of a file once it's scrolled by.

In addition, **more** gives you the ability to search for a specific text string, by typing:

```
/string
```

where *string* is the text string you want to search for.

Where Less is More than More

The **less** command isn't part of the standard UNIX distribution, but it's a very useful addition to the Linux command set. The **less** command provides more options when viewing a file—namely, the ability to move both forward and backward through a file. Again, to use **less** to view the file named **test**, you'd use the following command line:

```
gilbert:~$ less test
```

As with **more**, you can use the */string* option to search for text.

A big advantage to **less** is its ability to search backward through a file, by pressing **b**.

Using Head and Tail to View Portions of a File

If the file is especially large, you may want to load all of it and try to scroll through it, particularly if you're just interested in a quick glance at the contents of the file. In this case, you can use the **head** command to view the beginning of the file or **tail** to view the end of the file. For both commands, the default is to display 10 lines. Therefore, to display the first 10 lines of the file **report**, you'd use the following command line:

```
gilbert:~$ head report
```

To view the last 10 lines of the file **report**, you'd use the following command line:

```
gilbert:~$ tail report
```

To change the default of 10 lines, you'd specify the new number as an argument to the command; the following, for example, displays the first 20 lines of the file **report**:

```
gilbert:~$ head -20 report
```

Viewing an Octal Dump with Od

Finally, there's the **od** command, which allows you to view an octal dump of a file:

```
$ od filename
```

where *filename* is the name of the file to be viewed.

Finding the Magic Number with File

After you've been working on your Linux system for a while, you'll accumulate a lot of files if you do any serious work at all. If you're a careful worker, you'll be able to keep track of files by their locations and filenames. However, if you're not a careful worker, you may run into situations where you have no idea what a file contains. You don't want to view a binary file with **cat** or another command designed to view text files, because doing so will probably result in huge amounts of garbage being displayed to your screen (which may require you to relogin to your system).

Linux features a command, **file**, that will look at a file and return specific information about the contents of the file. (Well, most of the time, anyway.) The UNIX world of late has supported *magic numbers*, and in theory these numbers, found somewhere in the binary file, should match a database of magic numbers on your system. (These magic numbers can be found in the **/etc/magic** file.) To run **file** on a file named **45edfsdwe**, you'd use the following command line:

```
gilbert:~$ file 45edfsdwe
```

At the very least, **file** will tell you the file's type (executable, ordinary, etc.) and how it's compiled (such as *dynamically linked*). If you're lucky, the **file** command will also tell you if the file is related to your machine. However, if this file is merely text, you'll see the following information:

```
gilbert:~$ file 45edfsdwe
45edfsdwe                    text
```

Copying Files with Cp

The **cp** command is used for copying existing files. When you use the **cp** command, the original file is left intact. This is handy when copying files to another user's machine (provided you're networked, of course) or to another directory for backup purposes. (There are more formal ways to make system backups on your Linux system, but the **cp** command works well for single files or small groups of files.) The following command line copies a file named **textfile** to the **/home/eric** directory:

```
gilbert:~$ cp textfile /home/eric
```

When this command is run, the file named **textfile** will appear both in your home directory and *eric*'s home directory.

You may want to give **textfile** a new name when it's moved to the new directory. In this case, you're giving **textfile** a new name of **textfile.kr** when it's moved to the **/home/eric** directory:

```
gilbert:~$ cp textfile /home/eric/textfile.kr
```

WARNING

Linux will do exactly what you tell it to do. In some cases, this is a good thing. In other cases, this is a very bad thing—as can be the case with the **cp** and **mv** commands.

If (using the previous command-line example) there already were a file called **textfile.kr** in the **/home/eric** directory, the **cp** command would overwrite the existing file with the new file. The **cp** command, by default, doesn't check to see if there's a file already in that directory with the same name. (The same goes for the **mv** command; this will be covered in the next section, "Moving and Renaming Files with Mv.")

On the other hand, both the **cp** and **mv** commands have an option (*-i*) that prevents you from overwriting existing files, as seen in this command line:

```
gilbert:~$ cp -i textfile /home/eric/textfile.kr
cp: overwrite `textfile.kr'?
```

If you type **y**, **cp** will overwrite the existing **textfile.kr**. If you type anything else, **cp** will not overwrite the file.

Options to the **cp** command are listed in Table 5.8.

Table 5.8 Options to the cp command.

Option	Result
-d	Maintains a symbolic link as a link, rather than as a copy of original file
-i	Prevents overwriting of existing files with the same filename
-p	Retains the existing permissions
-r	Copies the entire directory structure, including subdirectories
-v	Runs in verbose mode; lists each file as it's copied

Copying Directories with Cp

Cp also has the power to copy entire directories (including all files and subdirectories), in the form of the *-r* option:

```
gilbert:~$ cp -r /users/data /users/eric
```

Moving and Renaming Files with Mv

The **mv** command is used to move files from one directory to another. This command doesn't leave a copy of the original file in the original location (for that, use the **cp** command); it deletes the original copy and inserts the new copy in the new location.

The following command line would move the **textfile** file to the new home (~) location:

```
gilbert:/usr$ mv textfile ~
```

If you were to run the **ls**, you'd find that **textfile** didn't appear in **/usr**, but was now located in your home directory.

In this example, **textfile** retains its current filename, no matter where you moved it. You can also use the **mv** command to rename a file. (In fact, it's one of the few ways to actually rename a file, since there's no command for doing so within Linux.) The following command changes the **textfile** filename to **aardvark** filename:

```
gilbert:~$ mv textfile aardvark
```

The following command line would move **textfile** to a new directory *and* give it a new filename of **aardvark**:

```
gilbert:/usr$ mv textfile ~/aardvark
```

Linux can be fairly harsh when you're moving and renaming files. For example, the **mv** command will overwrite an existing file with a renamed file and not warn you. For example, if you ran the following command line and a file named **aardvark** already existed in your home directory, you'd be ruined:

```
gilbert:/usr$ mv textfile ~/aardvark
```

as **mv** would overwrite the original **aardvark** file with the new **aardvark** file. To avoid this problem, use the *-i* option with the **mv** command:

```
gilbert:/usr$ mv -i textfile ~/aardvark
mv: overwrite `aardvark'?
```

Type **y** if you want to overwrite **aardvark, n** (or any other key, for that matter) if you do not.

A summary of the options to **mv** are listed in Table 5.9.

Table 5.9 A summary of the mv command options.

Option	Result
-f	Overwrites existing file
-I	Checks before overwriting existing files

Removing Files with Rm

The **rm** (short for *rem*ove) command removes files. Simple enough, eh? To remove a file, simply list it on the command line:

```
gilbert:~$ rm aardvark
```

Aardvark will then be swiftly and painlessly removed—so swiftly that you won't have a chance to confirm your choice. However, like the other commands listed in this chapter, you can tell Linux to confirm your file deletions, in the form of the *-i* option:

```
gilbert:~$ rm -i aardvark
rm: remove 'aardvark'?
```

Type **y** if you want to remove **aardvark, n** (or any other key, for that matter) if you do not.

Other options to the **rm** command are listed in Table 5.10.

Table 5.10 Options to the rm command.

Option	Result
-f	Removes the file without any input from you
-i	Runs in interactive mode
-v	Runs in verbose mode, which means files are listed as they are removed

Be warned that when you remove a file under Linux, you're *really* removing the file from existence.

If you're a PC or Macintosh user, you may have gotten spoiled by utilities like *The Norton Utilities*, which could "unerase" files that have been erased. At this time, no such utilities exist for Linux.

Be careful when you combine the **rm** command and wildcards, because a wildcard—especially an asterisk—in the wrong spot can wreak havoc on your system. For example, let's say that you wanted to delete all the files ending with *.golf* on your system. (Let's just say the boss is beginning to be a little suspicious about your afternoon field trips and you want to remove any incriminating evidence.) So you tell Linux to remove all files ending with *golf*—or you think you are, anyway:

```
gilbert:~/memos$ rm * golf
```

Disaster ensues. Because you placed a space between the asterisk wildcard and the rest of the command line, the **rm** command uses only the asterisk as an argument, ignoring the *golf* part of the command line. Since *every* file is returned by the asterisk wildcard, you've just removed all the files in your current directory. (By the way, the chance of this happening is an excellent argument for using the *-i* option at all times.)

Viewing Online-Manual Pages with Man

One of the handiest feature of UNIX—and by extension, Linux—is the existence of online-manual pages, which detail the workings of specific commands. These online-manual pages (commonly referred to as *man* pages) will list the purpose of a given command, any command-line options, and perhaps other information. (For example, **man** pages created by the FSF for use with GNU commands tend to be rather verbose, going into the entire purpose of the command, as well as listing any known bugs.) While this sort of information isn't as useful as a full online-help system (for example, you can't look up a man page for any topics at all; man pages are written for specific commands), it still can help you out a great deal, especially if you know a certain command can come close to doing what you want, but you still need to know the precise option that yields the desired behavior.

To view an online-manual page, you combine the name of the command with the **man** command:

```
gilbert:/$ man ls
```

You'll then see the information shown in Figure 5.1.

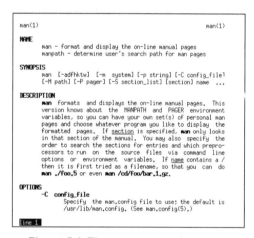

Figure 5.1 The **man** command in action.

The man page for **ls** is obviously a multipage document, as evidenced by the information at the bottom of the screen, since the bottom sentence isn't complete. To move up and down through the entire man page by entire pages, use the **PageUp** and **PageDown** keys; to move up and down the **man** page line by line, use the keyboard cursor keys (↑ and ↓). To quit the **man** command and get a command prompt, press the **q** key (short for *quit*).

There's an X Window equivalent of **man**, called **xman**, shown in Figure 5.2. You should use this command when running XFree86.

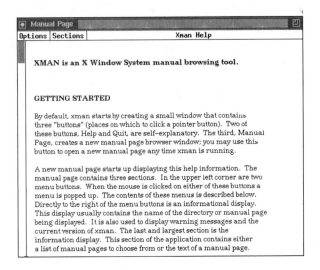

Figure 5.2 The **xman** command in action.

Finding Files

The **find** command included with Linux (actually the GNU **find** command) is very similar to the **find** command that ships with most other versions of UNIX—that is to say, the GNU version is maddeningly complex and nonintuitive to use. At its best, **find** will search your entire filesystem for a specific file. At its worst, **find** will return every file on the system, leaving you scratching your head about how to proceed with a useful search.

Still, you shouldn't run into too many problems with **find** if you remember one thing: You need to make sure all of the elements of the command line are properly organized. For example, you won't find the following command line to be very useful:

```
gilbert:~$ find *
```

as it returns the files in your current directory. Similarly, the following command line will list *every* file (at a dizzying speed, no less) on your Linux system:

```
gilbert:/$ find *
```

This move is guaranteed to give you a headache. (Remember, Linux does exactly what you tell it to do.)

Instead, you'll need to slow down and figure out exactly how to use the **find** command. Let's say you want to find out the directory location of a file named **test.bk**. First off, you need to tell **find** how to search for a file. Since we know the name of the file, we begin our command line by telling **find** to search via filename. We do so with the *-name* option:

```
gilbert:/$ find * -name
```

This is a start. Now we need to tell **find** what to look for. We do this by adding the name of the file:

```
gilbert:~$ find * -name test.bk
```

If you wanted, you could use a wildcard instead of listing the specific filename. With or without a wildcard, however, the command should work.

If you're working with a large filesystem, you may want to run the **find** command in the background. This is accomplished by adding an ampersand (&) to the command line:

```
gilbert:~$ find * -name test.bk &
```

Running this command in the background allows you to do more work while the **find** command searches for the file. For more information on running commands in the background, check out the section "Background Commands and Multitasking" later in this chapter.

When looking at other Linux texts, you'll be able to see who actually wrote the book using Linux, and who wrote the book with a knowledge of UNIX and not much experience with Linux, by the way the **find** command is explained. In most versions of UNIX, the **find** command requires that *-print* be added to the end of the command line, and that the name of the search be in quotation marks. The GNU version of **find** requires neither.

There's a lot more to the **find** command, as it encompasses an amazing amount of complexity that's more meant for large-scale systems than for the needs of the average Linux user. If you're interested in knowing more about the **find** command, use the following command line:

```
gilbert:~$ man find
```

Linking Files

Linux allows you to create links to other files. As a matter of fact, when you installed Linux, you unwittingly set up dozens of linked files (which you'd see if you did a **ls -l** listing of many of the XFree86-related directories). If you're a single user, you probably won't have much need to link files; after all, you're not sharing data with anyone else, and you're not necessarily trying to distribute data efficiently in limited disk space.

However, if you're using Linux on the network, you may find it advantageous to create a linked file or two. For example: You're working with Pat and Eric on a large project, and you want to share a file containing important addresses. This file is updated regularly by all of you. Instead of all three of you maintaining separate files and then trying to synchronize the changes regularly, the better move would be to create one main file and then create links to that file. In this way, all changes can be seen by the other user, and there's less of an administrative hassle in keeping the file current. It also cuts down on the hard-disk space needed, since there's only one file actually stored on the hard drive.

To link a file named **addresses** to Eric's home directory, you'd use the following command line:

```
gilbert:~$ ln addresses /home/eric
```

To link a file named **addresses** to Pat's home directory, you'd use the following command line:

```
gilbert:~$ ln addresses /home/pat
```

After this is done, Eric and Pat will see the file **addresses** in their directory. However, the actual file won't be in their directory; instead, the link to the file **addresses** in *your* home directory will be there. There's one drawback to this, however; you can't delete the original file **addresses** until the links have also been deleted, as Linux treats all hard links equally. Therefore, to get rid of **addresses**, you'd need to remove (with the **rm** command) **/home/eric/addresses** and **/home/pat/addresses** before you remove the **addresses** file in your directory. If you haven't created many links, you can probably keep track of this. If you have created many links, you may find that you haven't kept good track of the links and will be stymied in your attempt to delete the original file.

Some UNIX purists advise setting up links whenever possible, arguing that hard-disk space should be conserved at all times. However, we're not of this mindset. Indeed, the fewer links you can create, the better it will be for all of you. System administrators need to set up links occasionally, and so this practice should be mainly reserved for them. We present the mechanics of creating links, but we don't necessarily endorse the practice on a large scale.

Symbolic Links

In the above examples, we covered what are known as *hard* links. (After seeing what you need to go through to delete a linked file, you'll know why they're called *hard*.) Linux also supports *symbolic* links. These links, unlike hard links, don't need to be physically deleted if you want to delete the original linked file. (There are some other differences, of course, but they aren't important to this discussion.)

To set up a symbolic links, use the *-s* option to the **ln** command:

```
gilbert:~$ ln -s addresses /home/pat
```

Viewing a Calender with Cal

The **cal** command lists a one-month calendar:

```
gilbert:~$ cal
```

If you want to view a calendar for the entire year (in this case, 1995), enter the following command line:

```
gilbert:~$ cal 1995
```

To stop the scrolling, type **Ctrl-S**; to start it again, type **Ctrl-Q**. To stop the calendar entirely, type **Ctrl-D**.

Virtual Terminals

Linux allows you to be in more than one place at a time, with the notion of *virtual terminals*. UNIX inherently supports multiple users on a system at any given time. A virtual terminal allows you to login more than once on a Linux box. While this may not be something you would do commonly, there might be times when it will come in handy; for example, it's convenient to login as another user in order to kill some errant processes. While doing this, you'll still be logged in the initial terminal.

To move between virtual terminals, you type **Alt-F***n*, where **F***n* is the function key associated with the terminal. The initial login to a Linux system is always associated with the **F1** function key, so any additional logins will begin with the **F2** key.

When you're finished in the virtual terminal, you should logout with the following command:

```
logout
```

Linux and Passwords

When you added a user account, you set up a password for that account. Depending on your usage, the password you select may or may not be important. On the one hand, it's nice to have some security on a machine containing all your work, even if only to deter the mischievous actions of a fellow family member. On the other hand, you don't want to be messing with an obscure (and forgettable) password, especially if you won't be using Linux every day.

So the choice about your password is really yours. If you're installing Linux in a corporate environment, however, you should follow these basic rules regarding passwords:

- Your password must be longer than two characters, but generally not more than eight characters long. In addition, it must begin with a lowercase letter.

- Always use a password longer than six characters. The longer the password, the harder it is to hack.

- Don't use a password based on personal information. You may think it's clever to use your dog's name as a password, but anyone who knows you can make an informed guess about your password. Similarly, don't use your spouse's name, your lover's name (however romantic it may be), your middle name, your job title, or any other readily available information about you.

- Don't use a word that can be found in a dictionary. Hackers have been known to throw a computer-based dictionary at login prompts, waiting for one of the words to open the door.

- Make sure your password is memorable, yet meaningless to anyone but you. Let's say that Kirby Puckett is your favorite baseball player. You were ecstatic the last time the Twins won the World Series. Put them together and you have **puck1991** as a password.

- There's a time-honored trick in the UNIX world to combine an easily remembered password with the vagaries of system security. First, choose a word that you know you'll remember, like the aforementioned **kirby**. Then look at your keyboard. For your real password, use the keys to the upper left of the keys for our word. In this case, the password becomes **u84g6**.

- Never send your password over electronic mail, no matter how many times lovely spies named Natasha ask you for it.

- Don't scrawl your password on a Post-It note and then stick it next to your terminal.

Changing Your Password with Passwd

If you do want to change your password, you'd use the **passwd** command (not to be confused with the **pwd** command, covered earlier in this chapter):

```
gilbert:~$ passwd
Changing password for kevinr
```

```
Enter old password:
Enter new password:
Re-type new password:
Password changed.
```

When you type in the old and new passwords, the characters won't be shown on the screen.

Linux Shells

A *shell* acts as the intermediary between you and the raw operating system, interpreting your commands into a form the operating system can understand. In addition, a shell adds much of the functionality we've discussed in this chapter, and adds even more when (or if) you start programming your own shell scripts.

As you'll remember from Chapter 2, you set up a shell when you add a new user to your system, the default being **bash**. How much emphasis you put on the shell depends on your UNIX background and needs. On the one hand, if you're used to working with a particular shell, you should use that shell (or its equivalent) in Linux. On the other hand, if you're not experienced with any particular shell, you should stick with the default shell under Linux, **bash**.

Several shells ship with Linux:

- **Bash**, or the Bourne Again SHell. This contribution from the Free Software Foundation is the default Linux shell, and probably the most popular Linux shell. **Bash** is compatible with the Bourne shell (**sh**), which means it will run scripts written initially for the Bourne shell. In addition, **bash** adds some popular features not found in the original Bourne shell, such as the **history** command (while will be covered later in this section) and command-line editing. By and large, you'll want to stick with **bash** unless you have some reason to switch.

- **Csh**, the C shell. This widely available shell is also popular, and since it's available on most UNIX platforms, you may be familiar with it. The C shell originated the notion of command history, but it doesn't offer command-line editing. However, if you've written a passel of C-shell scripts and want to use them on your Linux box, this is your only alternative.

- **Sh**, the original Bourne shell. It offers compatibility with **bash** and other Bourne scripts from other implementations of UNIX. However, the original Bourne shell does not offer command history or command-line editing.

- **Tcsh**, an enhanced version of the C shell, supporting command-line editing.

- **Ash**, a trimmed-down shell used for when memory is extremely tight.

- **Zsh**, the Z shell. Yet another Bourne-compatible shell.

- **Pdksh**, the public domain Korn shell (found in the /**contrib** directory).

To list the shell you're using, use the following command line:

```
gilbert:~$ echo $SHELL
bash
```

As noted, the **bash** shell is very popular on Linux, and unless there's a reason to switch, you'll probably want to stick with it. (It also is POSIX-compliant, if that means anything to you.) However, if you do want to switch shells, Linux includes a command to do so: **chsh**.

```
gilbert:~$ chsh
Enter password:
The current shell is: /bin/bash
You can choose one of the following:
1. /bin/sh
2. /bin/bash
3. /bin/tcsh
4. /bin/csh
5. /bin/zsh
6. /bin/ash
Enter a number between 1 and 6: 4
```

```
Shell changed.
```

Because of the overwhelming popularity of **bash**, we're going to focus on it in our discussion of the shell in this chapter.

Your Environment

If you've been around UNIX and the X Window System long enough, you know that phrases sometimes have two different meanings, depending on their context.

One such word under UNIX is *environment*. On the one hand, your environment refers to the various tools you've configured, like your shell and your home directory. On the other hand, in a discussion of shells, *environment* means something a little different—the variables used by your system.

Variables

In Linux parlance, variables allow a user to define information with both a name and a value that may change over the course of time. This allows a vast number of users to do the same thing while doing it in different locations (for example, the $PS1 variable allows people to set their own prompt, while all the system needs to know is that there is a $PS! variable), while giving a lot of flexibility to users.

Under Linux, there are two kinds of variables: *environment* variables and *shell* variables. The difference is simple: an environment variable is set by the system and is available to all users, while a shell variable is managed by the shell and available only when the user is logged in to the system and running the shell.

For the most part, you'll use shell variables, even on a single-user Linux installation. Setting these variables is a matter of using a simple formula:

```
$ VARIABLENAME=VARIABLEVALUE
```

where *variablename* is the name of the variable and *variablevalue* is the value of the variable. Some popular shell variables are listed in Table 5.11.

Table 5.11 Useful shell variables.

Variable	Meaning
HOME	Your home directory
LOGNAME	Your login name
PATH	Lists the directories the shell will look to when searching for a command
PS1	Prompt
SHELL	Your shell, of course

Many of these variables were set when you installed Linux. (It's probably dawned on you by now that the Setup program in Chapter 2 did a lot more work under the hood than you ever thought.) There are some others, such as PS1, that you might want to change.

Variables can be best explained with a simple example that you might run across. When you run a command, Linux doesn't automatically know where to find the file; instead, the shell looks through a series of directories that are defined by the PATH statement. (This is why you may run into an error message when you throw a program into a nonstandard directory and try to run it when this nonstandard directory is not your current directory.) To see what's defined by the PATH statement, use the following command line:

```
$ echo $PATH

/usr/bin:/usr/local/bin:usr/bin/X11:.
```

The colons separate the directories searched by the shell when in search of an executable. (As you might expect, the PATH variable lists the most common locations for commands.) The listing ends with a dot, which tells the shell to look in the current directory for the command. (Interestingly, Linux doesn't assume that the current directory shouldn't automatically be searched.)

Background Commands and Multitasking

The shell also provides the capability to run multiple commands at one time. In computer parlance, this is called *multitasking*, and it's one of the prime selling points of the Linux operating system.

Multitasking merely means that the system can do more than one thing at a given time, while having the ability to set priorities among these different tasks. While this may be something that should be easily achieved given the power of the personal computer, it's not, as Macintosh and PC users are still waiting for an operating system that's truly multitasking (as opposed to merely being able to run more than one task at a given time). With the emergence of the X Window System, this capability isn't as important as it once was for the end user, even though X relies heavily on commands run in the background, as you'll see in Chapter 6, but there may be times when you'll need to run commands in the background yourself from the command line.

Running a command in the background is a simple matter—you simply add an ampersand (**&**) to the end of the command line. In fact, earlier in this chapter, the following command line as used as an example:

```
gilbert:~$ find * -name test.bk &
```

 For the most part, you don't need to run commands in the background when running X Window.

Not every command need be run in the background—performance under Linux is pretty snappy for most tasks. Some commands that might take a long time to complete, such as **TeX**, should be run in the background, especially if you're formatting a large document.

Processes

These multiple requests to the shell are called *processes*. As these requests are made, the shell numbers them. These numbers are important if you ever want to kill a process. To see a list of processes, use the **ps** command:

```
gilbert:/$ ps
```

There is always a minimum of three processes running when you use the **ps** command: the shell process (in this case, **bash**), the **init** process (which is the mother of all processes), and the **ps** process itself. However, you'll rarely see a **ps** command with only three processes. When the Linux system boots, it usually starts a series of processes, mostly related to networking and communications. A program may generate a series of processes. If you're running the X Window System, your list of processes will be considerably longer.

Standard Input and Output

The shell, technically, is responsible for the UNIX practice of standard input and output. You've stumbled across the practice several times in this chapter (a review of the **cat** command shows that), but now it's time to formally lay out the practice.

In general, Linux programs assume that input comes from the keyboard, and output goes to the monitor. (That's why it's *standard*.) To deviate from this standard practice, you need to specify the difference. This is done on the command line, mostly through the use of greater-than (>) and less-than (<) symbols.

For starters, you can redirect standard input to use an existing file as input for a program, rather than keyboard entry. In this case, you must point input from the file to the command in the following manner:

```
gilbert:/$ cat < data
```

Here, the file **data** is input for the **cat** command, as opposed to the normal keyboard entry.

In another variation of standard input/output, you can send the output of a command to a file. This is a *very* useful variation, as many commands generate output that's too voluminous to read as it whizzes by on your screen. For example, you may want to redirect the output of the **ls** command to a file and then look at that output with a text editor or a viewer like **less**. In this case, you'd direct output to a file:

```
gilbert:/$ ls > listings
```

In addition, you've already seen how standard input and output can be used to append information to an existing file:

```
gilbert:~$ cat >> memo
```

Table 5.12 lists the major input/output commands.

Table 5.12 Standard shell input/output commands.

Symbol	Usage	Result
>	command > filename	Output from command is sent to filename
<	command < filename	Input from filename is sent to command
>>	command >> filename	Output from command is appended to filename
|	command1 | command2	Run command1, and then send the output to command2

There are many places where redirection comes in handy. For example, you can send output from the command directly to a printer when using standard input/output:

```
gilbert:~$ ls | lp
```

Pipes

The previous example is a *pipe*. Redirection can only work with files and commands; a file can be used as input for a command, and a file is the recipient of output from a command. With a *pipe*, you can join commands, sending the output from one command to another command. A pipe is rather simple:

```
gilbert:~$ command1 | command2
```

Here, the output from *command1* is piped to *command2*. (Naturally, the entire command line is called a *pipeline*.)

You can combine a number of pipes on a command line, as in the following:

```
gilbert:~$ ls *.c | grep arg | lp
```

This command line would search for all the files ending with .c in your current directory and send that list to the **grep** command, which searches these files for the string *arg*, and sends all of these matching lines to the **lp** command, which goes directly the printer to spit them out.

Command History

Bash supports *command history*, which tracks which commands you've run and lets you choose among them when you need to run another command. For example, you may want to reuse a command you've recently run, but don't want to go through the trouble of typing it in. In this case, you could use the **history** command and scroll between a list of previous commands:

```
gilbert:~$ history
1. cal
2. ln -s addresses /home/pat
3. ln addresses /home/eric
4. history
```

With this list, you can press the up and down arrow keys (↑ and ↓) to move between the previous command lines. If there's a long list of previous commands and you want to run a specific one of the screen, you can enter its number and the command will appear on the command line.

Other shells do offer this capability, albeit in different forms.

Minimal Completion

Though you may not use the facility too often, the **bash** shell's ability to complete words on a command line may be convenient for you. For example, we've been working a lot with a file named **test** throughout this chapter. (In fact, you're probably sick of hearing about it.) Since we know you want to see this file again, we want you to run the **cat** command to view it one more time. However, instead of typing out the entire name of the file, stop when you have a command line that looks like this (*without* pressing the **Enter** key):

```
gilbert:~$ cat te
```

At this point, press the **Tab** key. Magically, the rest of the word *test* will appear on the command line. This is because you've given **bash** enough information to actually complete the command line for you. **Bash** actually goes through the directory and finds the filename that logically matches the beginning of the information you've entered. This capability can also be used to complete commands.

In our case, however, there were two files that actually met our conditions. If you see this you'll need to type in the rest of the desired filename yourself.

The Elvis/Vi Text Editor

In Linux, the chore of text editing falls on a few different editors, and these vary greatly in terms of capabilities. As you'll recall from Chapter 2, we presented some advice as to which text editors to install. We're going to follow this up by focusing on one of the text editors we advised installing, **elvis** (which installs automatically), while saving a discussion of **emacs** for Chapter 7, after you've had some experience with the X Window System. We're not going to get into a religious war about **vi** or **emacs**, as we'll present explanations of both.

Using the Elvis Text Editor

The full-screen **elvis** text editor is a clone of the **vi** text editor, which appears on most (but not all) UNIX systems. (Since you're technically not using the same **vi** found on other UNIX systems, we'll use the proper terminology here and refer to **elvis**. However, whenever you see **elvis** as part of a command, you can substitute **vi** if that's what you're used to.)

Elvis is used for editing text (ASCII) files, which have a wide application in the Linux operating system. Text files are used for shell scripts, input to text processors, input for electronic mail, and programming source-code files. **Elvis** works from the command line, and you can invoke it without a file loaded:

```
gilbert:/$ elvis
```

or with a file loaded:

```
gilbert:/$ elvis textfile
```

Without a file, **elvis** will look something like Figure 5.3.

Figure 5.3 Elvis without a file loaded.

With a file loaded, **elvis** will look something like Figure 5.4.

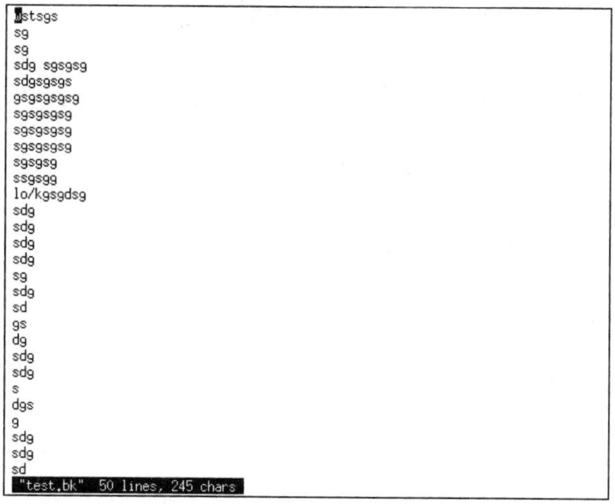

Figure 5.4 Elvis with a file loaded.

You can also invoke **elvis** using the following command lines:

```
gilbert:/$ vi
gilbert:/$ ex
gilbert:/$ view
gilbert:/$ input
```

These command-line variations can be a tad confusing, since they all call up the **elvis** editor. Basically, you can think of **vi** and **elvis** doing the same thing. If you run **view** with a file specified, you're starting **elvis** in read-only mode. (This is the equivalent of **elvis -R** run from the command line.) And if you run **input** with a file specified, you're starting **elvis** in input mode.

Input mode? Yes. **Elvis** works with two modes (as does **vi**): command and input (input mode is the same as insert mode, for you **vi** users out there). The two modes are pretty straightforward: command mode is used to send a command to **elvis**, while input mode creates the text making up the file. You'll notice the difference immediately if you load **elvis** from the command line and then assume you can begin typing immediately into the file—chances are good that you'll end up generating a series of annoying beeps, since **elvis** begins in command mode and won't accept most keyboard input. The exception is if you accidentally type **i**, which puts **elvis** in input mode.

When in input mode, you can go ahead and type away. When you do, you'll notice that **elvis** doesn't insert line breaks at the end of the line; the line shifts to the right, with previously input text scrolling off the page. Line breaks (in the form of an **Enter** keystroke) must be entered at the end of the line by you.

When you're ready to save the file, you must switch to command mode and enter the proper command. Pressing the **Esc** key will switch you to command mode; **elvis** by default won't tell you if it's in input or command mode. (If you're not sure you switched to command mode, go ahead and hit the **Esc** key again. If you are in command mode, the only damage you can do is generate an annoying beep.) To enter a command in **elvis**, you must preface it with a semicolon (:). For example, the following would save a file in **elvis**:

```
:w file
```

where *file* is the name of the file to be saved. To save a file and quit **elvis**, use the following command:

```
:wq file
```

where *file* is the name of the file to be saved. (The command **ZZ**—without a leading colon—does the same thing.) To quit **elvis** without saving a file, use the following command:

```
:q!
```

vi and Memory

There's one important thing to remember when dealing with **elvis**: As you edit a file, you're editing a file that's been loaded into your system's RAM (or, in **vi** parlance, a *buffer*). You're not making a single change to the copy of the file on your hard drive. You can delete all of the contents of the file loaded into RAM, or you can make a set of drastic changes, but the changes will be meaningless until you explicitly save the file to disk in the manner described in the previous section. If you're not happy with the changes, you can quit **elvis** without saving the file with the following command:

```
:q!
```

If you are happy with the changes, you save the file to disk, and the previous version of the file is gone. Poof.

Creating a Text File

Elvis can be as simple or as complex as you want to make it. On the one hand, it's really easy to create or edit a text file; all you need to know are the following steps:

- Launch **elvis** from the command line.
- Switch to insert mode by typing **i**.

- Type away.
- When you want to save the file and exit **elvis**, press the **Esc** key (which moves you to command mode), type :**wq** *filename* (use your own filename here), followed by **Enter**. The file is saved, and your command prompt reappears.

Moving through Your Document

If you're running **elvis** from the command line (as opposed to running it under the X Window System), you'll find that your mouse won't help you too much. If your documents get too long, you'll need to learn about some of the nifty shortcuts used to move through a document.

The easiest way to move through a document in **elvis** is to use the cursor and page-movement keys that exist on your keyboard (**PageUp**, **PageDown**). The **PageUp** and **PageDown** keys will move you up and down a single page; if there's less than a page of text to scroll to, you'll be placed at the beginning or the end of the file. Similarly, the up and down cursor keys (↑ and ↓) can be used to move the cursor through the document; if you press the up (↑) cursor key at the top of the screen, the previous line will scroll to the top.

However, there's one quirk with **elvis** (which maintains compatibility with **vi**, by the way): the left and right cursor keys (← and →) can be used only to maneuver through the current line of text. If you're at the end of the line and expect to use the right cursor key (→) to move to the following line, you'll be greeted by a beep and a cursor stuck on that last character, as only the up and down cursor keys (↑ and ↓) can be used to move between lines.

For the most part, the cursor and page-movement keys should serve your scrolling needs in **elvis**. However, should you require some additional capabilities, Table 5.13 list some useful additional cursor and scrolling commands.

Table 5.13 Elvis cursor and scrolling commands.

Command	Result
0 (zero)	Moves cursor to beginning of current line
b	Moves cursor to beginning of current word

Table 5.13 Elvis cursor and scrolling commands. (continued)

Command	Result
)	Moves cursor to end of document
$	Moves cursor to end of current line
e	Moves cursor to end of current word
w	Moves cursor to beginning of next word
*n*G	Moves cursor to beginning of line *n*
H	Moves cursor to beginning of file
G	Moves cursor to beginning of last line in file

Undoing the Last Command

Elvis can undo the last command (unless you've saved the file to disk, in which case all changes are set in stone); to do so, go to command mode with **Esc** and then type **u** (for *undo*).

More on Elvis

This is about all you'll need to know about **elvis**. To be honest, it's not a very complex application, and given your probable text-processing needs, there's little need to spend a ton of time mastering its every nuance. There are a lot of other options to **elvis**, but most of them are of interest only to the hardcore user. To see what additional actions you can take with **elvis**, use the following command line:

```
gilbert:~$ man elvis
```

Oh, and before we leave the discussion of **elvis**–we managed to cover the topic without making one cheap pun about the King.

Printing Files

When you install Linux, you were prompted about the location of the printer connected to your PC. If you're like 99 percebt of the PC users out there, you have a printed connected to your parallel port. If you're installing Linux on a UNIX network, you'll use the previously installed printer or set up a printer per the UNIX printing system (which varies considerably).

In this section, we'll assume you've installed the printer on the parallel port and told Linux of this installation. (If this isn't the case, check with a standard UNIX text to see how printers are treated on UNIX networks.) To see which printers Linux thinks are connected to the network, use **lpc**:

```
gilbert:/$ lpc
```

This command will present you with a series of options.

This section assumes that you're printing a file directly from the command line. Some other applications, primarily **ghostscript**, deal with printers on their own, which you'll learn in Chapter 7.

You'll use the standard **lpr** command to print files:

```
gilbert:/$ lpr filename
```

where *filename* is the name of the file you want to print. The command copies *filename* to a spool directory, and from there the file is actually printed. After you run the **lpr** command, you can edit the file you're printing, but the changes won't be reflected in the printed pages.

To check on the status of a print request, use the **lpq** command:

```
gilbert:/$ lpq
```

You'll be given information about the printer, the status of pending print jobs (what's being printed, what's next in line), and a job ID.

This ID becomes important if you want to cancel the print request; for this, you'd use the **lprm** command in conjunction with the job ID:

```
gilbert:/$ lprm 213
```

If you want to cancel *all* of the print requests (in other words, your printer jammed and you want to begin the print sequence from scratch), use the following command line:

```
gilbert:/$ lprm -
```

Summary

This long chapter covers the basic Linux commands and concepts, beginning with an explanation of how Linux organizes files and directories. There's nothing too obscure about these concepts, as Linux pretty much falls in line with the rest of the UNIX world. But these concepts are still worth reviewing, even if you're an experienced UNIX user.

A number of Linux commands are explained: **cd** (for moving between directories), **pwd** (which prints the current directory), **ls** (which lists the contents of the current directory or another specified directory), **mkdir** (which creates a directory), **rm** (which removes a file), **rmdir** (which removes a directory), and more.

Quite a lot of space is spent on permissions, since they can trip up even the most experienced UNIX user at times. Also covered are the commands that deal with permissions: **chmod** (which changes permissions) and **umask** (which defines how permissions are set when you create a file or directory).

How Linux deals with passwords is another important section of this chapter. When you installed Linux, you set up a password. Covered here is a further explanation of passwords, followed with coverage of the **passwd** command, used for changing passwords.

The many tools for viewing files are covered: **more** (used to scroll through a file), **less** (the more flexible successor to **more**), **head** (used to view the beginning of a file), **tail** (used to view the end of a file), and **od** (which displays an octal dump of a file).

The shell acts as the intermediary between you and the operating system. As such, the shell has a lot of power over your actions on the Linux operating system. It manages things like standard input and output, redirection, processes, and multitasking. The default shell under Linux is **bash**, from the Free Software Foundation.

The **elvis** text editor (a clone of **vi**) is a useful text editor. The basic operations in **vi** are covered, though the reader is advised to check out the online-manual pages for this command.

To print a file with Linux, use the **lpr** command. A set of utilities—
lpc, **lpq**, and **lprm**—assists in the task of managing print requests.

This chapter covers a lot of ground, but it barely scratches the surface
when it comes to useful Linux commands and concepts. In the next
chapter, we'll cover the X Window System and XFree86 configuration,
as well as a summary of some X applications.

Working with X on Linux

Topics in this chapter include:

- Setting up an X user account
- The X font server
- Setting a screen background image
- Configuring the **xterm** program
- X resource files
- The **fvwm** window manager
- Setting up an X login screen with **xdm**
- Troubleshooting X programs

Working With X In All the Wrong Places

This chapter covers working with X on Linux and covers basics about using X, X resource files, and troubleshooting X on Linux, as well as a nice set of handy utilities that come with Linux.

The X Window System is one of the neatest and also most complicated technologies to come from the UNIX world. It provided standardized graphics programs for UNIX in an era when each UNIX vendor had its own windowing system. X runs across networks and works on multiple operating systems, even DOS. X is also terribly difficult to configure and customize. We covered the tough task of configuring X in Chapter 4. In this chapter, we'll show you how to customize X to get the most out of your environment.

ON THE CD-ROM Luckily, the Slackware Linux defaults present you with a fairly reasonable default X environment. One of the first things you'll probably want to do, though, is customize the set of applications that appear when you start X.

Setting Up Your X Account

Depending on your preferences, there are a lot of different programs you may want to set up in your X environment. If you're new to UNIX, you may want to run a file manager program such as **xfm**, as shown in Figure 6.1.

If you're more familiar with UNIX, you'll probably want to run a number of shell windows with the program called **xterm**. **Xterm** presents a UNIX shell in a window, but allows you to specify the number of lines, the fonts and the colors used. You can also copy and paste between **xterm** windows, a handy feat with long, complicated UNIX command lines. (See the section on **xterm** below for more on this handy application.) Figure 6.2 shows **xterm**.

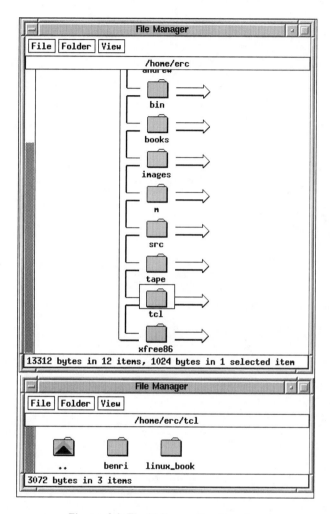

Figure 6.1 The X file manager in action.

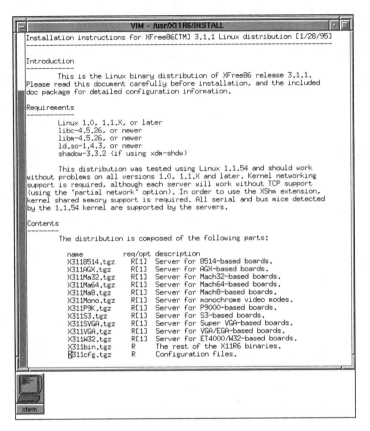

```
VIM - /usr/X11R6/INSTALL
Installation instructions for XFree86[TM] 3.1.1 Linux distribution [1/28/95]
---------------------------------------------------------------------------

Introduction
------------
        This is the Linux binary distribution of XFree86 release 3.1.1.
Please read this document carefully before installation, and the included
doc package for detailed configuration information.

Requirements
------------
        Linux 1.0, 1.1.X, or later
        libc-4.5.26, or newer
        libm-4.5.26, or newer
        ld.so-1.4.3, or newer
        shadow-3.3.2 (if using xdm-shdw)

        This distribution was tested using Linux 1.1.54 and should work
without problems on all versions 1.0, 1.1.X and later. Kernel networking
support is required, although each server will work without TCP support
(using the "partial network" option). In order to use the XShm extension,
kernel shared memory support is required. All serial and bus mice detected
by the 1.1.54 kernel are supported by the servers.

Contents
--------
        The distribution is composed of the following parts:

        name            req/opt description
        X3118514.tgz    R[1]    Server for 8514-based boards.
        X311AGX.tgz     R[1]    Server for AGX-based boards.
        X311Ma32.tgz    R[1]    Server for Mach32-based boards.
        X311Ma64.tgz    R[1]    Server for Mach64-based boards.
        X311Ma8.tgz     R[1]    Server for Mach8-based boards.
        X311Mono.tgz    R[1]    Server for monochrome video modes.
        X311P9K.tgz     R[1]    Server for P9000-based boards.
        X311S3.tgz      R[1]    Server for S3-based boards.
        X311SVGA.tgz    R[1]    Server for Super VGA-based boards.
        X311VGA.tgz     R[1]    Server for VGA/EGA-based boards.
        X311W32.tgz     R[1]    Server for ET4000/W32-based boards.
        X311bin.tgz     R       The rest of the X11R6 binaries.
        X311cfg.tgz     R       Configuration files.
```

Figure 6.2 The **xterm** program.

The **xterm** program is probably the most popular X program. It seems kind of funny to run a shell window program, which is what **xterm** is, in a fancy graphical environment. But we're still running X on top of Linux and still need access to the UNIX environment.

The neatest things about **xterm** are that you can:

- Run multiple shell windows (**xterms**) at once.
- Control the size of each **xterm** window.
- Control the fonts and colors used by the **xterm** program
- Copy and paste between **xterm** windows and other X programs.
- Use a scrollbar to view program output that has scrolled by.

With all of this, we find that **xterm** helps make the UNIX shell command line much more tolerable.

As we stated in Chapter 4, the file that controls which applications start up with X is the **.xinitrc** file in your home directory. You'll likely want to start a number of copies of **xterm** from this file.

Startup Applications

The **.xinitrc** file is a UNIX shell script and you can launch any number of X applications from this script. When the script exits, X quits. This usually means that when the last program in this file quits, the script quits, which quits X. For convenience, users generally start a window manager at the end of the file.

Before editing an **.xinitrc** file, it's important to maintain any assumptions that come with your system. Because of this, don't start from scratch. Instead, copy the system default **.xinitrc** file, **/usr/X11R6/lib/X11/xinit/xintrc** (with no leading period), to **.xinitrc** in your home directory. Remember to start the filename with a period (.) for the version in your home directory.

When you look at this file, you'll see some default shell commands in the beginning. You should normally leave these alone, unless you know what you're doing. (These lines set up the part of the environment that Slackware Linux expects.) What we usually do is modify the startup applications at the end.

Here's our customized **.xinitrc** file, originally based on the system file that comes with Linux:

```
#!/bin/sh
#
# Modified by Eric F. Johnson for Linux.
#
userresources=$HOME/.Xresources
usermodmap=$HOME/.Xmodmap
if [ x"$XWINHOME" != x ]; then
    XINIT_DIR=$XWINHOME/lib/X11/xinit
```

```
else
    XINIT_DIR=/usr/X11R6/lib/X11/xinit
fi
sysresources=$XINIT_DIR/.Xresources
sysmodmap=$XINIT_DIR/.Xmodmap

# merge in defaults and keymaps

if [ -f $sysresources ]; then
    xrdb -merge $sysresources
fi

if [ -f $sysmodmap ]; then
    xmodmap $sysmodmap
fi

if [ -f $userresources ]; then
    xrdb -merge $userresources
fi

if [ -f $usermodmap ]; then
    xmodmap $usermodmap
fi

# start some nice programs
xsetroot -solid bisque3
/usr/bin/X11/oclock -geom 100x100+0+6    &
/usr/bin/X11/xterm -ls -geom 80x24+3+372 &
/usr/bin/X11/xterm -ls -geom 80x48+264+13 &
exec fvwm
```

At the end of this file, we launch the following applications:

```
xsetroot -solid bisque3
/usr/bin/X11/oclock -geom 100x100+0+6   &
/usr/bin/X11/xterm -ls -geom 80x24+3+372 &
/usr/bin/X11/xterm -ls -geom 80x48+264+13 &
exec fvwm
```

Our **.xinitrc** file starts two **xterm** shell windows, a rounded clock program to tell the time **(oclock)**, sets the screen background color (via **xsetroot**) and then runs a window manager, **fvwm**. Note that we've changed the default **twm** window manager to **fvwm**, because we like that one better. (This is because **fvwm** looks and acts a lot more like the Motif window manager, **mwm**, we're used to with Hewlett-Packard and Silicon Graphics workstations at work.)

The **xsetroot** sets the screen background color. It can also set the screen background to a monochrome bitmap. (See the section on setting the screen background, below.) Our **.xinitrc** file sets the background color to **bisque3**. Other good screen background colors include **LightSteelBlue** and **MediumTurquoise**. You can see the whole list of X color names in the text file **/usr/lib/X11/rgb.txt**. This file contains a number of entries, such as:

```
255 239 213 PapayaWhip
255 235 205 BlanchedAlmond
 50 205  50 LimeGreen
```

Since the **.xinitrc** file is a UNIX shell script, all of the X programs (except for **xsetroot** and **fvwm**) run in the background. We run **xsetroot** in the foreground since it executes and quits quickly. We run **fvwm** in the background because when the **.xinitrc** shell script ends, X quits. If we ran all of these programs in the background, then you'd see X quickly start up and then exit. So, we arbitrarily pick one program to be the key program. When the key program quits, X quits. Since you always want a window manager around, using **fvwm** (or **twm** or **olwm**) as this key program is a good idea. Note that the default X setup uses an **xterm** program as this key program. We don't like that, since sometimes shells get locked up, and because we can never remember which **xterm** of the many on the screen is the key program.

We launch the **fvwm** window manager at the end of this file, and use the **exec** statement so that we don't have an extra copy of **sh** eating system resources.

NOTE

When we run **startx** after logging in, we see a number of applications launched from our **.xinitrc** file, as shown in Figure 6.3.

Figure 6.3 A set of startup X applications.

Starting X Automatically on Login

You'll need to type in **startx** after you login to get X and all these applications in your **.xinitrc** file started. If you don't like to enter in **startx** every time you log in, and you're sure that you really want to run X all the time when you login, you can put the **startx** command in your **.login** or **.profile** files (depending on the shell you use, **csh** or **ksh**). If you do, be sure that you're running from the console only. Otherwise, the **.login** or **.profile** files will error out if they get run from elsewhere (such as when you login over a serial line or from another virtual terminal).

The way to check for this is to check the result of the **tty** program. The **tty** program returns the current device file used for your terminal. When run from an **xterm** shell window, **tty** will print out something like **/dev/ttyp1** (for the first pseudo terminal device). But, when run from the console (from the first virtual terminal), **tty** will print out **/dev/tty1**. When run from the second virtual terminal, **tty** prints out **/dev/tty2**. So, we can check for **/dev/tty1**.

To do this, we can enter **tty** at the console (before starting X):

```
$ tty
/dev/tty1
```

Armed with this information, you can edit your **.login** file (presuming you use the C shell, **csh**, as your shell) to add the following lines:

```
if ( `tty` == "/dev/tty1" ) then
    startx
endif
```

This will start up X when you login at the console. You can also set up your account to log you out when you quit X. The vast majority of the time, we begin X at login and quit X when we want to log out. If this fits your pattern, you can change the **.login** file to contain the following:

```
if ( `tty` == "/dev/tty1" ) then
    startx
    logout
endif
```

Table 6.1 lists some common X programs.

Table 6.1 Common X programs on Linux.

Program	Use
iclass	C++ class browser from InterViews
oclock	Displays the current time in a round clock window
workman	Audio CD playing program
xcalc	A primitive calculator
xedit	Text editor
xeyes	The eyeballs follow your mouse
xfd	X font displayer—shows the characters in a font
xfm	A file manager for Linux
xfontsel	Program to help you choose a font
xload	Shows CPU load in a bar chart
xmahjongg	One of the better X games
xman	X front-end to UNIX online manual pages
xmh	X front-end to MH mail program
xsetroot	Changes screen background color
xtetris	Another game
xv	Displays GIF, TIFF, JPEG, and other image files

You can see these programs and more in the **/usr/bin/X11** and **/usr/openwin/bin** directories on your Linux system. Some of these programs, like **iclass**, come as part of an optional package (InterViews in this case), which you must have installed with Linux. We generally recommend you install all X-related packages.

The X Font Server

The X font server is a special program that can scale fonts. This ability dramatically increases the already-prolific set of X fonts available on your system (use the **xlsfonts** command to list these fonts).

To get the font server up and running, you must:

• Configure the font server and tell it where to get fonts.

- Configure the font server to start up before X does.
- Configure the X server to communicate with the font server.

To configure the font server, we need to tell it where to find the scalable fonts. Luckily, Linux comes with a workable preconfigured file, **/usr/X11R6/lib/X11/fs/config**.

To start the font server, you use the **xfs** (short for X font server) command. Enter the following command as *root*:

```
# xfs -port 7000 &
```

This uses the default configuration file, **/usr/X11R6/lib/X11/fs/config**, and runs on TCP/IP port 7000 (an arbitrary port to which the X font server defaults).

Once started, we can verify that the font server is running by using the **fsinfo** command:

```
gilbert:/$ fsinfo -server hostname:port
```

You need to fill in the *hostname* and *port* number. For example, with a hostname of *eric* and the default port number of 7000, the command would be:

```
gilbert:/$ fsinfo -server eric:7000
```

You should see output like the following:

```
name of server: eric:7000
version number: 2
vendor string:  X Consortium
vendor release number:  6000
maximum request size:   16384 longwords (65536 bytes)
number of catalogues:   1
        all
Number of alternate servers: 0
number of extensions:   0
```

Once you verify that the font server is running, you can then set up XFree86 to communicate with the font server. This is necessary so that X applications can take advantage of the font server's fonts.

To get the X server ready to accept the font server, you need to adjust its font path, or *fp* for short. Enter the following commands:

```
gilbert:/$ xset +fp tcp/eric:7000
gilbert:/$ xset fp rehash
```

In your case, you need to replace *eric* with your system's hostname. The first command tells the X server to use a TCP/IP port as a sort of font directory. The *tcp/hostname:port* syntax is the standard way to do this. The second command tells the X server to query again for all the available fonts.

If you're running **xdm** (see below), you should stop that, verify that things work manually and then set up **xdm** again. Problems with the font server may cause X to quit. If X quits, this may prevent an X-based login, leaving you in an unhappy situation.

Setting a Screen Background Image

In X, you can display a bitmap image, a solid color, or a graphics file as your screen background, depending on the program you use to accomplish this task.

The **xsetroot** program, mentioned above, can be used to set the screen background to a solid color or to a monochrome bitmap, stored in an X bitmap file. The syntax for setting the screen background to a bitmap is:

```
gilbert:/$ xsetroot -bitmap filename -fg fore -bg back
```

where *filename* is the name of the file containing the bitmap, and the *fore* and *back* are optional parameters that set the image's foreground and background color, respectively. Use the color names from the **rgb.txt** file explained above.

For example, if you have an X bitmap file named **prisoner.xb**, you can set it to be tiled over the screen background with the following command:

```
gilbert:/$ xsetroot -bitmap prisoner.xb
```

You'll see a result like that shown in Figure 6.4.

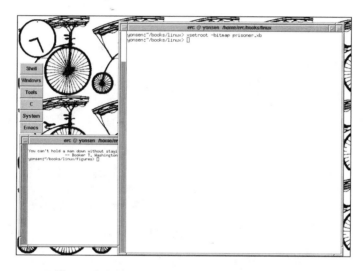

Figure 6.4 Using a bitmap as the screen background.

Because the image looks good in black and white, we skip the *-fg* and *-bg* options to **xsetroot** (and leave the famous penny-farthing bicycle alone).

If, instead of an X bitmap file, you have a GIF, TIFF, or JPEG image, you can use either **xv** or **xli** (short for X load image) to display the image. Both of these programs are meant to display an image in a window of their own, but with special command-line parameters, you can set it up to display an image on the screen background (technically called the *root window* in X).

For **xli**, use the following syntax:

```
gilbert:/$ xli -center -onroot filename
```

where filename is the name of the file you want to display.

For **xv**, use the following syntax:

```
gilbert:/$ xv -quit -root -max filename
```

where *filename* is the name of the file you want to display.

When you run this command on an image file, you'll see a result like the one in Figure 6.5.

Figure 6.5 Using **xv** or **xli** to set an image file for the screen background.

With complicated color images, you can soon fill up your colormap from the screen background image. This may lead to color flashing as X programs run out of colors in the default colormap and therefore create their own colormaps.

Configuring The Xterm Program

The most common X program you're likely to run is called **xterm**, which we've discussed previously in this chapter. **Xterm** is shown in Figure 6.6.

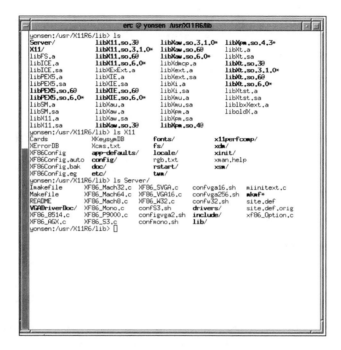

```
                    erc @ yonsen  /usr/X11R6/lib
yonsen:/usr/X11R6/lib> ls
Server/          libX11.so.3@        libXaw.so.3.1.0*    libXpm.so.4.3*
X11/             libX11.so.3.1.0*    libXaw.so.6@        libXt.a
libFS.a          libX11.so.6@        libXaw.so.6.0*      libXt.sa
libICE.a         libX11.so.6.0*      libXdmcp.a          libXt.so.3@
libICE.sa        libXExExt.a         libXext.a           libXt.so.3.1.0*
libPEX5.a        libXIE.a            libXext.sa          libXt.so.6@
libPEX5.sa       libXIE.sa           libXi.a             libXt.so.6.0*
libPEX5.so.6@    libXIE.so.6@        libXi.sa            libXtst.a
libPEX5.so.6.0*  libXIE.so.6.0*      libXmu.a            libXtst.sa
libSM.a          libXau.a            libXmu.sa           liblbxXext.a
libSM.sa         libXaw.a            libXpm.a            liboldX.a
libX11.a         libXaw.sa           libXpm.sa
libX11.sa        libXaw.so.3@        libXpm.so.4@
yonsen:/usr/X11R6/lib> ls X11
Cards            XKeysymDB           fonts/              x11perfcomp/
XErrorDB         Xcms.txt            fs/                 xdm/
XF86Config       app-defaults/       locale/             xinit/
XF86Config.auto  config/             rgb.txt             xman.help
XF86Config.bak   doc/                rstart/             xsm/
XF86Config.eg    etc/                twm/
yonsen:/usr/X11R6/lib> ls Server/
Imakefile        XF86_Mach32.c   XF86_SVGA.c     confvga16.sh    miinitext.c
Makefile         XF86_Mach64.c   XF86_VGA16.c    confvga256.sh   mkmf*
README           XF86_Mach8.c    XF86_W32.c      confw32.sh      site.def
VGADriverDoc/    XF86_Mono.c     confS3.sh       drivers/        site.def.orig
XF86_8514.c      XF86_P9000.c    configvga2.sh   include/        xf86_Option.c
XF86_AGX.c       XF86_S3.c       confmono.sh     lib/
yonsen:/usr/X11R6/lib> []
```

Figure 6.6 The **xterm** program.

Even though it's called **xterm,** the program isn't really a terminal emulator. It basically just provides you with a UNIX shell window. If you're interested in serial communications see Chapter 8.

Controlling the Size of the Xterm Window

The simplest way to control the size of an **xterm** window is through the *-geometry* command-line parameter:

```
gilbert:/$ xterm -geometry WidthxHeight &
```

With this parameter, the *Width* is the number of characters wide, almost always 80, and the *Height* is the number of lines to use. We find that 40 is a good number (the default is 24 lines).

Just about every X program supports the *-geometry* command-line parameter, but virtually every X program treats the *-geometry* command-line parameter different than **xterm** (**xterm** is the main exception, in other words). While you specify the width and height in terms of characters with **xterm**, just about every other X program treats the *-geometry* as the size in pixels. This is important to note if you create some really small windows.

For example, the command to start **xterm** with 80 columns (the default) and 40 lines is:

```
$ xterm -geometry 80x40 &
```

With the *-geometry* command-line parameter you can also specify the starting location, in pixels. The full syntax is:

```
-geometry WidthxHeight+X+Y
```

In this case, X and Y specify the location of the upper-left corner of the program's window, in pixels. In X, the origin is also in the upper left corner of the screen, so the following command creates an **xterm** window offset 10 pixels (in both X and Y) from the upper -left corner:

```
gilbert:/$ xterm -geometry 80x40+10+10 &
```

You can skip the size (width and height) or the location (x and y). The following are all valid commands:

```
gilbert:/$ xterm -geometry 80x40 &
gilbert:/$ xterm -geometry +10+10 &
gilbert:/$ xterm &
```

Setting Up a Scrollbar

By default, **xterm** does not provide for a scrollbar, although one is available. You can use the *-sb* command-line parameter:

```
gilbert:/$ xterm -sb &
```

This creates a scrollbar in the **xterm** window (usually in the left side).

 The **xterm** scrollbar is kind of tricky. Use the middle mouse button to move the position to the place you want. The right mouse button (assuming you have a three-button mouse), moves back, while the left mouse button moves forward. We almost always just use the middle mouse button.

In addition to the *-sb* command-line parameter, you can request a scrollbar for **xterm** in an X resource file.

X Resource Files

X resource files provide a powerful mechanism to customize just about every X application. There are a lot of options both within a resource file and the locations on disk in which you can place these resources files. Because many options conflict, it's easy to get lost in all the details.

Stripped to its basics, an X resource file is an ASCII text file that specifies some option for a program or programs. For example, you can specify in an X resource file that all **xterm** programs should start up with the scrollbar turned on, which we'll show how to do below. You can also control fonts, colors and a lot of the text displayed by most X programs.

To set up the scrollbar commands for **xterm** in a resource file, create a file named **XTerm** (note the capitalization) in your home directory. Both the file name, **XTerm**, and the location (your home directory) are essential. Put in the following lines:

```
XTerm*scrollBar: True
XTerm*saveLines: 1000
```

The above X resource commands tell **xterm** to use a scrollbar and to save 1000 lines in its scroll buffer.

Save this file and start another **xterm** program. You should see a scrollbar.

For more on X resource files, see the book list in Appendix A.

Controlling Fonts and Colors

Like most options, you can control **xterm**'s choice of fonts and colors from both command-line parameters and from X resource files. What we usually do is set up the options we always want in an X resource file and then use the command-line parameters only for options we rarely need.

Normally, we're happy with **xterm**'s color defaults: black text on a white background. It's the font we'd like to change. By default, **xterm** uses the font named *fixed*, a fixed-character-size font (as opposed to a proportional font). We find this font far too small, so we'd like to use a larger font.

For setting the font, you can use the *-font* command-line parameter or set the *font* resource. To do the latter, you can add the following line to your **XTerm** file created above:

```
XTerm*font: -*-courier-medium-r-normal—14-140-75-75-m-90-*
```

This sets up a much more pleasing (to our eyes at least) and larger font for **xterm**.

To get a list of the available fonts, use the program **xlsfonts**, which will present you with a huge listing. For **xterm**, you want a fixed-width font. The courier fonts typically are fixed-width, as are the Lucida typewriter fonts. In the very long font names, the fixed-width fonts should have an *m* or *c* as shown below after the two 75s:

```
-adobe-courier-medium-r-normal—14-140-75-75-m-90-iso8859-1
```

As usual, to test this, save the **XTerm** file and start another **xterm** program.

For our XTerm file, we set the following resources:

```
!
!  XTerm resource file
!
XTerm*foreground:  black
XTerm*cursorColor: black
XTerm*background:  white
```

```
XTerm*scrollBar:    True
XTerm*saveLines:    1000
XTerm*font: -*-courier-medium-r-normal—14-140-75-75-m-90-*
```

Lines beginning with an exclamation mark (!) are comments.

We list the most-used **xterm** command-line parameters in Table 6.2.

Table 6.2 Commonly used xterm command-line parameters.

Parameter	Meaning
-bg *color*	Sets background color; defaults to white
-cr *color*	Sets color of text cursor; defaults to black
-display *hostname:0*	Sets name of X display to which to connect
-e *program [args]*	Runs *program* instead of shell
-fg *color*	Sets foreground color; defaults to black
-fn *fontname*	Uses the given font
-font *fontname*	Uses the given font
-geometry *geom*	Uses given size and location
-ls	Turns shell into login shell
-sb	Turns on scrollbar

Copying and Pasting Between Xterm Windows

One of the best benefits of **xterm** over the console terminal is that you can copy and paste text between **xterm** windows. This is very handy if you edit documents. You can view one document in one **xterm** window and edit another in a different **xterm** window, copying and pasting between them both.

Xterm is highly configurable, but in the default configuration, you select text by holding down the left mouse button and dragging over the text you want to select. Double clicking over a word selects just that word. Triple clicking anywhere in a line selects the entire line.

To paste, press the middle mouse button. The text will be inserted just as if you typed it.

Xterm just presents a shell window. Inside the **xterm** window, you run text-based shell programs, few of which know anything about the mouse and selecting text. Therefore, you have to ensure that the program you run within the **xterm** window is ready for the pasted text. In the **elvis** text editor, for instance, you should enter input mode by typing i in command mode.

Elvis does not support middle-mouse button pastes. This is highly annoying. To paste in **elvis**, you must hold down the **Shift** key while you press the middle mouse button.

Our fix is to use a different **vi** clone that comes with Linux, called **vim**. **Vim** fully supports mouse pasting in **xterm** windows without the hassle of **elvis**.

Other Shell Window Programs

In addition to the ubiquitous **xterm**, Linux ships with a few other shell programs, including **color_xterm**, **rxvt**, and **shelltool**.

If you want a shell with color, use **color_xterm**. This program acts just like **xterm**, but presents a lot more color. For example, when you make a directory listing with **ls**, **color_xterm** presents directories in one color and ordinary files in another.

The **rxvt** program is very similar to **xterm**. Many claim that **rxvt** uses a smaller memory footprint than **xterm**, but we find its quirks aren't worth the difference (particularly with Linux shared libraries, which reduce **xterm**'s memory footprint to a reasonable level).

If you use Open Look applications on a Sun system at work, you will find yourself right at home with **shelltool**, found in **/usr/openwin/bin**.

You must have loaded the Open Look applications when you installed Linux to have this program. We recommend you install these programs, which also include the **olwm** and **olvwm** window managers.

All in all, we tend to only use **xterm** instead of other shell window programs, because **xterm** remains constant on all the UNIX systems we use, at home and at work.

The Fvwm Window Manager

The window manager is one of the most important applications you'll run, as it sits around each and every application window on the screen and can influence how the windows work. The *de facto* window manager for Linux is called **fvwm**.

This window manager provides a great deal of control over the way you interact with X, especially since **fvwm** supports a host of configuration options. While you can run any window manager you want, **fvwm** seems the most popular in the Linux world. In addition, it's not documented in many places or X books, so we'll show you how to set up **fvwm** for your Linux system.

You can run only one window manager at a time.

Configuring Fvwm

Most window managers under X support a configuration file. Usually, this file is located in a dot file in your home directory. Most window managers also follow a naming convention for their configuration file. For the **mwm** window manager, the file is named **.mwmrc**. For **twm**, it's **.twmrc**. For **fvwm**, it's **.fvwmrc**.

At start-up time, **fvwm** will look for your customizations in a file named **.fvwmrc** in your home directory. If you have no **.fvwmrc** file (which is likely when you start out), **fvwm** will look for a system file named **/usr/lib/X11/fvwm/system.fvwmrc**. If that file, too, is missing, **fvwm** will exit.

You may find that the **fvwm** system directory is **/var/X11R6/lib/fvwm** rather than **/usr/lib/X11/fvwm**.

Because **fvwm** is a very complex window manager, you should copy the **system.fvwmrc** file, or one of the example files, to your home directory and name this file **.fvwmrc**. By starting from a working example, you'll find it a lot easier than creating a **.fvwmrc** file from scratch.

Once you find the **fvwm** system directory, you'll see a number of sample configurations in the **sample_configs** directory. It's easiest to configure **fvwm** from a working model. So you can either copy the **system.fvwmrc** or one of the files in the **sample_configs** directory. We happen to like the **4Dwm.fvwmrc** file, as this was the closest to the Motif window manager behavior that looked good. (There's also a **mwm.fvwmrc** in the directory, but the **4Dwm.fvwmrc** file, based on Silicon Graphics' **4Dwm** window manager, looked more professional.) See the section below on a Motif-like look and feel for more on this.

Once you have copied a working configuration file into your home directory, the next step is to start customizing.

The **.fvwmrc** file is very long, so we'll provide an overview of the areas you're most likely to customize, and then provide an example **.fvwmrc** file—a very long example—that you can use. Just browsing this example should give you plenty of ideas. In addition to our example, you may want to look at the **fvwm** example files mentioned above and also look at **fvwm**'s online-manual page.

In the **.fvwmrc** file, the order of items is very important. It's best to start with a working example and then search for the items we mention. Change the item's value, but leave the item itself in the same relative position in the **.fvwmrc** file.

Configuring Fonts and Colors

The foremost area you'll likely customize in the **.fvwmrc** file is fonts and colors.

Each window manager, **fvwm** included, allows only one application at a time to get keyboard input. This window, usually called the *active window* or the *keyboard focus window*, is usually highlighted by the window manager. In the **.fvwmrc** file, the **HiForeColor** sets the text foreground color for the active window's title. The **HiBackColor** sets the active titlebar color. We use the following colors:

```
HiForeColor   Yellow
HiBackColor   RoyalBlue
```

 Window managers usually support two policies for selecting which window is made active: click-to-focus and focus-follows-mouse. **Fvwm** defaults to activating whatever window is underneath the mouse. To change this to click-to-focus mode, uncomment the following line in the **.fvwmrc** file:

```
#ClickToFocus
```

Since a # character is a comment in the **.fvwmrc** file, simply remove the #:

```
ClickToFocus
```

For fonts, we use the following:

```
Font         -*-helvetica-medium-r-*-*-12-*-*-*-*-*-*-*
WindowFont   -*-helvetica-bold-r-*-*-12-*-*-*-*-*-*-*
IconFont     -*-helvetica-medium-r-*-*-10-*-*-*-*-*-*-*
```

The asterisks (*) in the font names are wildcards. We only specify the minimum amount of data necessary to get Helvetica fonts at 10 and 12 point.

Testing Your Fvwm Configuration

Now that we've made a change to our **.fvwmrc** file, it's time to test our new configuration. To do this, you need to restart **fvwm**. You can either quit X and restart everything or call up **fvwm**'s root window menu where hopefully you'll find a restart **fvwm** menu choice. (This choice may be on a submenu.) You can access **fvwm**'s root menu by holding down the left mouse button over the screen background.

Turning Off the Virtual Desktop

Both XFree86 and **fvwm** provide the ability to use virtual screen space, screen space beyond the confines of your monitor's resolution. XFree86 calls this a *virtual screen*, and **fvwm** calls this a *virtual desktop*.

These two methods tend to conflict and frankly, we don't really have much use for either kinds of virtual screen space, as we don't run that many X applications at once and we can iconify windows to get them out of the way. Furthermore, it's easy to accidentally warp to one of **fvwm**'s virtual desktop spaces, which tends to get annoying.

Because of all this, we turn off **fvwm**'s virtual desktop in our .fvwmrc file with the following:

```
DeskTopSize 1x1
```

You specify the desktop value in units of the screen size. 1x1 means no virtual desktop.

Placing Icons

Fvwm's defaults result in bizarrely placed icons, with hidden icons strewn throughout the screen. We want to change this. To do so, use the **IconBox** command in the **.fvwmrc** file. We like our icons to go across the top of the screen but start from an offset of about 130 pixels, to leave room for the round **oclock** window we place in the upper left corner of the screen. (See our .xinitrc file, above.)

The **IconBox** specifies a rectangular area where you want the icons to appear. Here's our area:

```
IconBox 130 5 600 150
```

Configuring the Good Stuff

Fvwm also supports something called *modules*, add-ons that you can configure and run. The most-popular add-on is called **GoodStuff**, and it places a window on your screen from which you can launch applications or menus, sort of like a toolbar or the Windows 95 command area at the bottom of the screen.

With **GoodStuff** on, our start-up screen looks like the picture shown in Figure 6.7.

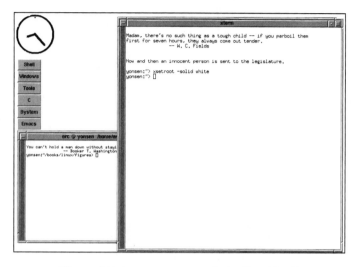

Figure 6.7 At start-up time with the **GoodStuff**.

You can turn on the **GoodStuff** in a number of ways. First, **fvwm** must be able to find this module, so you need to set up a **ModulePath**:

```
ModulePath /var/X11R6/lib/fvwm:/usr/bin/X11:/usr/local/bin
```

Then you can turn on the **GoodStuff**:

```
# Turn on the GoodStuff toolbar.
Module GoodStuff
```

You can alternatively fill in the **InitFunction** section:

```
Function "InitFunction"
    Module  "I" GoodStuff
EndFunction
```

Either way works. The **InitFunction** section allows you to specify a set of X applications to launch at **fvwm** startup as well. Since this overlaps with the **.xinitrc** file, we typically skip starting any applications in the **InitFunction** section.

Toward a Motif-Like Look and Feel

One of **fvwm**'s claims to fame is that it is a free window manager that looks a lot like the Motif window manager, **mwm**, used on just about every commercial version of UNIX. Unfortunately, while **fvwm** looks like Motif, it doesn't act as much like **mwm** as you'd expect. The similar look of **fvwm** can fool you.

Take heart, though, as there are a few things you can do to make **fvwm** look and act more like **mwm**. Take a look at our **.fvwmrc** file, below, and you'll see a lot of **mwm**-like behavior.

Putting It All Together

To put all this together, the following is our **.fvwmrc** file. You can use this as a base for your modifications. We don't expect you to type this in. Instead, we provide it as a source of ideas and information for configuring **fvwm** to your liking:

```
# Eric's .fvwmrc file, modified from 4Dwm example.
#
# Unfortunately, order does matter in this file.
# The correct order for inserting configurations is:
# 1. Colors
# 2. Assorted configuration parameters such as
#    ClickToFocus, or MWMBorders
# 3. Path setup (ModulePath, PixmapPath, IconPath)
# 4. Style settings, including the default
#    style Style "*" ...
# 5. InitFunction and ResetFunction definitions.
# 6. Other Functions. Functions cannot be forward
#    referenced from other functions, but they can
#    be backward referenced.
# 7. Menus definitions. Same caveats about forward
#    referencing
# 8. Key and Mouse Bindings.
# 9. Module options.
```

```
# The order of steps 5, 6, and 7 is not critical,
# as long as there are no forward references to
# functions or menus.

# If you get it wrong, the most common problem is
# that color or font settings are ignored

###################################################
# Modified by Eric Johnson, from the 4Dwm example.
#
# Here's nation@rocket.sanders.lockheed.com's MWM
# like configuration, # with several changes to make
# it more 4Dwm like by tabaer@magnus.acs.ohio-state.edu.
# Perhaps some mwm fans can fix this up a little, and
# mail the changes to:
#
#        nation@rocket.sanders.lockheed.com
#
###################################################
# Set up the colors.
#
# This is used for non-selected windows,
# menus, and the panner

# 4Dwm is an mwm derivative, so this should look as
# "mwm" as possible without sacrificing any of the
# functionality I like. —tabaer@magnus
MWMButtons
MWMDecorHints
MWMFunctionHints
MWMMenus

# Placement. Use fvwm's defaults.
SmartPlacement
```

```
RandomPlacement

#
# GoodStuff is a "module" of fvwm that places
# a toolbar window on the screen.
#
ModulePath /var/X11R6/lib/fvwm:/usr/bin/X11:/usr/local/bin

# You must specify the proper size.
*GoodStuffGeometry 62x181+5+120
*GoodStuffColumns    1
*GoodStuffFont   -adobe-helvetica-bold-r-*-*-12-*-*-*-*-*-*-*
*GoodStuffFore   Black
*GoodStuffBack   LightGray

# A minor complaint about the GoodStuff button:
# the GoodStuff window doesn't size itself
# width-wise correctly, so it chops off the
# last letters on a couple of the button labels.
# I'd like to see GoodStuff with the button text
# left-justified and the icons right-justified,
# like in SGI's toolchest, but I'll have to hack that
# out myself when I get the time. Also, is there any
# way to get the popup menus to cascade off the buttons,
# rather than appearing over them? —tabaer@magnus
#
#*GoodStuff Button  Icon  Command
*GoodStuff   Shell   "" Exec  "" xterm -ls -geom 80x32 &
*GoodStuff   Windows "" PopUp "Windows"  Windows
*GoodStuff   Tools   "" PopUp "Tools"    Tools
*GoodStuff   C       "" Popup "C"     C
*GoodStuff   System  "" PopUp "System"    System
*GoodStuff   Emacs   "" Exec  "" emacs -i &

#
```

```
# Note: The names must all match above,
# e.g., C, "C" and C.-Eric
#
# this is used for the selected window
HiForeColor        Yellow
HiBackColor        RoyalBlue


PagerBackColor     #5c54c0


# Menu colors
MenuForeColor      Black
MenuBackColor      grey
MenuStippleColor   SlateGrey


##################################################
# Now the fonts - one for menus/icons,
# another for window titles
Font         -*-helvetica-medium-r-*-*-12-*-*-*-*-*-*-*
WindowFont  -*-helvetica-bold-r-*-*-12-*-*-*-*-*-*-*
IconFont     -*-helvetica-medium-r-*-*-10-*-*-*-*-*-*-*
##################################################
# Set up the major operating modes
#
# Normally, we'll be in focus-follows mouse
# mode, but uncomment this for mwm-style
# click-to-focus
#ClickToFocus


# Place icons near the top left, but leave
# space for the clock window.
IconBox 130 5 600 150


ButtonStyle 1 50x22
ButtonStyle 2 50x50
ButtonStyle 4 22x22
```

```
################################################
# Virtual Desktop and Pager

# Set the desk top size in units of
# physical screen size. A 1x1 size
# means no virtual desktop.
DeskTopSize 1x1

# And the reduction scale used for
# the panner/pager.
DeskTopScale 32

# Flip by whole pages on the edge
# of the screen.
EdgeScroll 100 100


################################################
# Icon paths
#
# The pixmap dir does not exist on many systems-Eric
#PixmapPath /usr/include/X11/pixmaps/
IconPath   /usr/include/X11/bitmaps/


################################################
# Set the decoration styles and window options
# Order is important!!!!
# If compatible styles are set for a single
# window in multiple Style commands, then the
# styles are ORed together. If conflicting styles
# are set, the last one specified is used.

# These commands should be defined before any
# menus or functions are defined,
# and before the internal pager is started.
```

```
# Change the default width.
Style "*" BorderWidth 1, HandleWidth 7, Color Black/LightGray,Icon
xlogo32


Style "Fvwm*"      NoTitle, NoHandles, Sticky,
WindowListSkip,BorderWidth 0
Style "Fvwm Pager" StaysOnTop
Style "FvwmPager"  StaysOnTop
Style "FvwmBanner" StaysOnTop
Style "GoodStuff"  NoTitle, NoHandles, Sticky,
WindowListSkip,BorderWidth 0
Style "*lock"      NoTitle, NoHandles, Sticky, WindowListSkip
Style "matlab"     StartsOnDesk 3
Style "xterm"      Icon terminal, Color black/grey


#################################################


# Stuff to do at start-up


Function "InitFunction"
    Module  "I" GoodStuff
EndFunction


Function "RestartFunction"
    Exec    "I" xsetroot -solid "#266294"
    Module  "I" GoodStuff
EndFunction


#################################################
# Now define the menus - defer bindings until
# later. The first three menus are very basic
# and are used in several places.
# —tabaer@magnus


# This menu is invoked as a sub-menu - it allows
# you to quit, restart, or switch to another WM.
```

```
Popup "Quit-Verify"
    Title   "Really Quit Fvwm?"
    Nop "This may log you out!"
    Nop ""
    Quit    "Yes, Really Quit"
    Restart "Restart fvwm" fvwm
    Restart "Start twm" /usr/bin/X11/twm
    Restart "Start olwm"    /usr/openwin/bin/olwm
    Restart "Start olvwm"   /usr/openwin/bin/olvwm
    Nop ""
    Nop "No, Don't Quit"
EndPopup


PopUp   "WindowManagers"
    Restart "Restart fvwm" fvwm
    Restart "Start twm" /usr/bin/X11/twm
    Restart "Start olwm"    /usr/openwin/bin/olwm
    Restart "Start olvwm"   /usr/openwin/bin/olvwm
EndPopUp


# This menu checks to make sure you REALLY want to log out,
# assuming killing the WM will kick you out of X.
PopUp   "Logout-Verify"
    Title   "Do You REALLY want to log out?"
    Nop ""
    Quit    "Yes, log me out."
    Nop "No, cancel that."
EndPopUp


#
# A menu for the GoodStuff that has a bunch of tools
# I use a lot for X software development.
# -Eric
PopUp "C"
    Title   "Software Development"
```

```
     Nop       ""
     Exec      "Online Manuals"    exec xman &
     Exec      "Colormap Viewer"   exec xcmap &
     Exec      "Bitmap Editor"    exec bitmap &
     Exec      "Clipboard"     exec xclipboard &
     Exec      "Event Tracker"    exec xev &
EndPopUp


# A menu of various and sundry background graphics.
PopUp "Pixmaps"
     Title   "Backgrounds"
     Nop ""
     Exec    "Bisque"    exec xsetroot -solid bisque3
     Exec    "SlateGrey" exec xsetroot -solid SlateGrey
     Exec    "Blue"      exec xsetroot -solid "#266294"
EndPopUp



PopUp   "Windows"
     Title    "Windows"
     Nop ""
     PopUp   "Set Background"    Pixmaps
     Nop "Set Screen Saver"
     PopUp   "Window Managers"   WindowManagers
     Nop ""
     CirculateUp "Shuffle Up"
     CirculateDown   "Shuffle Down"
     Refresh "Refresh All"
EndPopUp


PopUp   "Tools"
     Title    "Tools"
     Nop ""
     Exec    "File Manager"  exec xfm &
     Exec    "Calculator"    exec xcalc &
```

```
    Exec    "Clipboard" exec xclipboard &
EndPopUp


# Note: You must have installed the Open Look
# apps to run meminfo. -Eric


PopUp   "System"
    Title "System
    Nop ""
    Exec    "System Load"   exec xload &
    Exec    "Memory Usage"  exec meminfo &
    Nop ""
    Exec    "Lock Terminal" exec xlock -mode random &
    Nop ""
    PopUp   "Log Out"   Logout-Verify
EndPopUp


# The next few menus are mostly used in the root window.
# They control basic things like window placement,
# iconification, and logging out.
# —tabaer@magnus


# This defines the most common window operations
# As with the key bindings (see below), these were
# appropriated from a stock SGI .4Dwmrc file
Popup "Window Ops"
    Move    "Move    (Alt-F7)"
    Resize  "Resize  (Alt-F8)"
    Iconify "Minimize (Alt-F9)"
    Maximize    "Maximize (Alt-F10)"
    Raise   "Raise   (Alt-F1)"
    Lower   "Lower   (Alt-F3)"
    Nop ""
    Destroy "Close   (Alt-F4)"
    Delete  "Quit    (Alt-F2)"
```

```
EndPopup

# 4dwm-ish root window menu
PopUp "RootMenu"
    Title   "FVWM"
    Nop   ""
    Exec   "Lock Terminal" exec xlock -mode random &
    PopUp   "Log Out"   Logout-Verify
EndPopUp

#4dwm-ish long root window
PopUp "LongRootMenu"
    Title   "FVWM"
    Nop   ""
    Exec   "New Window"   exec xterm -ls -geom 80x32 &
    CirculateUp "Shuffle Up"
    CirculateDown   "Shuffle Down"
    Refresh "Refresh All"
    Nop   ""
    Restart "Restart fvwm"  fvwm
    PopUp   "Quit fvwm" Quit-Verify
    Nop   ""
    Exec   "Lock Terminal" exec xlock -mode random &
    PopUp   "Log Out"   Logout-Verify
EndPopUp


###################################################
# Now define some handy complex functions

# This one moves and then raises the window
# if you drag the mouse, only raises the window
# if you click,  or does a RaiseLower if you double
# click.
Function "Move-or-Raise"
    Move        "Motion"
```

```
    Raise       "Motion"
    Raise       "Click"
    RaiseLower  "DoubleClick"
EndFunction


# This one moves and then lowers the window
# if you drag the mouse, only lowers the window
# if you click,  or does a RaiseLower if you double
# click.
Function "Move-or-Lower"
    Move        "Motion"
    Lower       "Motion"
    Lower       "Click"
    RaiseLower  "DoubleClick"
EndFunction


# This one resizes and then raises the window
# if you drag the mouse, only raises the window
# if you click,  or does a RaiseLower if you double
# click.
Function "Resize-or-Raise"
    Resize      "Motion"
    Raise       "Motion"
    Raise       "Click"
    RaiseLower  "DoubleClick"
EndFunction


Function "Move-or-Iconify"
    Move        "Motion"
    PopUp       "Click" Window Ops
    Iconify     "DoubleClick"
EndFunction


# This does the Motif/MSWin thing of killing the
# window when you double-click the top left button.
```

```
# Very useful if you're used to Windows 3.1, SGI
# machines, or both (like me).  —tabaer@magnus
Function "Die-on-DoubleClick"
    Destroy     "DoubleClick"
    PopUp       "Click" Window Ops
EndFunction


##################################################
# This defines the mouse bindings

# First, for the mouse in the root window
# I use the AnyModifier option for the modifier
# field, so you can hold down any shift-control-whatever
# combination you want!

#       Button    Context Modifi  Function
Mouse 1    R       A         PopUp "LongRootMenu"
# Mouse button 2 calls up the Tools menu in case GoodStuff doesn't
work
Mouse 2    R       A         PopUp "Tools"
Mouse 3    R       A         PopUp "RootMenu"


# Now the title bar buttons
# Any button in the left title-bar button gives
# the window ops menu Any button in the right
# title-bar button Iconifies the window
# Note the use of "Mouse 0" for AnyButton.

#       Button    Context Modifi  Function
Mouse 0    1       A         Function "Die-on-DoubleClick"
Mouse 0    2       A         Maximize
Mouse 0    4       A         Iconify


# Now the rest of the frame
# Here I invoke my complex functions for
```

```
# Move-or-lower, Move-or-raise,
# and Resize-or-Raise.
# Button 1 in the corner pieces, with any
# modifiers, gives resize or raise
Mouse 1    FS  A   Function "Resize-or-Raise"
Mouse 2    FS  A   Function "Resize-or-Raise"
Mouse 1    T   A   Function "Move-or-Raise"
Mouse 2    T   A   Function "Move-or-Raise"
Mouse 1    I   A   Function "Move-or-Iconify"
Mouse 2    I   A   Function "Move-or-Iconify"


###############################################
# Now some keyboard shortcuts.

# I don't use (or compile in, for that matter)
# the virtual stuff, so the Scroll keybindings
# are pretty useless to me.  I shut them
# off.  —tabaer@magnus

# Arrow Keys
# press arrow + meta key, and scroll by 1/10 of a page
Key Left   A   M   Scroll -10 +0
Key Right  A   M   Scroll +10 +0
Key Up     A   M   Scroll +0   -10
Key Down   A   M   Scroll +0   +10

# press shift arrow + control anywhere, and
# move the pointer by 1% of a page
Key Left   A   SC  CursorMove -1 0
Key Right  A   SC  CursorMove +1 +0
Key Up     A   SC  CursorMove +0   -1
Key Down   A   SC  CursorMove +0   +1
```

```
# press shift arrow + meta key, and move
# the pointer by 1/10 of a page
Key Left    A    SM   CursorMove -10 +0
Key Right   A    SM   CursorMove +10 +0
Key Up      A    SM   CursorMove +0   -10
Key Down    A    SM   CursorMove +0   +10


# Keyboard accelerators
# These are "borrowed" from the .4Dwmrc file on
# an SGI I use, except for AltF2 and AltF6 which
# I added for completeness.
# I think the other are standard Motif. —tabaer@magnus
Key F1      WFST    M    Raise
Key F2      WFST    M    Delete
Key F3      WFST    M    Lower
Key F4      WFST    M    Destroy
Key F5      WFST    M    Raise
Key F6      A    M    WindowList
Key F7      WFST    M    Move
Key F8      WFST    M    Resize
Key F9      WFST    M    Iconify
Key F10     WFST    M    Maximize


# Turn on the GoodStuff toolbar.
Module GoodStuff


# end of .fvwmrc file.
```

Exiting X from Fvwm

To exit from **fvwm** and usually quit X (if **fvwm** is the last X application in your **.xinitrc** or **.xsession** file), you usually call up the **fvwm** root menu and quit. The default choices are *Exit Fvwm*, which invokes a submenu to confirm, and *Yes, Really Quit*.

Setting Up an X Login

Up to now, we've been running **startx** to begin an X session. You still need to log in at the console and start X yourself (or use the automatic method we described above). In addition to this method, there's also a way to set up an X login screen, using XDM. XDM stands for the *X Display Manager* and is a means to control an X session. As such, XDM is generally much nicer on the user, as it automatically starts the X server and it presents a graphical login window, such as the one shown in Figure 6.8.

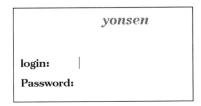

Figure 6.8 A graphical login window.

The X Display Manager is run from a program called **xdm**. While **xdm** takes a little getting used to, we like it better than the **startx/xinit** that we've been running so far. This is because **startx** (which runs **xinit**) requires you to login to a text screen and only then start up X (via **startx**). **Xdm** allows you to log directly into an X session.

 Xdm also allows one program to control your workstation's console as well as a number of X terminals. If you're interested in this, look in Appendix A for books that cover **xdm**.

To set up **xdm**, you need to edit at least one system file. This is a key file used when booting Linux, so it is a serious endeavor. Always back up any system file before you edit it. (It's probably a good idea to make a general backup now, too.)

UNIX Run Levels

Xdm is usually set to trigger off what is called a *run-level*. With a few exceptions, run-levels in UNIX an arbitrary concept that mostly follows ancient UNIX traditions. The run-level "S" implies a single-user standalone system.

In Linux, run-level 1 and higher is multiuser. This means that more than one user is allowed to login. On many systems, run-level 3 starts up networking. For Linux, the default run-level is 5. Linux also has special run-levels for power-fail (which shuts the system down) and the Vulcan death-grip (**Ctrl-Alt-Backspace**).

You can get some ideas about run-levels by looking in the **/etc/inittab** file. In **/etc/inittab**, one of the first entries will be something like the following:

```
# Default runlevel.
id:5:initdefault:
```

This states that the default system run-level is level 5. When Linux boots up, it will boot into run-level 5. Later on in the **/etc/inittab** file, you'll find something like:

```
x1:6:wait:/etc/rc.d/rc.6
```

This states that on entry to run-level 6, run **/etc/rc.d/rc.6**. This file, then, starts up the X Display Manager, which will present an X login screen.

On our system, **/etc/rc.d/rc.6** starts the following program:

```
# Call the "xdm" program.
exec /usr/X11/bin/xdm -nodaemon
```

This is what starts up **xdm**. To get **xdm** up and running, all you should really have to do is edit the **/etc/inittab** as root as change the following line:

```
id:5:initdefault:
```

to:

```
id:6:initdefault:
```

After making these changes, when you next boot Linux, you'll boot into run-level 6 rather than run-level 5. The process of going into run-level 6 will start **xdm**, because of what's in the **/etc/rc.d/rc.6** file.

Before doing this, though, make a copy of **/etc/inittab**. You also should test out **xdm** before setting the system to boot into it, because you always want to be able to boot Linux. (Making a mistake in **/etc/inittab** can result in a Linux that won't boot.) To test **xdm** out, you can type in the following command as root, to change to run-level 6 now:

```
# init 6
```

This will jump you to run level 6. Be patient, as this command takes a while.

 Ensure that X is *not* running when you do this. You should be logged in as *root* at the console.

If you set up your **.login** or **.profile** file to automatically call **startx** when you login (see "Starting X Automatically" above), you must disable this first. These two methods for starting X conflict. Quit X, then comment out those lines you added to the **.login** or **.profile** file, for example:

```
if ( `tty` == "/dev/tty1" ) then
#    Commented out.
#    startx
endif
```

After a while, you should see a graphical login screen. It is best to test **xdm** using **init 6** first, to see if everything is set up. Try to login and see what happens. If this works, you're in business and you can confidently modify the **/etc/inittab** file.

The **xdm** configuration files are in **/usr/lib/X11/xdm**. You probably won't have to edit anything there, especially for a stand-alone Linux system without X terminals on the network. (If your needs are more demanding, you'll need to look into a book specifically on X, such as *The UNIX System Administrator's Guide to X*. See Appendix A for more on this.)

User Accounts Under Xdm

While you probably won't have to edit any of the **xdm** system files in **/usr/lib/X11/xdm**, it's likely you'll have to edit files in your home directory. By default, **xdm** runs a file named **.xsession** from your home directory, instead of the **.xinitrc** that is run by **startx** (and **xinit**).

To create this file, you can start by copying your **.xinitrc** file to **.xsession** in your home directory. (Remember to put in the leading period on the file name in your home directory.) Then, modify this file like you changed the **.xinitrc** file, above.

Here's a copy of our **.xsession** file:

```
#!/bin/sh
#
# Modified by Eric F. Johnson, for Linux.
#
userresources=$HOME/.Xresources
usermodmap=$HOME/.Xmodmap
if [ x"$XWINHOME" != x ]; then
    XINIT_DIR=$XWINHOME/lib/X11/xinit
else
    XINIT_DIR=/usr/X11R6/lib/X11/xinit
fi
sysresources=$XINIT_DIR/.Xresources
sysmodmap=$XINIT_DIR/.Xmodmap

# merge in defaults and keymaps

if [ -f $sysresources ]; then
    xrdb -merge $sysresources
fi

if [ -f $sysmodmap ]; then
    xmodmap $sysmodmap
fi
```

```
if [ -f $userresources ]; then
    xrdb -merge $userresources
fi

if [ -f $usermodmap ]; then
    xmodmap $usermodmap
fi

# start some nice programs
xsetroot -solid SteelBlue
/usr/bin/X11/oclock -geom 100x100+0+6   &
/usr/bin/X11/xterm -ls -geom 80x24+3+372 &
/usr/bin/X11/xterm -ls -geom 80x48+264+13 &
exec fvwm
```

Troubleshooting X Programs

In the last section of this chapter, we cover a number of common X-related problems and how to deal with them.

Finding Information on X

It's hard sometimes to find where in the mass of X files lies the truth you want to find. One very useful application is **xman**, a graphical manual-page browser, as shown in Figure 6.9.

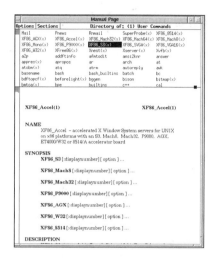

Figure 6.9 The **xman** man-page viewer.

Online-manual pages of particular interest for the X Window System are listed in Table 6.3.

Table 6.3 *X-related manual pages of interest.*

Man Page	Description
XF86Config	File format description
XFree86	Implementation of X on Linux
XF86_Accel	X servers for accelerated graphics cards
XServer	The program X itself
startx	Program that starts X
fvwm	A window manager
xdm	X Display Manager
xfs	X font server
xlsfonts	Lists fonts
xset	Controls settings in X server
xsetroot	Controls screen background
xterm	UNIX shell window

Killing X the Hard Way

If for some reason your X display hangs and you can't do anything, there are a number of things you can try before you hit the hardware-reset button. First, try the magic Vulcan death grip for X: **Ctrl-Alt-Backspace** (unless you disabled this in your **XF86Config** file, as was mentioned in Chapter 4). This key sequence should terminate all running X programs, as well as the X server.

If the Vulcan death grip doesn't work, then try to switch to another virtual console, by typing **Ctrl-Alt-Fn** (like F2). Login at this virtual console, use the ps command to search for X-related processes, and then kill them with **kill -9**. Don't do this unless you have to.

Xmodmap and the Delete Key

Under some versions of XFree86, both the **Delete** key and the **Backspace** key are configured to send the same virtual key in X (called a *KeySym*). This may cause problems with Motif programs (if you have Motif installed, that is). To change this, you can put the following line into a file named **.Xmodmap** in your home directory:

```
keycode 22 = Backspace
```

This changes the KeySym that X sends to applications when you hit the Backspace key.

Shared Libraries for X11 R5 and R6

To save on RAM, Linux makes heavy use of shared libraries, particularly for large X Window applications. There's a problem, though, in that there was a major change to the X libraries between X11 Release 5 and Release 6, which correspond on Linux to XFree86 versions 2 and 3.

ON THE

CD-ROM

A lot of older applications—Motif-based applications like NCSA Mosaic for X Window in particular—expect the older Release 5 X libraries, not the newer Release 6 ones. Because of this, you should load both sets of libraries when you install Slackware Linux.

The version numbers are kind of odd, but you should have two numbered copies of each shared X library in **/usr/X11R6**. For example, for **libX11.a**, you should see something like:

```
libX11.so.3
libX11.so.3.1.0
libX11.so.6
libX11.so.6.0
```

ON THE
CD-ROM

There are really two shared libraries (**libX11.so.3.1.0** and **libX11.so.6.0**) and two symbolic links (**libX11.so.3** and **libX11.so.6**). Note the large version-number increase with the new libraries (version 6 as compared with version 3). You need the new libraries for all the applications that come with Slackware Linux and the old libraries for older Motif applications.

What About Motif?

While we covered how to make **fvwm** look more like Motif window manager **mwm**, the fact remains that none of Motif (programs, programming libraries or window manager) ship with Linux. This is because these programs require the Motif library, **libXm.a**, to compile. Since Motif isn't free, you have to pay extra to a vendor of Motif on Linux to get this library.

That's not much fun, as a lot of neat programs, like Mosaic, require the Motif libraries (such as **libXm.a**) to compile. Luckily, you can get Mosaic precompiled for Linux, but this isn't true of most other Motif programs.

What is Motif?

There are a lot of confusion amongst UNIX users as to what Motif really is. We see Motif as a number of things, including:

- A look-and-feel style guide. You don't necessarily need the Motif libraries to follow this style guide in your programs.

- A window manager, **mwm**, that places distinct (and Windows-like) borders around application windows. The program inside the border remains the same and may be based on Motif, Open Look, or any other interface style.

- A set of programming libraries, including **libXm.a**, and header files (most located in **/usr/include/Xm**) to allow you to develop Motif programs. These libraries include a User Interface Language, called UIL.

When people ask if you have Motif, they mostly mean the Motif libraries that allow you to compile Motif programs. See Appendix A for more on Motif and Chapter 10 for more on programming in Linux.

If you don't have the Motif libraries or header files, you can't compile any Motif programs. Don't worry, though, as the more popular programs like NCSA Mosaic are available in binary format for Linux.

If you want Motif, you must purchase it from a Motif vendor.

Improving X Performance

The number-one way to improve X performance is by adding RAM. Simply put, X is a RAM pig. Shared libraries help, but unless you have 16 MB of RAM, or hopefully more, you'll likely face very slow X performance.

Accelerated local bus graphics cards also help, but the number-one determinant remains RAM.

Summary

Chapter 6 covers working with X on Linux and covers basics about using X, X resource files, troubleshooting X on Linux and a nice set of handy utilities that come with Linux.

There are many neat X-based programs that ship with the Slackware distribution. One of the handiest, however, is **xterm**, an admittedly blah program that gives you a UNIX-like terminal (and, by extension, access to the UNIX command line). We find that most Linux users make heavy use of **xterm**, making it one of the most popular X Window applications. In this chapter we discuss **xterm**, as well as how to configure and use it.

X runs through a series of configuration files after it's launched. Some of these files control what applications begin when X begins, while other files add functionality in the form of the X Display Manager.

The **fvwm** window manager is advertised as being Motif-like, and it is—on the surface, anyway. When you start using it for a while, you'll learn that it doesn't respond to the same commands as does the Motif window manager (**mwm**), and all in all, it works differently than does **mwm**.

The chapter ends with a discussion of X troubleshooting, including an explanation of why other Linux programs may interfere with X and how to avoid problems posed by shared libraries.

In the next chapter we cover additional Linux tools, both character-based and X-based.

Additional Linux Tools

This chapter covers:

- Using **emacs**
- Text-processing tools: **groff**, **TeX**, **texinfo**, and **sed**
- Printing with Ghostview
- Compressing your files with **gzip**
- Archiving your files with **tar**
- Using the MTools
- System-administration tools
- More on multiprocessing
- Setting up additional swap files
- Emulating DOS and *Windows*

A Wealth of Features

In the past two chapters you've been exposed to a lot of what Linux has to offer in your daily work. However, those chapters barely scratched the surface of Linux's many, many tools—particularly the tools found in the Slackware distribution.

In this chapter, we extend our discussion of Linux tools, focusing on some specific topics. We begin with an overview of the **emacs** text editor. However, we're not going to cover every single Linux tool, especially not those tools that can be found in most distributions of UNIX. Here, we'll discuss tools that are unique to Linux or (in the case of **gzip** and **tar**) come in versions that are slightly different than they are in the rest of the UNIX world. (You'll see what we mean when we discuss **tar** and its compression capabilities.) Since Linux does contain most of the standard commands in the UNIX world, we strongly advise that you purchase another guide to UNIX (many are listed in Appendix A) to use as a guide to the more common UNIX commands; we won't spend time here covering useful commands like **grep**, for exmaple, as they're adequately covered in other texts, and there's very little to distinguish the Linux versions of these commands from the mainstream UNIX versions.

With that in mind, it's time to cover the many tools that make Linux unique both when compared to other operating systems, but to other versions of UNIX as well.

Using Emacs

The **elvis/vi** text editor covered in Chapter 5 was a pure text editor; all it did was allow you to open or create a text file and edit it in a full-screen layout. (It also performed this basic capability in a very confusing manner, forcing you to distinguish between command and input modes.)

The **emacs** text editor goes a little further in its capabilities, while being easier to use. Created by Richard Stallman and controlled by the Free Software Foundation, **emacs** has evolved into an essential piece of software for most UNIX users, even though **emacs** ships with relatively few commercial implementations of UNIX; its appeal is such that system administrators are willing to go the extra mile and obtain it for use on their systems.

Though we're not going to get into the religious war that separates **vi** and **emacs** editors, we do think that **emacs** is worth checking out, especially if you've not used either text editor extensively. **Emacs** offers many things not found in **vi**:

- **Emacs** allows you to edit more than one file at a time, with the added ability to cut and paste between files.
- **Emacs** features online help—a rarity in the Linux/UNIX world.
- A spelling checker, based on the UNIX **spell** command, can be accessed from a pull down menu.
- With pull down menus and a graphical interface (though, sadly, without what-you-see-is-what-you-get capabilities), **emacs** comes closest to a true word processor in the Linux world.

Beginners will probably get a little more out of **emacs** than other Linux text-editing tools, if only because the basic commands are always available in pull down menus. In addition, **emacs** can be used for a host of other functions, including the reading of electronic mail and Usenet news, and the editing of source-code files for C, Lisp, and TeX.

NOTE

This discussion will center around the X Window version that ships with the Slackware distribution of Linux—version 19.28. If you've decided to forego the joys of X, you should have installed the non-X version of **emacs** that was available during the Linux installation process. You can go back and install that version if you're not using X; however, if you installed the X Window version of **emacs**, you should remove that version from your system before installing the non-X version.

If you do use the non-X version of **emacs**, you'll still be able to follow along with this section of the chapter, for the most part. We'll provide keyboard equivalents to the commands listed here.

To launch **emacs** without a file loaded, type the following command line in an **xterm** window:

```
gilbert:/# emacs
```

as seen in Figure 7.1.

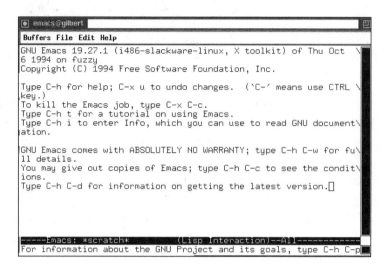

Figure 7.1 Emacs without a file loaded.

You can also load **emacs** with a file loaded, specifying the file on the command line:

```
gilbert:/# emacs filename
```

where *filename* is the name of the file. (Remember that if *filename* isn't found on your PATH or in the current directory, you'll need to list an absolute filename.)

If you've used any other computing system or another X Window application, you'll feel fairly comfortable in **emacs**. There are some changes in terminology that might throw you off; for instance, you don't edit separate files (you edit buffers), and the mechanism for showing your position in a document is not called the *cursor*, but the point. (In this chapter, we'll use the term cursor.)

Emacs and Commands

With **emacs**, there is usually more than one way to perform a command, especially with the X Window version of **emacs**.

One method is through keyboard shortcuts. Every **emacs** function can be performed via the keyboard, usually in conjunction with the **Ctrl** and **Alt** keys. (In some **emacs** documentation, there will be references to the **Meta** key and not the **Ctrl** key; this reference is more for the users of other UNIX systems that lack a **Ctrl** key on their keyboard. This is of course not the case with Linux.) Most of the time the **Ctrl/Alt** keys are literally shortcuts for full commands, which you could enter if you were truly inclined.

There's one thing to note when working with keyboard sequences: When you see notation like **Ctrl-x Ctrl-f**, this means you hold down the **Ctrl** key and then press the **x** and **f** keys in sequence. (No, you don't need to release the **Ctrl** key between the **x** and **f** keys.)

The other method is through a pulldown menu. As you can see from Figure 7.2, **emacs** provides some pulldown menus (Buffers, File, Edit, and Help). Be warned that these menus don't work the same way as pulldown menus in the Microsoft *Windows*, Macintosh or OS/2 environments. In these situations, a menu choice acts as a gateway to another action, either a dialog box or another menu.

Essentially, pulldown menus in the **emacs** environment act as gateways for the **emacs** command line, which can be found on the bottom of the screen. For instance, go ahead and choose **Open File** from the File pulldown menu (or the keyboard equivalent of **Ctrl-x Ctrl-f**) You won't see a fancy dialog box that allows you to choose from a list of existing files. Instead, you'll see a line at the bottom of the emacs window that lists the current directory, as shown in Figure 7.2.

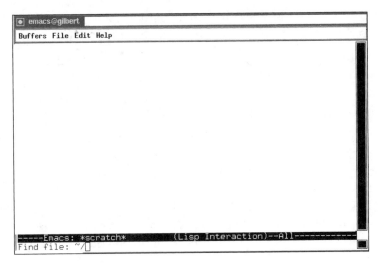

Figure 7.2 Emacs before loading a file.

Here is where you can choose your directory. After doing so, you'll see a listing of files, as shown in Figure 7.3.

Figure 7.3 Emacs with the listings of a directory.

If you look at Figure 7.3 closely, you'll see that the pulldown-menu choices have dramatically increased. Depending on the context, **emacs** will display varying sets of pulldown menus.

The listings from Figure 7.3 are meant as a way to show your options; the contents are read-only, and you can't scroll between them to actually select a file or directory; instead, you continue to choose **Open File** from the File menu (**Ctrl-x Ctrl-f**) and manually insert the file or directory name. In short, the **Open File** menu choice is actually a shortcut both to the **emacs** command line and to the **ls -l** command line.

After you choose a file, you'll see something like Figure 7.4— assuming, of course, that your file contains more than the gibberish shown in the figure.

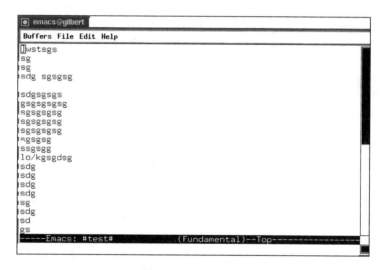

Figure 7.4 Emacs with a file loaded.

Again, you'll note that the menu bar for emacs has slightly changed, in reaction to the context of editing a simple text file. In Figure 7.4, **emacs** gives us the name of the file (**test**), the mode (*Fundamental*), and the amount of the file is displayed on the screen (in this case, 22 percent).

You'll also notice that the status bar on the bottom of the **emacs** window has also changed. In the previous screen shots, the status bar listed *Lisp Interaction*, without the name of a file (which made sense, since we didn't have a file loaded). This leads us to a major feature of **emacs**: modes.

The Many Modes of Emacs

You've already seen **emacs** change behavior when presented with a different context—the example being different pulldown menus for different chores. Another sign of **emacs'** flexibility is in its support of *modes*, which essentially changes **emacs** depending on the usage.

For instance, the first screen shots in this section showed **emacs** in *Lisp Interaction* mode. If you were a Lisp programmer, this mode might be important to you. However, most of you will be interested in other **emacs** modes—particularly the mode found in Figure 7.4, *Fundamental* mode. This is the mode used to edit ASCII files. There are other modes for **emacs** that you may end up using, however, such as the modes for editing C and TeX source-code files.

Creating and Editing Files

Most of what **emacs** does is pretty straightforward; as you've already learned, most actions can be done from the pulldown menu or from keyboard equivalents.

After you launch **emacs** from a command line, you're presented with a blank screen. If you're creating a new file, you can go ahead and type away. **Emacs** will wrap words at the end of a column, but in an unusual manner, displaying a slash (/) to indicate that a word is continued on the following line (as shown in Figure 7.5).

With the version of **emacs** found on the accompanying CD-ROM, **emacs** performs just like any other text editor when it comes to cursor commands and such; there are a few quirks to watch for, however:

Figure 7.5 Emacs displaying text.

- The cursor keys (↑, ↓, ←, and →) are used slightly differently than you'd think. The up arrow (↑) moves the cursor to the beginning line of the current paragraph; pressing it twice moves the cursor to the beginning of the file. The down arrow (↓) moves the cursor to the end of the current paragraph; pressing it twice moves the cursor into the following paragraph. However, the left and right arrow keys (← and →) work as you would expect them to.

- The **PgUp** and **PgDn** commands apply to the position of the document in the **emacs** buffer. If the entire document is displayed in a window, these commands simply won't do anything.

- The **Home** and **End** keys are used to mark text, in addition to positioning the cursor at the beginning or end of a document.

- The **Backspace** and **Delete** keys should work as you'd expect. (This is one of the advantages of Linux on the PC architecture; Linux assumes that there's standard PC equipment present, and by and large that assumption will be valid. There are mechanisms for remapping keys should Linux not work as you'd expect, but these sorts of problems are minimized under Linux and XFree86.)

In addition, there are a host of keyboard commands for maneuvering through a document, as listed in Table 7.1.

Table 7.1 Emacs cursor commands.

Command	Result
Ctrl-v	Moves the document ahead one page
Alt-v	Moves the document back one page
Alt-<	Moves the cursor to the beginning of the document
Alt->	Moves the cursor to the end of the document

Buffers

In UNIX parlance, a *buffer* is a portion of memory set aside for a specific task. In **emacs**, a buffer can contain an existing file or a new file in progress. When a file is in a buffer, it exists separately from something stored on the hard disk; you can make changes to the buffer, but they won't be reflected in the version stored on disk. Only when you explicitly save the file to disk will the changes be made permanently.

Emacs allows you to view multiple buffers, as well as cutting and pasting between the buffers. To see what buffers are currently open, select **Buffers** from the menu bar (or type **Ctrl-x Ctrl-b**). You'll see something like Figure 7.6.

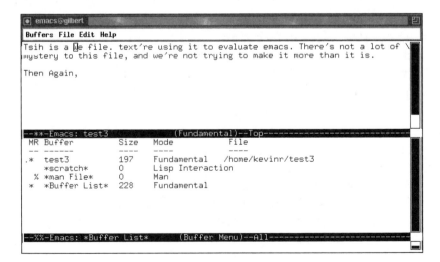

Figure 7.6 Buffers in emacs.

Emacs and Help

There's also one addition area where **emacs** is superior to most other Linux text-editing tools: the presence of true online help. To access the online help, you can choose **Help** from the pulldown menu, which gives you a list of selections. Some of the help is context-sensitive, responding to what you're doing at the moment (such as the help for modes), while there are general help topics and a tutorial.

A good place to start with the online help is with the **Info** menu choice (**Ctrl-h I**), which provides a general overview of **emacs** online help (as shown in Figure 7.7). And **Ctrl-h t** provides a decent tutorial.

```
emacs@gilbert
 Buffers File Edit Help
File: dir          Node: Top        This is the top of the INFO tree
  This (the Directory node) gives a menu of major topics. Typing "d"
  returns here, "q" exits, "?" lists all INFO commands, "h" gives a
  primer for first-timers, "mTexinfo<Return>" visits Texinfo topic, etc.
  --- PLEASE ADD DOCUMENTATION TO THIS TREE. (See INFO topic first.) ---
* Menu: The list of major topics begins on the next line.

Developing in C and C++:
========================
* GCC: (gcc).           Information about the gcc Compiler
* CPP: (cpp).           The C Preprozessor
* Make: (make).         The GNU make Utility
* GDB: (gdb).           The GNU Debugger

Libraries and program generators:
=================================
* glibc: (libc).        The standard C runtime library.
* iostream: (iostream). The GNU C++ iostream library.
* Libg++: (libg++).     The G++ Library
* gmp: (gmp).           GNU MP arbitrary precision arithmetic library.
* Regex: (regex).       The GNU regular expression library.
* Termcap: (termcap).   The termcap library, which enables application progr\
--%%-Info:  (dir)Top        (Info Narrow)--Top------------------------------
menu-bar help info
```

Figure 7.7 The emacs help screen.

NOTE

There will be further discussion of the **emacs** help system in a section later in this chapter entitled "Using Texinfo."

A Basic Emacs Tutorial

A good share of Linux users won't care about **emacs'** bell and whistles—they only care about creating and editing a document. In that spirit, we present this minitutorial that covers the creation and editing of text files under **emacs**.

You already know how to load **emacs**. If you want to create a new file, you can go ahead and type away. If you want to load an existing file and didn't specify the file on the command line, you can open it by selecting **Open File** (**Ctrl-x Ctrl-f**) from the File menu.

To edit the file, you can use the basic movement and editing keys on the keyboard. When it comes time to save your file, you can select **Save Buffer** (**Ctrl-x Ctrl-s**) from the File menu; if you're working with an existing file, you should select **Save Buffer As** (**Ctrl-x Ctrl-w**) from the File menu, but using the existing filename.

To quit **emacs**, select **Exit Emacs** from the File menu, or else type **Ctrl-x Ctrl-c**. If you haven't saved any changes to the file, **emacs** will make sure you want to quit and give you the option of saving the file at that time.

The Undo Command

Emacs also allows you to undo your most recent action; naturally enough, the **Undo** menu selection from the Edit menu does just this. (The keyboard equivalent is **Ctrl-_**.)

Editing Text

When you edit existing text, you can go one of two ways. Old-time UNIX and **emacs** users make a big deal about the scads of commands that are used to delete and edit text. Since we're modernists (relatively speaking), we're into the more recent (and handier) methods to do things.

For instance: To cut and copy text, there's a host of commands for cutting existing text, saving it to a buffer, and then reinserting the buffer either in the existing file or a new file. We find it's a lot easier to use the mouse to mark a section of text, and then use the menu choices in the Edit menu to make the changes (cut, copy, and paste). If you're used to this trinity of choices from the *Windows*, Macintosh, or OS/2 worlds, you'll feel comfortable with them under Linux:

- The **Cut (Ctrl-w)** menu choice cuts the marked text and saves it to another buffer.

- The **Copy (Alt-w)** menu choice copies the marked text to a buffer, leaving the marked text intact.

- The **Paste (Ctrl-y)** menu choice pastes the text in the buffer to where the cursor is positioned on the page.

There are two things to note here: The keyboard equivalents for these mechanisms aren't the same as the keyboard equivalents under *Windows*, Macintosh, or OS/2; and that marked text is grayed when you select it with the mouse, but isn't grayed when you release the mouse. Still, the text is marked; you just have no way to tell.

Deleting text involves the same sort of mechanisms: Marking text with the mouse and then using the **Clear** menu choice (no keyboard equivalent, interestingly enough) from the Edit menu to delete the text. (You can't use the **Backspace** or **Delete** keys to delete marked text.) There are also a host of keyboard commands for deleting text (if you're a devoted touch-typist and can't bear the thought of actually using a mouse), as listed in Table 7.2.

Table 7.2 Delete commands in emacs.

Command	Result
Delete	Deletes the character to the left of the cursor
Backspace	Deletes the character to the left of the cursor
Ctrl-d	Deletes the character beneath the cursor
Ctrl-k	Deletes all characters to the end of the line
Alt-d	Deletes to the beginning of the next word
Alt-Delete	Deletes all characters to the beginning of the previous word

Finally, **emacs** features a slew of keyboard commands for changing existing text. Most of these selections aren't found in a menu, so you'll need to perform them from the keyboard. We list them in Table 7.3.

Table 7.3 Additional emacs editing commands.

Command	Result
Ctrl-t	Transposes the character under the cursor with the character before the cursor
Alt-t	Transposes the word under the cursor with the word before the cursor
Ctrl-x Ctrl-t	Transposes the current line with the next line in the document. Remember that under emacs a line can be a paragraph, if there's no carriage return at the end of a line
Alt-l (ell)	Changes the case of a word to lowercase. However, there's a twist; if your cursor is positioned in the middle of the word, emacs only changes the case of the letters in the remainder of the word
Alt-u	Changes the case of a word uppercase. However, there's a twist; if your cursor is positioned in the middle of the word, emacs only changes the case of the letters in the remainder of the word
Alt-c	Capitalizes the word, provided the cursor is at the beginning of the word

Searching and Replacing

When it comes to searching and replacing text, **emacs** is not a very sophisticated player, but you'll probably have little need for the more extensive search-and-replace facilities found in a commercial word processor.

To search for a specific string, select **Search** from the Edit menu. The bottom of the window will feature the following input mechanism:

```
Search:
```

At that point you can enter the string of text to look for, moving forward through the document from the current cursor position, *not* from the beginning of the file.

If you choose **Ctrl-s** from the keyboard, you'll get a slightly different search mechanism, as you'll see by the bottom of the window:

```
I-search:
```

The search is incremental, which means that **emacs** is moving through the document based on your first keystroke (if you type **t**, it will move to the first *t* it finds).

To perform a search-and-replace operation, use **Query-Replace** from the Edit menu. **Emacs** will prompt you for the text to search, followed by the text to replace. Armed with this, **emacs** will then move to the first occurrence of the search text in the buffer, asking you if you do want to replace the text (type **y** or **n** to choose).

Spell-Checking

Emacs features a spelling checker that's really an extension of the UNIX **spell** command, **ispell**. If you select **Spell** from the Edit menu, you'll see a host of choices that allows you to check the spelling in the buffer, a spelling of a particular word, or to check the spelling using a different or foreign-language dictionary. This menu also allows you to make changes to a dictionary (a good thing, especially if you're writing a book and use a lot of words that aren't in the standard dictionary).

Linux also supports the spell command, if you wish to run it from the command line.

Printing in Emacs

To print a file in **emacs**, select **Print Buffer** from the File menu (no, there's no keyboard equivalent). This has the same effect as running **lpr** from the command line.

There's a lot more to **emacs** than what we list here; realistically, all we can do is offer you an overview of **emacs** and let you poke around the rest, figuring out which of **emacs** many capabilities best fit your situation.

Text-Processing Tools

Like the UNIX operating system as a whole, Linux offers many tools for text processing, in addition to the text-editing tools already covered in this chapter and in Chapter 5. This split requires a little background first, however.

As you've been told repeatedly through the course of this book, UNIX (and by extension, Linux) is built upon a set of specialized commands, as computing chores are divided between many small-scale, specific commands. To create a document, for instance, you can't merely call on a word processor like *WordPerfect* and create a document from beginning to end, with fancy layouts and such. While **emacs** does do many of the things a good *Windows* or Macintosh word processor would do, it's still limited when it comes to page layouts and such.

That weakness is actually inherent in the UNIX operating system, which delegates small tasks to small commands. Traditionally, creating a document within UNIX has involved three sets of tools:

- Text editors, such as **vi** or **emacs**
- Text processors, such as **groff** or **tex**
- Printing commands, such as **lpr**

In this chapter and in Chapter 5, you've learned about the major text editors in Linux. In this section, we'll run down the major text processors in Linux, followed by a discussion of printing in Linux.

Groff: The Traditional Standard

Early on in its history, UNIX was viewed as the perfect front-end to a robust printing system. (This is how early UNIX development was justified at Bell Labs, as a matter of fact.) As a result, there are many text-processing tools in UNIX. Some of them have been superseded by commercial what-you-see-is-what-you-get text editing/processing packages in the commercial world (such as *FrameMaker, Island Write,* and *WordPerfect*), but since these tools haven't yet been released for Linux at this point (never say never—if Linux grows, it will get the attention of commercial software developers), you'll need to made do with the existing text-processing tools.

Roff was an original text-processing tool from the Bell Lab days of UNIX, which then evolved into various other tools (like **troff** and **psroff**). **Roff** and its descendants were viewed as text-processing filters, which would take the output of a text editor (properly formatted with **roff** commands, of course) and then send it to a specific printer. These formatting commands could include columns, fonts, boxes, and other layout elements.

The Slackware version of Linux features **groff**, the Free Software Foundation version of **troff**. **Groff** and its accompanying utilities allow you to format documents for a wide range of devices, including PostScript printers (using the ps device driver), TeX, X Window programs, and other line printers.

Using Groff

As mentioned, **groff** is a text processor, which means it takes input from a text editor (like **vi** or **emacs**) and prepares it for output on another device. For your part, you must input **groff** formatting commands into your text document.

Groff formatting commands begin with a backslash (\) or a period (.). **Groff** then takes these commands and interprets them for the output device. For instance, you may want to input the text found in Figure 7.8, using **vi** or **emacs**, saving the file as **rules** in your home directory.

```
.po 1i
.ce1
\s12\fBLinux Rules!\fR


\s10This monthly issue of \fILinux Rules!\fR features 20 more reasons
why Linux is the ultimate operating system. Some of the reasons
include:
.in 5
* Linux is way cool!
* Linux is better than DOS at \fIeverything\fR.
* Only smart people like us use Linux.


\s10Do we need to say more?
```

Figure 7.8 Input for the groff text processor.

You can run the **rules** file and see the result on the screen using the following command line:

```
gilbert:~/$ groff rules
```

After running the text in Figure 7.8 through **groff**, the result will look like Figure 7.9.

Linux Rules!

This monthly issue of *Linux Rules!* features 20 more reasons why Linux is the ultimate operating system. Some of the reasons include:

    * Linux is way cool!
    * Linux is better than DOS at *everything*.
    * Only smart people like us use Linux.

Do we need to say more?

Figure 7.9 The document after it was run through groff.

You can also send the **groff**-formatted document to the default printer, using the following command line:

```
gilbert:~/$ groff rules | lpr
```

There are some things to note when using **groff**:

- **Groff** automatically fills to the right margin, even if you insert your own carriage returns in the text document. To stop this from happening, insert **.nf** at the beginning of the document; this is short for *no fill*.

- **Groff** automatically justifies the text; spaces between words are increased to allow the text to be stretched across the page. We're not fans of this spacing, since it results in some awkward looking lines, especially when you're working with longer words. We usually tell **groff** to stop justifying the text, which means inserting the **.ad** command at the beginning of the file.

- As you can tell from Figure 7.8, we tagged some bold and italic words with commands that begin with \f; for instance, the \fB command turns on the bold formatting, while the \fI command turns on the italic formatting. These commands stay in effect until you explicitly turn them off with the \fR command.

- The first line of the little message is in 12-point type, as opposed to the 10-point type used in the rest of the message. The \s command, followed by a number, enters the point size. (This is valid only for devices that can handle different point sizes, of course; older line printers do not, for instance.)

- Dot commands must appear on their own line; these lines won't appear at all in the document. Backslash commands, on the other hand, can appear anywhere in the document.

Some useful **groff** commands are listed in Table 7.4.

Table 7.4 Useful groff formatting commands.

Command	Result
.ad	Turns off text justification
.bp	Inserts a page break
.ce *n*	Centers the next n lines. If no number is specified, only the following line will be centered
.fi	Tells **groff** to fill the text lines. (Counters **.nf**)
.ft *n*	Changes the font to *n* (**B** for bold, and so on)
\f*n*	Changes the font to *n* (**B** for bold, and so on)
.in *n*	Indents the following lines by *n* spaces
.ls *n*	Sets the line spacing on a document; for example, **.ls 2** would change the spacing to double-spaced. The default is single-spaced
.na	Turns on text justification. (Counters **.ad**)
.nf	Tells **groff** not to fill the lines of text
.pl *n*	Sets the number of lines on a page to *n*. The default is 66 lines to a page

Table 7.4 Useful groff formatting commands. (continued)

Command	Result
.po *ni*	Sets the left margin; **1i** (*one ell*) would set the left margin to 1 inch. You must set this, or else the printing will begin at the absolute left of the page. (You can also use centimeters instead of inches by using **c** instead of **i**)
.ps *n*	Changes the point size to *n*
\s*n*	Changes the point size to *n*
.sp *n*	Sets the number of lines to skip by *n*. To skip a specific space, using *ni* for inches or *nc* for centimeters
.ti *n*	Indents the first line of the following paragraphs by *n* spaces
.un *n*	Underlines the following line. If a number (*n*) is specified, then *n* lines will be underlines. It must be used with entire lines; you can't just underline a specific word

As always, you can check out the online-manual page for a command by specifying it on the command line:

```
gilbert:~/$ man groff
```

Creating Man Pages with Groff

Programmers or system administrators on larger systems will want to check out the use of **groff** to create online-manual pages. To create them, you'd go through the same document-creation process found in the previous section: Formatting pages in **elvis** or **emacs** and then running the documents through the **groff** text processor. However, to create an online-manual page, you'd need to run the page through groff with two options: -*Tascii* (which tells **groff** to output in ASCII text, rather than formatting for a printer; the default is PostScript) and -*man* (which tells **groff** to use the manual-page macros).

Groff is also capable of outputting for other devices and software applications. An option of -*Tdvi* produces files in the TeX device-independent DVI format.

Using TeX

Biblical scholar and programming whiz Donald E. Knuth developed TeX (pronounced *tech*) to handle the tough typesetting chores that other computer tools couldn't handle at the time, such as mathematical and foreign-language formatting. **TeX** works like **groff**: You create the source file in **elvis** or **emacs**, and then you run the file through **TeX**. Linux also features **LaTeX**, a series of useful macros for use with **TeX**, as well as scads and scads of fonts for use with **TeX**. (Academics will find that these fonts are worth the price of Linux on their own; the fonts cover all major and most minor dialects, even descending into the world of fantasy with fonts for Klingon.)

In this book, we're not going to spend a lot of time covering **TeX**. When you installed Linux from the CD-ROM, you were prompted about whether you wanted to install **TeX** and the accompanying fonts. If you didn't do so at the time, you can run the Setup program again and install the **TeX** disk sets. the usage of **TeX** is somewhat involved; if your work involves this sort of precise mathematical formatting, you will definitely want to check out one of the many books covering **TeX**. On the top of that list would be Knuth's own *The TeXbook*. In addition, Leslie Lamport (the creator of **LaTeX**) documented LaTeX in *LaTeX User's Guide and Reference Manual*.

Using Texinfo

Hypertext meets Linux with the **texinfo** text-formatting program, courtesy of the same folks who brought us **emacs**. **Texinfo** is a relatively new attempt in the UNIX/Linux world to provide useful documentation for users of all sorts. The goal is **texinfo** is to create Info files that be access from help systems within applications, from the command line, or printed in a traditional manual. The benefit, of course, is that documentation need be changed only on one source file. Since this makes the creation of useful online documentation easier, we certainly applaud the effort—UNIX has a reputation for being too cryptic, and **texinfo** is a way to bring online help to the masses.

The nice thing is that the Free Software Foundation practices what it preaches, placing most of its online help in **texinfo** files. In fact, if you use **emacs**, you'll want to check out the **texinfo** files that **emacs** uses in the Help menu (you can also access these files by typing **Ctrl-h I**).

We show the top-level of the info files in Figure 7.10.

```
emacs@gilbert
Buffers File Edit Help
File: dir       Node: Top       This is the top of the INFO tree
   This (the Directory node) gives a menu of major topics. Typing "d"
   returns here, "q" exits, "?" lists all INFO commands, "h" gives a
   primer for first-timers, "mTexinfo<Return>" visits Texinfo topic, etc.
       PLEASE ADD DOCUMENTATION TO THIS TREE. (See INFO topic first.) ---
* Menu: The list of major topics begins on the next line.

Developing in C and C++:
-----===================
* GCC: (gcc).            Information about the gcc Compiler
* CPP: (cpp).            The C Preprozessor
* Make: (make).          The GNU make Utility
* GDB: (gdb).            The GNU Debugger

Libraries and program generators:
--------------====================
* glibc: (libc).         The standard C runtime library.
* iostream: (iostream).  The GNU C++ iostream library.
* Libg++: (libg++).      The G++ Library
* gmp: (gmp).            GNU MP arbitrary precision arithmetic library.
--%%-Info:  (dir)Top      (Info Narrow)--Top--------------------------------
Composing main Info directory...done
```

Figure 7.10 The Info mode for emacs.

Though you can't see the entire page from the figure, this portion of the **emacs** documentation actually acts as the documentation for *all* of the offerings of the Free Software Foundation, most of which are found within the Slackware implementation of Linux. For instance, if you scroll down the Info page, you'll actually run into the documentation for **texinfo** itself, as we show in Figure 7.11.

NOTE

You don't need to access these Info files through **emacs**. You can do so by using the following command line:

```
gilbert:/$ info
```

The result is shown in Figure 7.12.

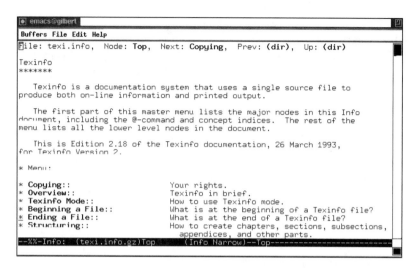

Figure 7.11 Online documentation for the texinfo system.

Figure 7.12 The info command in action.

As you can see from Figure 7.11, the documentation for **texinfo** is completely online, which makes further coverage in this chapter somewhat redundant. The files listed in Figure 7.11 can tell you anything about the creation of **texinfo** pages that you'll ever want to know.

Using Sed

The **sed** (streams editor) command isn't really a text editor, nor is it really a text processor. However, it can be used as a text processor—or rather, as an *interactive* text processor. Or else you can think of **sed** as a filtering text editor; procedurally, you use the **sed** command with the following steps:

- Read in text from file
- Make changes in the text
- Display new text on screen or save to file

These procedures are specified all in one command line. A typical **sed** command line should look something like this:

```
gilbert:~$ sed -n -e operation -f scriptfilename filename
```

where *-n* refers to a specific line or lines, *operation* refers to one of the many available **sed** operations, *scriptfilename* refers to a file that contains a longer list of **sed** operations, and *filename* refers to the file that **sed** works upon.

The various command-line options are explained in greater detail in Table 7.5.

Table 7.5 Sed command-line options.

Command	Result
-e	Explicitly tells **sed** that what follows is an operation. If you only use one operation, then you can omit the **-e**
-f	Specifies a script file. If you plan on using many operations and use them regularly, then it's best to save them in a script file for future use
-n	Specifies a specific line number or a range of line numbers to use

Go ahead and create a text file called **test**:

```
This is a test of the Emergency Linux system. This is a test.
If this were an actual document, we probably would take it
more seriously than we do this flippant, unorganized memo.
```

Let's begin by using **sed** to display only a portion of the file test, like the second and third lines. Do so with:

```
$ sed -n '2,3p' test
```

On your display, you'd see the following:

```
If this were an actual document, we probably would take it
more seriously than we do this flippant, unorganized memo.
```

If we wanted to write the results of our command to a file, we could do so as follows:

```
$ sed -n '2,3p' w filename test
```

where *filename* is the name of a file.

Some things to note in our little examples:

- Because we used only one operation, we omitted the *-e* option.
- We listed the command within single quotes, which tells **sed** that everything contained in the quotes is part of the same operation.
- We specified certain lines for **sed** to work on. If no lines are specified, **sed** assumes that it is to work on the entire file.

Printing, of course, is not the only operating available to **sed** users. We list the major operations in Table 7.6.

Table 7.6 Sed operations.

Operation	Result
a*string*	Adds the *string*
c*string*	Changes specified lines to the specified string
d	Deletes specified lines or strings
i	Inserts specified string before specified lines
l	Lists the file or specified portions thereof. Useful because it displays characters normally used for formatting; for instance, tabs are printed with the > character
p	Prints to standard output—unless specified otherwise, your screen
r *filename*	Inserts an entire file after a specific line
s/*string1*/*string2*/	Substitutes *string1* for *string2*
w *filename*	Writes specified lines to *filename*

Like most UNIX commands, **sed** can be used with pipes and other commands. If you want more information about **sed**, we suggest that you consult the other references cited in Appendix A. You can also see some more information about **sed** from the online-manual page:

```
gilbert:~$ man sed
```

Printing with Ghostview under Linux

Printing and Linux isn't a very intuitive topic to grasp. (Of course, neither is printing on any PC, for that matter, thanks to a lack of standards between hardware and software.) Most standalone Linux users are going to connect their printers to their PC's parallel port, as this is the accepted way of doing things in the PC world. Of course, some PC owners will be stubborn and use a serial port for a printer, despite all the headaches this will cause.

On one level, printing with Linux is a simple matter, as long as your printer is connected to the parallel port and you don't want to do more than printing simple ASCII text. (When you installed Linux, you were asked where the printer was installed; if your printer was connected to the first parallel port, the answer would have been **LPT1** in DOS parlance.) For this level, the basic Linux printing tools (**lpr**, **pr**) will work just fine, which is how the topic was covered in Chapter 5. The problem becomes a little more pronounced when you want to print graphics and fonts, especially those formatted with PostScript.

Additional information about printing and Linux can be gleaned from Grant Taylor and Brian McCauley's excellent **Printing-HOWTO**, contained on the accompanying CD-ROM.

Using Ghostview

Many UNIX documents are distributed in the PostScript format (even the Linux Documentation project uses PostScript-formatted documents). PostScript, as we all know, is a commercial product under the watchful eye of Adobe. Since Adobe doesn't give away PostScript for free, it's clear that in order to access PostScript files on the non commercial Linux operating system, a work around was needed. Once again the Free Software Foundation came to the rescue with Ghostscript and Ghostview.

Ghostview, the program for viewing PostScript-formatted documents, is an X Window application.

To view PostScript a file with Ghostview, just specify the file on the command line:

```
$ ghostview file.ps
```

The menu selections for Ghostview are pretty self-evident.

Unlike a normal Linux application, which can write directly to the printer, it takes a little bit more work to print a PostScript-formatted file, especially on most PC-based printers. Unlike the UNIX and Macintosh printer worlds, PostScript isn't the *lingua franca* of the PC printer world. Printers listed in Table 7.7 are supported by Ghostview.

Table 7.7 Printers supported by Ghostview.

Name	Printer
appledmp	Apple dot-matrix Imagewriter
bj10e	Canon BubbleJet BJ10e
bj200	Canon BubbleJet BJ200
cdeskjet	HP DeskJet 500C with 1 bit/pixel color
cdjcolor	HP DeskJet 500C with 24 bit/pixel color and dithering
cdjmono	HP DeskJet 500C, black only
cdj500	HP DeskJet 500C (same as cdjcolor)
cdj550	HP DeskJet 550C
declj250	Alternate DEC LJ250 driver
deskjet	HP DeskJet and DeskJet Plus
dfaxhigh	Digiboard DigiFAX software format
dfaxlow	DigiFAX low (normal) resolution
djet500	HP DeskJet 500
djet500c	HP DeskJet 500C
epson	Epson-compatible dot matrix printers (9- or 24-pin)
eps9high	Epson-compatible 9-pin, interleaved lines (triple resolution)
epsonc	Epson LQ-2550 and Fujitsu 3400/2400/1200 color printers
escp2	Epson ESC/P 2 language printers, including Stylus 800
ibmpro	IBM 9-pin Proprinter
jetp3852	IBM Jetprinter ink-jet color printer (Model #3852)
laserjet	HP LaserJet
la50	DEC LA50 printer
la75	DEC LA75 printer
lbp8	Canon LBP-8II laser printer
ln03	DEC LN03 printer

Table 7.7 Printers supported by Ghostview. (continued)

Name	Printer
lj250	DEC LJ250 Companion color printer
ljet2p	HP LaserJet IId/IIp/III with TIFF compression (achieved via an add-on cartridge)
ljet3	HP LaserJet III with Delta Row compression (achieved via an add-on cartridge)
ljet4	HP LaserJet 4
ljetplus	HP LaserJet Plus
m8510	C.Itoh M8510 printer
necp6	NEC P6/P6+/P60 printers
nwp533	Sony Microsystems NWP533 laser printer (Sony only)
oki182	Okidata MicroLine 182
paintjet	HP PaintJet color printer
pj	Alternate PaintJet XL driver
pjxl	HP PaintJet XL color printer
pjxl300	HP PaintJet XL300 color printer
r4081	Ricoh 4081 laser printer
sparc	SPARCprinter
t4693d2	Tektronix 4693d color printer, 2 bits per R/G/B component
t4693d4	Tektronix 4693d color printer, 4 bits per R/G/B component
t4693d8	Tektronix 4693d color printer, 8 bits per R/G/B component
tek4696	Tektronix 4695/4696 inkjet plotter
trufax	TruFax facsimile driver (UNIX only)

Ghostview also supports a number of graphic file formats, as listed in
Table 7.8.

Table 7.8 Graphical file formats supported in Ghostview.

Format	Explanation
bmpmono	Monochrome Microsoft *Windows* .BMP bitmap file format
bmp16	4-bit (EGA/VGA) Microsoft *Windows* .BMP file format
bmp256	8-bit (256-color) Microsoft *Windows* .BMP file format

Table 7.8 Graphical file formats supported in Ghostview. (continued)

Format	Explanation
bmp16m	24-bit Microsoft *Windows* .BMP file format
gifmono	Monochrome GIF file format
gif8	8-bit color GIF file format
pcxmono	Monochrome PCX file format
pcxgray	8-bit gray scale PCX file format
pcx16	Older color PCX file format (EGA/VGA, 16-color)
pcx256	Newer color PCX file format (256-color)
pbm	Portable bitmap (plain format), as grabbed by **pbm**
pbmraw	Portable bitmap (raw format), as grabbed by **pbm**
pgm	Portable graymap (plain format) as grabbed by **pbm**
pgmraw	Portable graymap (raw format) as grabbed by **pbm**
ppm	Portable pixmap (plain format) as grabbed by **pbm**
ppmraw	Portable pixmap (raw format) as grabbed by **pbm**
tiffg3	TIFF or Group 3 fax

Compressing and Archiving Your Files

When you start poking around the Internet and see that most of the files end with cryptic suffixes like *gz* and *tar*, you know you've wandered past your background in older versions of UNIX—or past the PC and Macintosh worlds, for that matter.

These suffixes are important, however, if you plan on grabbing software from an FTP site and installing it on your Linux system. In addition, you may find the tools responsible for these suffixes to be very useful as you archive files or prepare them for transmission to other system, either directly or via the Internet.

Essentially, a suffix of *gz* means that a file has been compressed using the GNU **gzip** utility. **Gzip** is not the only UNIX/Linux utility for compressing files; the traditional **compress** command is also supported.

Both commands essentially do the same thing: They take an ASCII or binary file (or a defined set of files) and shrink them into a smaller file. This file can then be sent via the Internet or electronic mail faster. Most UNIX systems come with both **compress** and **pack** (and their uncompression counterparts, **uncompress** and **unpack**).

Since **gzip** comes with your Linux system, it's probably the command you'll want to concentrate on. **Gunzip** (the uncompression counterpart to **gzip**) can be used on files compressed with **compress** and **pack**, which means that it will work with the vast majority of compressed files in the UNIX world. You don't need to know what command the file was compressed with (in other words, you don't need to worry about an extension of *.z* versus *.Z* versus *.gz*—**gzip** will work on them all. If you're working with compressed files for distribution to the rest of the world, you'll want to be careful about using **gzip**; after all, not all UNIX users have **gzip**, though most Internet users seem to (judging by the number of **gzip**-compressed files on various FTP sites).

 Extended documentation on **gzip** can be found in the GNU **texinfo** documentation discussed earlier in this chapter. This section will cover **gzip** fundamentals.

Using Gzip

The **gzip** command works in the following steps:

- Compress the specified file
- Save the compressed file to disk, adding a *gz* to the old filename; compressing a file named **test** will yield a new filename of **test.gz**.
- Delete the original file.

For instance, you may begin with a directory that contains the following files:

```
#test#   fig7_10.xwd   fig7_12.xwd   test.bk
#test3#  fig7_11.xwd   test          test3
```

Let's say you want to compress the file named **test**. You'd do so with the following command line:

```
gilbert:/home/kevinr# gzip test
```

A listing of the current directory would yield the following result:

```
#test#   fig7_10.xwd   fig7_12.xwd     test.gz
#test3#  fig7_11.xwd   test.bk test3
```

The file **test** has been replaced by **test.gz**. If you're used to working in the PC or Macintosh worlds, you may be used to working with PKZip from PKWare. However, **gzip** and PKZip don't work exactly the same. For starters, **gzip** won't compress multiple files into a single archive via wild cards in the way PKZip does. If you run the following command line:

```
gilbert:/home/kevinr# gzip te*
```

A listing of the current directory would yield the following result:

```
#test#   fig7_10.xwd   fig7_12.xwd     test.gz
#test3#  fig7_11.xwd   test.bk.gz      test3.gz
```

The original files beginning with *te* have replaced by individual files beginning with *te* and ending with *.gz*.

To see to what extent a file has been compressed, use the *-l* (ell) option to **gzip** on a compressed file:

```
gilbert:/home/kevinr# gzip -l test.gz
compressed   uncompr.   ratio  uncompressed_name
       122    245        59.5%  test
```

The 59.5 percent is actually a tad low for a file compressed with **gzip**; however, since we started out with a relatively small file, the compression factor isn't as extensive as it would be with a larger file.

However, some large files that are already compressed (namely graphics files in the JPEG and GIF formats) can't be compressed to a great extent by **gzip**.

Using Gunzip

The **gunzip** command can be used to uncompress any compressed file, no matter if the compression was performed with the **gzip**, **compress**, or **pack** commands. It's simple to use—just combine it with the name of the compressed file:

```
gilbert:/home/kevinr# gunzip test.gz
```

When you uncompress a file, the compressed file is automatically deleted from the system. If you're uncompressing a file and you're not quite sure about its contents, you may want to copy the file into another directory, leaving the original compressed file intact.

Using Tar

As noted, the **gzip** command doesn't work with a set of files, working only on a single specified file. If you want to compress a set of files, you'll first need to create an archive of files, and then compress the archive. The UNIX/Linux **tar** (*t*ape *a*rchive) command does just this.

Tar doesn't actually compress any files in the archive. It merely combines the files and retains the directory structure in one large archive.

Again, if you're wandering around the Internet and various FTP sites, you'll probably run into files that end with *.tar.gz*; this means that a set of files have been archived with **tar** and then compressed with **gzip**. And if you ever decide to do system backups—which we strongly advise that you do—the **tar** command is the first step in creating that archive.

The **tar** command is somewhat involved; it's not that it's difficult to use, but rather that its options tend to the obscure side. However, a few examples of **tar** in action should clear things up for you.

Let's say you want to backup all the files in an important directory—**/home/patrick**—to make sure your work isn't lost to the world. Before you use **tar**, make sure your current directory is **/home/patrick**, and then use the following command line to backup the contents of the directory:

```
gilbert:~/patrick tar cvf archive.tar .
```

This command line will create an archived file name **archive.tar** in the current directory, through the use of the following functions and options:

- **c**, which *c*reates the archive file;
- **v**, which tells **tar** to be *v*erbose (that is, report on the files being archives) as it archives the contents of the directory;
- **f**, which specifies that **archive.tar** is the *f*ilename of the archive.

It doesn't matter too much what order the functions and options are in; older versions of **tar** required that a function immediately follow the command in the command line, but the version of **tar** that ships with Linux lacks this requirement. However, it's usually a good idea to put *f* as your final option, since this is where you specify a filename.

Tar also leaves the existing files in the directory intact (unlike **gzip**, which removes the original file).

Tar doesn't require the usage of a hyphen (-) before functions and options. However, you can use one if you please, as it won't cause any effect to the command line.

The command line ends with a period (.), which tells **tar** to use all of the contents of the current directory as input for the archive file. (**Tar** will also archive hidden files.) You can also use **tar** with wildcards (using **c*** instead of **.** at the end of the command line would archive all files in the current directory beginning with *c*). In addition, you can specify a directory to be archives, giving either a pathname (**home/patrick**) or a pathname relative to the current directory (for instance, you can specify **patrick** if the current directory is **/home**). However, you cannot use absolute filenames to create an archive; **tar** will remove the leading slash (/) from the pathname, to make sure that important files aren't overwritten when the file is unarchived. (You'll see why later in this section.) When you specify a directory to be archives, **tar** will also archive any sub directories and maintain the directory structure. In fact, it's considered good practice to create a sub directory specifically for the archived material; in that way, users won't have problems when unarchiving your materials on their systems.

After you run **tar**, you end up with another Linux file, subject to the same rules that all Linux files must follow. You could copy this file to a floppy disk, you could copy it to another directory in the Linux file system, you could save it to a tape drive or recordable CD-ROM drive, or you could compress it using **gzip** (as explained earlier in this chapter). Since all UNIX users have access to the **tar** command, you can pass the file along to other users and know that they can unarchive your archive. In addition, there are versions of **tar** for the MS-DOS and Macintosh operating systems, so your archive can be used by the vast majority of computer users.

Functions and Options

When we used **tar** in the previous section, we specified *cvf* on the command line. This bears some further explanation.

Tar requires the use of *functions* as well as *options* on the command line. If you enter a command line lacking a function, **tar** will report an error. In our sample command line, we used *c* as the obligatory function, following it up with the optional *v* and *f* options.

Important **tar** functions and options are listed in Tables 7.9 and 7.10. We present them in case you'll need some of the more obscure functions; for the most part, the only functions you'll use are *c, x,* and *t.*

Table 7.9 Important functions in tar.

Function	Result
A	Appends files to an existing archive
c	Creates a new archive
d	Compares existing files in the file system to the files in the archive, making sure that no existing files are overwritten
r	Appends specified files to the end of an existing archive
t	Lists of the contents of an existing archive
u	Updates files in the file system if the archive contains newer versions
x	Extracts files and directories from the archive

Table 7.10 Important options in tar.

Function	Result
f *filename*	Specifies a *filename* for the archive
k	Keeps existing files
M	Creates a multivolume archive
v	Works in verbose mode, which means that **tar** lists the files being archives or unarchived; we always use this option to make sure **tar** is really archiving the files we want archived
z	Zips a file (using **gzip**) while also creating the archive. (This option will be explained later in this chapter)

NOTE These are the major functions and options for **tar**, but there are a host of other functions and options that may apply to other situations. For a full list of the functions and options for the GNU version of **tar**, use the following command line:

```
gilbert:~$ man tar
```

or else use the **info** command to view the **texinfo** explanation of **tar**.

Unarchiving an Archive

You'll also use **tar** to unarchive a **tar** file, using a command line that looks like the following:

```
gilbert:~$ tar xvf archive.tar
```

This will unarchive the files, as well as create any subdirectories found in the archive. However, these subdirectories will be created as a subdirectory of the current working directory. In the above command line, if there's a directory named **stuff**, it will be created as a subdirectory of the user's home directory. When files are archived, **tar** automatically strips the leading slash (/), which denotes an absolute pathname. If you've been a good UNIX citizen, you've created an archive based on a new subdirectory, so all the files that are unarchived will be in their own subdirectory.

To see what files are in an archive, use the t function with **tar**:

```
gilbert:~$ tar tvf archive.tar
drwxr-xr-x kevinr/users        0 Apr 23 00:57 1995 home/kevinr/
-rw-r--r-- kevinr/users      164 Mar 30 02:59 1995 home/kevinr/.kermrc
-rw-r--r-- kevinr/users       34 Jun  6 15:16 1993 home/kevinr/.less
-rw-r--r-- kevinr/users      114 Nov 23 19:22 1993 home/kevinr/.lessrc
drwxr-xr-x kevinr/users        0 Mar 29 09:31 1995 home/kevinr/.term
-rwxr-xr-x kevinr/users     2730 Mar 30 02:59 1995
                                                home/kevinr/.term/termrc
-rw-r--r-- kevinr/users     3016 May 13 16:39 1994 home/kevinr/.emacs
 -rw-r--r-- kevinr/users     471 Apr 20 03:12 1995
                                                home/kevinr/.bash_history
 -rw-r--r-- root/root        197 Apr 21 00:04 1995 home/kevinr/test3
 -rw-r--r-- root/root        247 Apr 20 03:33 1995 home/kevinr/#test#
 -rw-r--r-- root/root        197 Apr 21 00:18 1995 home/kevinr/#test3#
 -rw-r--r-- root/root     268399 Apr 22 11:48 1995
                                                home/kevinr/fig7_10.xwd
 -rw-r--r-- kevinr/users     122 Apr  6 10:13 1995 home/kevinr/test.gz
 -rw-r--r-- root/root     325889 Apr 22 12:03 1995
                                                home/kevinr/fig7_11.xwd
 -rw-r--r-- root/root     252107 Apr 22 12:01 1995
                                                home/kevinr/fig7_12.xwd
 -rw-r--r-- kevinr/users     245 Apr  8 09:22 1995 home/kevinr/test.bk
```

The t function merely tells **tar** to display the contents of the archive; there's no extraction of files. Armed with this knowledge, however, we could go ahead and unarchive a specific file or files. For example, to unarchive the file **test.bk**, you'd use the following command line:

```
gilbert:~$ tar xvf archive.tar home/kevinr/test.bk
```

Using the Z Option

As we've mentioned repeatedly here, you'll probably use the **tar** command in conjunction with the **gzip** command, creating an archived and compressed file. Because Linux works with tools from the Free Software Foundation, you can expect some integration of similar tools (as you've seen with **emacs** and **texinfo**). This integration is extended with an option unique to the GNU versions of **tar** and **gzip**: the z option. This handy function allows you to both archive and compress a file or set of files by using the z options with **tar**. For example, you could use the following command line to both archive and compress a set of files:

```
gilbert:~$ tar cvzf archive.tar.gz .
```

You must specify the *tar* and *gz* extensions when creating an archive using the z option, as opposed to the separate use of **gzip** where a gz extension is added automatically.

To both unarchive and uncompress a file, you'd use the following command line:

```
gilbert:~$ tar xvzf archive.tar.gz
```

Making System Backups

In our discussion of **tar** and **gzip**, we didn't really get into making backups of your systems. If you've been exposed at all to computing (and by the time you're at this point, you should be). Computing systems fail, though not as often as they did in the past, and you should always make it a point to back up critical data.

Of course, what constitutes critical data depends on your viewpoint. Some users feel comfortable with backing up their entire system, particularly if they've made a ton of configuration changes to their Linux installations. (This would include recompiling the kernel.) Others may feel comfortable in backing up only selected system files, knowing that Linux is on a CD-ROM and can be easily reinstalled.

Backups really fall in two categories: *system* files and *data* files. The system files, of course, are the configuration files that you've adapted for your own particular usage; these would include any hidden configuration files, as well as the configuration files used for the X Window System. On the other hand, data files are your actual work; if you've been programming an application, for example, you'll want to save those data files in a backup frequently. And you'll probably want to save the files—both hidden and public—in your home directory, and the home directories of your users if you're a system administrator.

Our larger point is that there's no size to fit all the circumstances surrounding a backup. If you're a system administrator and need to save a large number of files, you should be using **tar**, **gzip**, and a tape drive to archive files. If you're just looking at saving a few smaller files or a single directory, you can use **tar** and **gzip** to create a smaller file that can be copied directly to a floppy disk.

Using a Floppy for Backups

Linux allows you to directly write to a floppy disk. You don't need to mount the disk drive or create a Linux file system before writing to it. Even if the diskette is formatted with MS-DOS, Linux will write over the existing contents of the file. (In other words, if you've got important files on a diskette and don't want them to be wiped out by Linux, don't use a device driver to access the floppy. Later in this chapter we'll discuss Linux commands for accessing the MS-DOS-formatted floppy.)

Linux assumes that the first disk drive on a PC is **/dev/fd0**. You can use the **tar** command to send its output to this drive, instead of to a file:

```
gilbert:~$ tar cvf /dev/fd0 .
```

If the contents of the archives files are too large to fit on one floppy, you'll need to create a multivolume archive; you can do so with the *M* (remembering that case counts in Linux; using *m* instead of *M* will yield a different result!) option to **tar**, as in the following command line:

```
gilbert:~$ tar cvMf /dev/fd0 .
```

In this instance, you'll want to keep careful track of your floppies; if they get out of order or you accidentally lose a diskette, you run the risk of ruining the entire archive.

Of course, if you use the *z* option to **tar**, you may be able to fit an entire archive on a single floppy.

Using a Tape Drive for Backups

You can write to a tape drive for a backup directly with the **tar** command. However, which device you write to depends on your system setup.

If you're using a tape drive that runs from the floppy controller (as is the case with most QIC-type drives, for example), you'll need to specify **/dev/rft0** as your device:

```
gilbert:~$ tar cvf /dev/rft0 .
```

This creates an archive on the tape drive.

NOTE There's a little more to creating this tape archive that might appear. For instance, if you're using a QIC-type tape drive, there's no way to format these tapes under Linux; you'll need to use the DOS utilities to format a tape (see, there was a reason to keep that DOS partition!), or else buy preformatted tapes.

In addition, there's the sticky issue of exactly how much data you can throw on a tape. Most newer QIC-type drives rewind automatically every use. However, Linux can't deal with this rewinding, and there's no way to create a marker on the tape to place multiple backups on the same tape. How wasteful this seems depends on who is paying for the tape; quite honestly, you can get by with just two tapes, performing weekly backups revolving the two tapes and reformatting between.

Another option is to use a non rewinding tape device driver, which can be specified as **/dev/nrft0** (or another number in the sequence, depending on your system setup). Your command line would look something like this:

```
gilbert:~$ tar cvf /dev/nrft0 .
```

In this manner you could create several archives.

When using **/dev/nrft0** you'll have to rewind the tape on your own and then look for separate archives. To rewind the tape after you're done creating archives, use the **mt** command:

```
gilbert:~$ mt /dev/nrft0 rewind
```

The **mt** command is a wonderful thing. If you're worked with tape drives at all, you know that they can run into problems when they're only partially used; they become "loose" and can jam. The **mt** command allows you to forward a tape to the end and then rewind, in a command line like the following:

```
gilbert:~$ mt /dev/nrft0 retension
```

Finally, the **mt** command allows you to specify files on a tape drive, in case you don't want to use **tar** to unarchive all of them. This gets you into some tricky ground, however, since Linux still can't recognize the file makers on a tape drive, and your efforts are in effect tricking Linux into accessing the correct files. Let's say you've rewound the tape, but you want to grab the second file on the tape. In this case, you must tell Linux to look for the *next* file on the tape—or in **mt** parlance, the first file past the current file. You'd use the following command line:

```
gilbert:~$ mt /dev/nrft0 fsf 1
```

The same thing could be used to move the tape placement to the third or fourth files on the tape, using the following command lines (respectively):

```
gilbert:~$ mt /dev/nrft0 fsf 2
```

and

```
gilbert:~$ mt /dev/nrft0 fsf 3
```

In addition, there's another twist to **mt**. You can't move between sequential files on a tape drive and then try to grab more than one file; with **mt**, you must move to the first file in question, and then move to the next file in question. If you want to grab the fifth and sixth files in a tape, you must first move to the fifth file, use **tar** to unarchive it, and then move to the sixth file separately, remembering that **mt** moves in relation to the current file. Therefore, you'd use a sequence like the following:

```
gilbert:~$ mt /dev/nrft0 fsf 4
```

remembering that you're moving in relation to the first file on the tape; after you use **tar**, you'd use the following command line:

```
gilbert:~$ mt /dev/nrft0 fsf 1
```

remembering that the sixth file is the first file after the fifth file.

You can also backup to a tape drive, such as a QIC or DAT tape drive, connected to a SCSI board. In this case, you'll use a command line like the following:

```
gilbert:~$ mt /dev/rst0 .
```

if you want to use a rewinding device and the SCSI device is numbered *0*, or:

```
gilbert:~$ mt /dev/nrst0 .
```

for a rewinding device and the SCSI device is numbered *0*.

The **mt** command also allows you to access tapes made by different devices. For the most part, you shouldn't have problems reading a DAT tape created on another system. However, you can run into problems if the other UNIX system used a different block size when creating the tape. In this case, your attempts to read the file will result in error messages. To avoid these, you'll need to use **mt** to specify a new block size, as in the following command line:

```
gilbert:~$ mt setblk blocksize
```

There are a host of additional options to the **mt** command; as always, you're encouraged to peruse the online-manual page:

```
gilbert:~$ man mt
```

Commands Specific to the PC Architecture: MTools

The **mt** command is but one of many Linux commands that are expressly designed for the many quirks of the PC architecture—and specifically on DOS-formatted floppy disks. The MTools commands are designed to take these quirks into account when performing many routine tasks.

In short, the need for the m-series of commands exists because DOS files and UNIX files are structured a little differently, which is something that you'll need to watch for, especially if you're using floppy drives. In fact, you can wipe out a good DOS floppy disk by using a UNIX command to copy a file to it. (We learned this the hard way.) Therefore, you'll want to check out the m-series of commands, used specifically to deal with the quirks of the DOS and Linux architectures and the differences between them.

Using Mdir to View the Contents of a DOS Directory

This straightforward command is used to list the contents of a DOS directory:

```
gilbert:~$ mdir
```

The default for **mdir**, as well as the rest of the Mtools, is A:. Since a DOS partition can be mounted from Linux, the m-series of commands don't accept C: as an input.

Using Mcd to Change Directories

The **mcd** command changes directories on the floppy drive (the default is the root directory on A:). Without an argument, it displays the current device and working directory:

```
gilbert:~$ mcd
A:/
```

Using Mcopy to Copy Files

As noted, the UNIX **cp** command can be destructive to a MS-DOS file structure on a floppy. To copy a file from within Linux to a DOS floppy, you'll want to use the **mcopy** command:

```
gilbert:~$ mcopy -t textfile a:textfile
```

As you probably noticed, the **mcopy** command uses the DOS convention of naming floppy drives (as opposed to the UNIX **dev** designations). Here **mcopy** was used to copy a file named **textfile** (presumably containing text) to the A: floppy drive. The *-t* option was used because UNIX and DOS have different ways of dealing with line feeds, and this option is specifically for text-file translation.

There are only a few other command-line options to **mcopy**. In a show of mercy on the part of its designers, **mcopy** will warn you if you're overwriting an existing file. In order to ignore this mercy, you'd need to run **mcopy** with the *-n* option:

```
gilbert:~$ mcopy -n textfile a:textfile
```

If you want to be told about each file movement as it happens, use the verbose mode, as launched by the *-v* option:

```
gilbert:~$ mcopy -v textfile a:textfile
```

Also, remember that you must always conform to the DOS eight-dot-three naming convention when working with DOS files.

The **mread** and **mwrite** commands also do the same thing.

Using Mren to Rename DOS Files

The **mren** command renames DOS files:

```
gilbert:~$ mren oldfile.nam newfile.nam
```

Remember that you must always conform to the DOS eight-dot-three naming convention when working with DOS files.

Using Mdel to Delete DOS Files

The **mdel** command, predictably enough, is used to delete files from a DOS directory. For instance, to delete **textfile** from the A: floppy drive, you'd use the following command line:

```
gilbert:~$ mdel a:textfile
```

Using Mtype to View a DOS File

If you want to view the contents of a DOS file on a floppy, use the **mtype** command to display the file:

```
gilbert:~$ mtype filename
```

If you're viewing an ASCII file, use the *-t* option:

```
gilbert:~$ mtype -t filename
```

Using Mmd to Create a DOS Directory

You can create a DOS directory with the **mmd** command:

```
gilbert:~$ mmd newdirec.tor
```

Remember that you must always conform to the DOS eight-dot-three naming convention when working with DOS directories.

Using Mrd to Remove a DOS Directory

If you're not happy with the directory you created with **mmd**, you can delete it with the **mrd** command:

```
gilbert:~$ mrd newdirec.tor
```

Using Mread to Copy a DOS File to Linux

The **mread** command transfers a DOS file to a Linux file, making appropriate conversions if necessary. This command actually works on two different levels: It can be used to transfer a single file to a UNIX file, or it can be used to transfer a set of DOS files to a Linux directory. In the first usage, you'll need to specify both the DOS and UNIX filenames:

```
gilbert:~$ mread dosfile unixfile
```

To copy a set of files to a specific UNIX directory, specify the DOS files (yes, you can use wildcards) and then the UNIX directory:

```
gilbert:~$ mread *.* /home/kevinr
```

If a file of the same name already exists in the destination directory, **mread** will warn you before overwriting the file.

There are a few useful options to **mread**:

- *t*, which converts a DOS text file to a UNIX text file, which strips DOS carriage returns from the destination file.
- *m*, which preserves the time stamps on the original DOS files.

- *n*, which removes the overwriting-prevention mechanisms.

 The **mcopy** command will also copy files between DOS and Linux.

Using Mwrite to Write a UNIX File to DOS

The **mwrite** command writes a UNIX file to a DOS-formatted diskette:

```
gilbert:~$ mwrite unixfile dosfile
```

If a file of the same name already exists in the destination diskette, **mwrite** will warn you before overwriting the file.

There are a few useful options to **mwrite**:

- *t*, which converts a UNIX text file to a DOS text file, which adds DOS carriage returns to the destination file.
- *m*, which preserves the time stamps on the original Linux files.
- *n*, which removes the overwriting-prevention mechanisms.

 The **mcopy** command will also copy files between DOS and Linux.

Using Mformat to Format a Diskette

The **mformat** command adds the basics of a DOS file system (FAT, boot sector, and a root directory) to a UNIX-formatted diskette. To format a diskette in drive A:, you'd use the following:

```
gilbert:~$ mformat a:
```

Mformat also supports a number of options:

- *t*, which sets the number of tracks (*not* sectors).
- *h*, which sets the number of heads.
- *s*, which sets the sectors per track.
- *l*, which sets the volume label.

The **mformat** command will work only with a diskette that's already been formatted for UNIX. Its usefulness is actually more limited than may appear at first glance.

Using Mlabel to Designate a Volume Label

The **mlabel** command displays a current DOS volume label and then asks you for a new label; if you don't enter anything at the prompt, **mlabel** merely removes the existing volume label without adding a new one. The only option to **mlabel**, *-v*, runs the command in verbose mode (always a good thing if you're working with an unfamiliar command).

Using Mattrib to Change the DOS File Attributes

If you're exchanging files with a DOS machine, you may (however, the chance is pretty remote) run into conflicts with the file's attributes (which are akin to the Linux file permissions). A DOS file can have be read-only (*r*), archived (*a*), system (*s*), or hidden (*h*). You can use **mattrib** to change these permissions—+ to add the attribute (highly unlikely) or - to remove the attribute (which is more likely, though in all honesty you probably won't be messing too much with DOS file attributes). For instance, to change a file from hidden to unhidden, you'd use the following command line:

```
gilbert:~$ mattrib -h filename
```

To remove the read-only designation from a file, use a command line like the following:

```
gilbert:~$ mattrib -r filename
```

To make the file a regular file and not a system file, you'd use a command line like the following:

```
gilbert:~$ mattrib -s filename
```

To make the file a file that can be archived (how DOS allows files to be archived is a rather twisted and sordid tale; let's just leave it at that), you'd use a command line like the following:

```
gilbert:~$ mattrib -a filename
```

To add the attributes in the above examples, you'd substitute **+** for **-**.

The above commands assumes that you're working with drive A. If you're working with a file on your hard drive, you can designate an absolute filename on the command line (using the DOS practice of a backslash between directories), but be sure and enclose the absolute filename in quotation marks, or else your Linux shell will choke on the filename.

System-Administration Tools

If you're working on a standalone Linux system, you're wearing two hats: the hat of a user and the hat of a system administrator. Of course, when you installed Linux in Chapter 2 and set up a user account, you were fulfilling the role of a system administrator. Congratulations!

In fact, setting up and maintaining accounts is one of the more important tasks you have as a system administrator. If you plan on letting other people (i.e., the family or a co-worker) use your Linux system, you should set up user accounts for them, complete with passwords, groups and home directories.

Using the Passwd File

Linux stores information about users in the **/etc/passwd** file (not to be confused with the **passwd** command, of course). As a matter of fact,

Linux stores a lot of system-configuration information in this file, as is evidenced by the following excerpt:

```
root::0:0:root:/root:/bin/bash
bin:*:1:1:bin:/bin:
daemon:*:2:2:daemon:/sbin:
adm:*:3:4:adm:/var/adm:
lp:*:4:7:lp:/var/spool/lpd:
sync:*:5:0:sync:/sbin:/bin/sync
shutdown:*:6:0:shutdown:/sbin:/sbin/shutdown
halt:*:7:0:halt:/sbin:/sbin/halt
mail:*:8:12:mail:/var/spool/mail:
news:*:9:13:news:/usr/lib/news:
uucp:*:10:14:uucp:/var/spool/uucppublic:
operator:*:11:0:operator:/root:/bin/bash
games:*:12:100:games:/usr/games:
man:*:13:15:man:/usr/man:
postmaster:*:14:12:postmaster:/var/spool/mail:/bin/bash
nobody:*:65535:100:nobody:/dev/null:
ftp:*:404:1::/home/ftp:/bin/bash
root:/IoSosasKKS83:0:0:root:/root:/bin/bash
kevinr:/AoIoaPOSU80c:501:100:Kevin Reichard:/home/kevinr:/bin/bash
```

Most of these commands specify the paths associated with specific commands, such as the path for **man** pages. If you want to change these defaults (for instance, if you're using **uucp** to connect to other systems and other systems are connecting to yours, this would be the place to change the **uucp** default path), here's the place to do it.

Our real concern, however, is with the final line of the file, concerning the configuration for the user **kevinr**:

```
kevinr:/AoIoaPOSU80c:501:100:Kevin Reichard:/home/kevinr:/bin/bash
```

We'll break this line down:

- *kevinr* refers to the user name, obviously.

- *AoIoaPOSU8Oc* is an encrypted form of the password. If the password begins with an asterisk (*), this means that the account is disabled (something you'll learn about later in this chapter).

- *501* is the user ID, a numeral the system uses to track the account. Instead of dealing with *kevinr* when working with file permissions and such, the system deals with 501, or the equivalent user ID.

- *100* is the group ID. (Again, you'll learn about groups later in this chapter.)

- *Kevin Reichard* is the full name of the user. It can contain additional information about the user.

- */home/kevinr* refers to the user's home directory.

- */bin/bash* refers to the user's default shell.

Not every field needs to be used, but there needs to be spaces left for them (:).

As you can see from the previous example, the root user has a slightly different line than does a normal user; in this case, zeroes (0) are used in the user ID and group ID fields.

This file is where you'd check for the current user configuration, not to add new users. The **adduser** command, which you first encountered in Chapter 2, can be used to add users. This command can be run by the root or superuser at any time:

```
gilbert:/# adduser
```

You can make changes to this file that will be reflected in the system as a whole; for instance, you can give the user a new ID by merely changing the appropriate number in the user ID field. However, there are ramification to doing this; since the system tracks file ownership and group membership by user ID and not by user name, this change will mean that all the files that the user used to own would be in ownership limbo; you'd need to manually change the ownership of the files with the **chown** command. Unless you absolutely, positively have to change the user ID for a user, you're best off avoiding this maneuver.

Deleting Accounts

The flip side of adding accounts is, of course, deleting accounts. If you're working on a smaller system, you don't need to worry too much about deleting accounts, unless you have a situation where a disgruntled employee may have the opportunity to wreak havoc on your system.

Deleting an account is a multifaceted affair, however, as you must delete any reference to the user in the Linux system. This means removing the user's entry from **/etc/passwd**, removing the user's home directory, transferring ownership of the removed user's files, deleting references to the user from any group files (which you'll learn about in the next section), and making sure that the mail subsystem doesn't continue to acknowledge the user's existence.

You may also want to disable an account, rather than delete it outright. In this case, you'd merely throw an asterisk (*) in front of the user's password in the **/etc/passwd file**. The following would temporarily disable *kevinr's* account:

```
kevinr:*/AoIoaPOSU80c:501:100:Kevin Reichard:/home/kevinr:/bin/bash
```

Managing Groups

In the UNIX world, *groups* have a long history as a mechanism for dividing access to certain files. Anyone who's worked with a network of any sort realizes that giving only some members access to a set of files enhances security and makes organizational chores go that much easier.

Linux supports groups; each file is owned by both a user and a group. By using the **ls -l** (that's *ell*, not one) command line, you can get the full permissions line for a file:

```
gilbert:~$ ls -l
-rwxrw-r—  1 kevinr users    87619 Apr 23 23:39 addresses.dat
```

This tells us that the file **addresses.dat** is owned by both the individual user *kevinr* and the group *users*, that *kevinr* can read, write, and execute the file, while the *users* group can read and write the file. All other users can only read the file.

Here are the contents of a typical **/etc/group** file:

```
root::0:root
bin::1:root,bin,daemon
daemon::2:root,bin,daemon
sys::3:root,bin,adm
adm::4:root,adm,daemon
tty::5:
disk::6:root,adm
lp::7:lp
mem::8:
kmem::9:
wheel::10:root
floppy::11:root
mail::12:mail
news::13:news
uucp::14:uucp
man::15:man
users::100:kevinr,pat,erc
execs::101:kevinr,pat
nogroup::-1:
```

As you can see, most of the listings in a **/etc/group** file have very little to do with user group, and have more to do with applications and other ownership issues. You can tell which lines have to do with user groups, as they are numbered above 100 (this is a Linux convention). In the above example, these two lines are reserved for user groups:

```
users::100:kevinr,pat,erc
execs::101:kevinr,pat
```

This is actually an incomplete listing, as evidenced by the double colon, meaning a field has been left out. Normally the lines in the **/etc/group** file are listed in the following format:

```
groupname:password:groupID:users
```

This field is blank because most systems don't bother setting up passwords for groups; whether or not this is a huge security breach is debatable, and to be honest setting up a password for a group is a pain.

Logging in as Su

When you want to work as the root user (for the purposes of adding and deleting users, for example), you don't need to logoff the system and then login again as **root**; instead, you can login as the *superuser*:

```
gilbert:~$ su
gilbert:/home/kevinr#
```

Note that the previous home directory was listed as ~, but is changed to **/home/kevinr** after logging in as superuser.

In addition, there's another important reason to login as *su* (as well as having others on your Linux system login as superuser, in instances where there are multiple administrators on the network): When someone is logged in as *root*, the system only notes that *root* logged on the system. However, when someone uses **su** to login for root privileges, there's a record of the login in the file **/var/adm/messages:**

```
Apr 27 22:06:30 gilbert su: kevinr on /dev/tty1
```

To quit using the system as superuser, using **exit** or **bye**:

```
gilbert:/home/kevinr# exit
exit
gilbert:~$
```

More on the Messages File

The **/var/adm/messages** file can be a very useful tool if you're trying to track down problems with your Linux system, as it logs all system activity, including the system configuration when boot Linux. The

following section shows the messages logged to **/var/adm/messages**
when Linux is booted:

```
Kernel logging (proc) started.
Console: colour EGA+ 80x25, 1 virtual console (max 63)
Serial driver version 4.00 with no serial options enabled
tty00 at 0x03f8 (irq = 4) is a 16450
tty01 at 0x02f8 (irq = 3) is a 16450
lp_init: lp0 exists, using polling driver
ftape: allocated 3 buffers aligned at: 00230000
SBPCD version 2.6 Eberhard Moenkeberg <emoenke@gwdg.de>
SBPCD: Looking for a SoundBlaster/Matsushita CD-ROM drive
SBPCD:
SBPCD: = = = = = = = = = W A R N I N G = = = = = = = = = =
SBPCD: Auto-Probing can cause a hang (f.e. touching an ethernet card).
SBPCD: If that happens, you have to reboot and use the
SBPCD: LILO (kernel) command line feature like:
SBPCD:
SBPCD:     LILO boot: linux sbpcd=0x230,SoundBlaster
SBPCD: or like:
SBPCD:     LILO boot: linux sbpcd=0x300,LaserMate
SBPCD: or like:
SBPCD:     LILO boot: linux sbpcd=0x330,SPEA
SBPCD:
SBPCD: with your REAL address.
SBPCD: = = = = = = = = = = END of WARNING = = = = = = = = = =
SBPCD:
SBPCD: Trying to detect a SoundBlaster CD-ROM drive at 0x230.
SBPCD: - Drive 0: CR-563-x (0.80)
SBPCD: 1 SoundBlaster CD-ROM drive(s) at 0x0230.
SBPCD: init done.
Calibrating delay loop.. ok - 25.04 BogoMips
scsi : 0 hosts.
Memory: 14652k/16384k available (976k kernel code, 384k reserved,
  372k data)
```

```
This processor honours the WP bit even when in supervisor mode. Good.
Floppy drive(s): fd0 is 1.44M
FDC 0 is a 8272A
Swansea University Computer Society NET3.017
Swansea University Computer Society TCP/IP for NET3.017
IP Protocols: ICMP, UDP, TCP
PPP: version 0.2.7 (4 channels) NEW_TTY_DRIVERS OPTIMIZE_FLAGS
TCP compression code copyright 1989 Regents of the University of
  California
PPP line discipline registered.
SLIP: version 0.7.5-NET3.014-NEWTTY (4 channels)
CSLIP: code copyright 1989 Regents of the University of California
eth0: 3c505 not found
eth0: D-Link DE-600 pocket adapter: not at I/O 0x378.
D-Link DE-620 pocket adapter not identified in the printer port
Checking 386/387 coupling... Ok, fpu using exception 16 error
  reporting.
Checking 'hlt' instruction... Ok.
Linux version 1.1.59 (root@fuzzy) (gcc version 2.5.8) #5 Sat Oct
  29 15:50:31 CDT 1994
Partition check:
  hda: WDC AC2340H, 325MB w/128KB Cache, CHS=1010/12/55,
  MaxMult=16
  hda: hda1 hda2
VFS: Mounted root (ext2 filesystem) readonly.
Max size:332509   Log zone size:2048
First datazone:152   Root inode number 155648
ISO9660 Extensions: RRIP_1991A
gilbert login: ROOT LOGIN ON tty1
```

Most of this code is pretty self-evident, but we'll take a few minutes to explain what a few of the lines mean, in order of appearance. The first line of the code, obviously, shows that the system started logging actions. The next line:

```
Console: colour EGA+ 80x25, 1 virtual console (max 63)
```

tells what resolution Linux is running in. This resolution applies only to Linux running in text mode, not when running the X Window System. The lines:

```
tty00 at 0x03f8 (irq = 4) is a 16450
tty01 at 0x02f8 (irq = 3) is a 16450
```

both refer to the serial devices on the PC, and their corresponding IRQs. As you'll recall from Chapter 2, **tty00** is the equivalent of COM1 (in other words, the first serial port). This also tells us that the serial port features a 16450 UART chip, which you'll find useful for high-speed communications.

The next set of lines beginning with *SBPCD* refer to configuration factors when using a SoundBlaster Pro sound card/CD-ROM drive, as the system automatically polls the device to make sure it's functional. The line:

```
Memory: 14652k/16384k available (976k kernel code, 384k reserved,
    372k data)
```

refers to the amount of RAM the system has. In this case, as 16MB of RAM are indeed installed on the PC, this means that Linux can see all of it. The line:

```
Floppy drive(s): fd0 is 1.44M
```

refers to the floppy drive, which Linux does recognize as a high-density 3.5-inch drive on **fd0**. The line:

```
eth0: 3c505 not found
```

refers to an unsuccessful search for an Ethernet card—no surprise, since this particular machine is lacking such a device. However, the following lines:

```
Swansea University Computer Society NET3.017
Swansea University Computer Society TCP/IP for NET3.017
```

```
IP Protocols: ICMP, UDP, TCP
PPP: version 0.2.7 (4 channels) NEW_TTY_DRIVERS OPTIMIZE_FLAGS
TCP compression code copyright 1989 Regents of the University
   of California
PPP line discipline registered.
SLIP: version 0.7.5-NET3.014-NEWTTY (4 channels)
CSLIP: code copyright 1989 Regents of the University of
   California
```

shows that this machine supports the SLIP and PPP remote-login protocols, which means that this machine could login to an Internet host. The line:

```
ISO9660 Extensions: RRIP_1991A
```

tells us that the CD-ROM drive supports the ISO-9660 extensions. Finally, the line:

```
gilbert login: ROOT LOGIN ON tty1
```

tells us that a root user logged in the system.

Error Messages

The previous section relied on a small section of the **/var/adm/messages** file; if you take a look, you'll see a *very* large file if you've been using Linux for any amount of time. For instance, you'll see who logged on and off the system, even if the login was unsuccessful, as in the following line:

```
Mar 31 14:48:51 gilbert login: 1 LOGIN FAILURE ON tty1, root]
```

Scheduling Events

Linux features a number of system-administration tools that allow you to schedule events at specific times; for instance, you may want to schedule a system backup in the middle of the night. These tools are covered in the next few sections.

The Nice Command

Sometimes you'll run a command and not care too much when it's completed, such as when you issue a command right before you leave for lunch. When time is not of the essence—especially on large, multiuser systems that may not contain quite enough hardware firepower to support so many users—you may want to use the **nice** command in conjunction with other commands, so named because you're being *nice* to the system. Use it at the beginning of the command line:

```
gilbert:~$ nice command filename
```

For instance, if you're performing an extremely complicated sort with many files, you may want to launch the sort using **nice** before that typical two-hour lunch.

The At Command

Of course, some lunches can expand to three or even four hours, depending on the libations involved. If you're not sure you'll be back to the office in time to run an important command, you can use the **at** command.

Seriously, you're more likely to use the **at** command to relieve pressure on the system by running system-intensive commands in the middle of the night, to send mail messages involving long-distance charges when rates are lowest, or to backup a large hard disk at some regular interval.

Using **at** is simple, as you first specify a time for execution, followed by the command line. To set up a specific command, type the following:

```
gilbert:~$ at 11am
```

At is very flexible about defining the time when the command is to be run; you can use a time as in our example, or you can use a more precise number based on military time.

After you hit the **Enter** (or **Return**) key, you'll be placed on the following line, without a prompt. As you recall, this is the Linux method of asking you for additional input. (Usually, anyway; there are exceptions.) This is where you provide the command that at is to execute; end each command by hitting the **Enter** (or **Return**) key. When you're through, type **Ctrl-D**.

The system's response is a single line of information that confirms when the command (designated by the system with a job-ID of many digits) will be run. This job-ID is very valuable information. Should you need to see a list of pending job-IDs, use **at** with the -*l* option:

```
gilbert:~$ at -l
```

If you want to cancel a pending command scheduled with **at**, use **at** with the -*r* (remove) option:

```
gilbert:~$ at -r job-ID
```

For procedures you need to perform again and again, **cron**, covered later in this chapter, is likely to be a better tool than **at**.

The Batch Command

The **batch** command combines many commands into one command line, which is then run in the background without any prompting on your part. Use **batch** as follows:

```
gilbert:~$ batch
```

End the command by hitting the **Enter** (or **Return**) key. As with **at**, you'll be placed on a new line, as **batch** waits for additional input. Go ahead and type in the commands, ending each by hitting the **Enter** (or **Return**) key. When you're finishing entering commands, type **Ctrl-D**.

You'll then be presented with a command prompt, so go ahead with your other work as your **batch** commands are quietly executed by the system. If your commands require some sort of confirmation message or output delivered to you, the message will be conveyed as a mail message; you won't find messages popping up on your screen while you're in the middle of some other action.

Elsewhere in this book, we have discussed running programs in the background using the ampersand. There are some fundamental differences between background tasks and **batch**:

- Commands issued to **batch** are accorded even less priority than commands run in the background.

- With **batch**, commands will continue to execute even if you logoff the system. Background tasks are killed if you logoff the system.

- Background tasks will interrupt you should your background command specify some kind of output or confirmation. **Batch** does not; as we noted, confirmation or output is sent as a mail message.

The Cron Command

System administrators have all the fun—or used to, anyway, as evidenced by the **cron** command. **Cron** started life as a tool for system administration, allowing the system administrator to schedule regular tasks unattended.

Why use **cron**? As we said above, it allows you to schedule regular tasks unattended. You may want to backup your data to tape drive weekly or even daily. You may want to send yourself a mail message to remind you of important, non computer chores. Or you may want to send electronic mail to other UNIX systems late at night when the long-distance rates are lower.

NOTE

In some ways, the **at** command accomplishes the same as the **cron** command. So why use **cron**? Because you can set it up to perform regular tasks. With **at**, you can only set up a single task to be performed at one specific time. Because **at** is much easier to use, we recommend using it in one-time situations, and **cron** in repetitive situations.

There are two parts to **cron**: The **crontab** file and the actual **cron** command. We'll cover each.

Creating a Crontab File

As we said earlier, the **crontab** file contains the tasks that are to be performed regularly. You have your own personal **crontab** file, stored in the **/usr/lib/crontab** directory. Such a file is not created automatically when you install Linux; instead, it's up to you to create the file—though not directly. The **crontab** file installation, as well as the structure of the actual file, can be a tad confusing.

You can use **vi** or **emacs** to create a **crontab** file. However, you can't save the file directly in the **/usr/lib/crontab** directory; instead, you must save it under a different name and use the cron command to install it. We'll guide you through a typical file creation and installation.

There are six fields to a **crontab** file, each separated by a space. The first five fields specify exactly when the command is to be run; the sixth field is the command itself.

Let's say that we wanted to run a command every morning at 8:30 a.m. The structure of the **crontab** line looks something like this:

```
30 8 * * * command
```

The exact values associated with the five fields are listed in Table 7.11.

Table 7.11 Fields in a crontab line.

Field	Meaning
1	Minutes after the hour
2	Hour, in 24-hour format
3	Day of the month
4	Month
5	Day of the week

Some things to note when creating a **crontab** file:

- Asterisks (*) are used to specify when commands are to be run in every instance of the value of the field. An asterisk in the third field means to run the command every day of every month, an asterisk in the fourth field, means to run the command every month, an asterisk in the fifth field means to run the command every day of every week.

- Days of the week are notated somewhat strangely. The week begins with a 0 for Sunday and ends with a 6 for Saturday. (Computer people, especially on UNIX, are famous for starting to count with 0 rather than the more common 1 used by others)

- Times are specified in military (24-hour) time. Thus 10 p.m. is specified as 22.

- Ranges can be specified, instead of specific days and times. For instance, you can perform the command only on the 15th and 30th days of the month by using 15,30 in the third field. (Just make sure you adjust it in February.) Or you can specify that a command be run only the fall months by using 10-12 in the fourth field. These two methods can be combined: running a command in spring and all means using 4-6,10-12 in the fourth field.

After creating our **crontab** file (which must be saved under a filename of anything but **crontab**; we'll call it **ourfile**), we can then install it, using the **crontab** command:

```
gilbert:~$ crontab ourfile
```

Cron then takes **ourfile**, copies it, and saves the copy under our username in the **/usr/lib/crontab** directory, with a filename of **/usr/lib/crontab/***ourname*. If we want to make changes to our **cron** configuration, we must edit our original file (which still exists—remember, **cron** only makes a copy) and then reinstall it using **crontab**. If we want to totally remove the file, we must use the **crontab** command with the *-r* option:

```
$ crontab -r
```

To prevent mischief or some unintended damage, we are allowed access to only our own **crontab** file.

Some Crontab Examples

The **crontab -l** command lists out the **crontab** entry for your username. For example:

```
gilbert:~$ crontab -l

15 3 * * * sh /u/erc/my_backup
```

In this example, every night at 3:15 a.m., cron will invoke the Bourne shell, **sh**, and execute a shell script called **my_backup** that is stored in the **/u/erc** directory. Presumably, this script will back up certain directories to tape. The reason it's performed at 3:15 is because at this time, the machine is mostly idle.

If you only wanted to back up on Mondays, you'd use the following **crontab** entry:

```
15 3 * * 1 sh /u/erc/my_backup
```

Again, we've left the time to execute the script at the arbitrary time of 3:15 a.m.

If you wanted to only perform backups on the first and fifteenth of each month, you could use the following **crontab** entry:

```
15 3 1,15 * * sh /u/erc/my_backup
```

The Bc Command

Even though the proliferation of ubiquitous and inexpensive calculators have made this command somewhat obsolete, the **bc** command—especially in the Free Software Foundation version included with

Linux—can still be used as a very functional calculator. Use it as follows:

```
gilbert:~$ bc
1+1
2
quit
```

The preceding example was performed on a 486-based PC, not a Pentium.

This simple equation shows how to use **bc**: Type it as a command line, hit **Enter** (or **Return**), enter your equation, hit **Enter** (or **Return**), read the calculation, and type quit when you're through. Obviously, other more advanced features are available, such as square roots, converting numbers from one base to another, determining prime factors, control statements for writing programs, and more. Consult your system documentation or the online **man** page for further information.

More on Multitasking

We discussed running commands in the background briefly in Chapter 5. This is where we extend that discussion.

Multitasking is a fancy computer-speak way of saying the operating system can do more than one thing at a time. While this may seem like a simple matter, it's really not; personal-computer users have been screaming for a multitasking operating system for (seemingly) years (though, ironically, they for the most part ignore OS/2, which handles multitasking in much the same manner as Linux).

Linux documentation doesn't actually often use the term *multitasking* (even though the rest of the computer world uses it); instead, Linux is said to be *multiprocessing*—the same thing described differently. When you run a Linux command, like **ls** or **cat**, you're running a *process*. When you boot the Linux operating system, you are actually launching a series of processes without consciously doing so. (If you use a graphical user interface like the X Window System, you're launching many, *many* processes.) On a large multiuser system, there may be literally thousands of processes running at a given time.

These processes compete with each other for computing resources. Running programs in the background, as described earlier, is a way for the Linux user to allocate resources efficiently. Such allocation is necessary for to keep the system from bogging down, especially a large multiuser system with less-than-adequate resources. If there are more processes running than can fit in your system's random-access memory (RAM), then Linux uses a hard disk as extended RAM in a action called *swapping* to disk. (You've already leaned about a swap partition in Chapter 2; later in this chapter we'll discuss how to set up a swap file.) However, hard disks are much slower than RAM, so swapping to disk is not the most desirable of solutions; but on the PC, bit may be the only solution you have.

As we said, it's important for the Linux system and user to efficiently allocate resources. Linux does this (as it does almost everything else) in hierarchical fashion: Processes beget other processes (much as directories containing sub directories), with one process at the top of the pyramid. When a process launches another process, it uses a system call entitled a *fork*, which creates the new process.

When you boot a Linux system, the first process (process 1) launches a program called **init**, which then launches other processes. **Init** is the mother of all Linux processes—or, as referred to in Linuxdom, **init** is a *parent* to other resources, which in turn can act as parents to additional resources, called *child* processes. It is, ultimately, the ancestor of all processes running on the system.

When we described the shell and its importance in running programs for you, we were referring to the shell acting as the parent and managing other child processes. Unless you tell it otherwise (by issuing the **kill** command), the shell waits while you run a child and returns with a prompt after the child process is finished, or *dies*. (Telling it otherwise is accomplished through several means, background being the most common.) If a child process dies but this fact is not acknowledged by the parent, the child process becomes a *zombie*. What macabre imagery!

It's up to the operating system to keep track of these parents and children, making sure that processes don't collide. This means scheduling processes to within a fraction of a second, ensuring that all processes have access to precious CPU time. It's also up to the operating system, through the init program, to manage child processes that have been abandoned by their parents. These abandoned processes are called *orphans*. (Family values obviously play as important a role in the Linux operating system as they do in the Republican Party.)

Though we have mockingly referred to the high level of abstraction associated with the UNIX operating system, using names like *parent*, *orphan*, *zombie*, and *child* to describe the various stages of processes is a very useful thing; it helps both users and programmers visualize very intangible actions.

To see what processes are running on your system, use the **ps** command:

```
gilbert:~# ps
  PID TTY STAT  TIME COMMAND
   49 v02 S     0:00 /sbin/getty tty2 38400 console
   50 v03 S     0:00 /sbin/getty tty3 38400 console
   51 v04 S     0:00 /sbin/getty tty4 38400 console
   52 v05 S     0:00 /sbin/getty tty5 38400 console
   53 v06 S     0:00 /sbin/getty tty6 38400 console
   73 v01 S     0:01 bash
   57 v01 S     0:00 sh /usr/X11/bin/startx
  258 v01 S     0:00 xinit /usr/X11R6/lib/X11/xinit/xinitrc −
  260 v01 S     0:00 twm
  262 v01 S     0:00 /usr/bin/X11/oclock -geom 100x100+0+6
  263 v01 S     0:00 /usr/bin/X11/xterm -ls -geom 80x24+3+372
  264 v01 S     0:00 /usr/bin/X11/xterm -ls -geom 80x48+264+13
  265 pp1 S     0:01 -bash
  266 pp0 S     0:00 -bash
  293 pp1 R     0:00 ps
   48 v01 S     0:00 -bash
```

Because we used the command on a single-user Linux machine running X Window, our list of running processes is not very long (relatively speaking, of course). If you're working on a large, multiuser system and ask for the all the processes running, your list may be pages long. The fourth field, which covers the time the processes have run, may be of interest if there are some inordinately large numbers present. Most Linux commands, even very complex ones, don't take tons of time to complete.

We're using the **ps** command in its simplest form. Should you need more information than provided in the manner discussed here, use the **ps** command in the long form:

```
gilbert:~# ps -l
```

or in the full form:

```
gilbert:~# ps -f
```

which provides a lot of neat information, including which processes are children of other processes:

```
gilbert:~# ps -f
PID TTY STAT  TIME COMMAND
 49 v02 S     0:00 /sbin/getty tty2 38400 console
 50 v03 S     0:00 /sbin/getty tty3 38400 console
 51 v04 S     0:00 /sbin/getty tty4 38400 console
 52 v05 S     0:00 /sbin/getty tty5 38400 console
 53 v06 S     0:00 /sbin/getty tty6 38400 console
 48 v01 S     0:00 -bash
 73 v01 S     0:01  \_ bash
257 v01 S     0:00      \_ sh /usr/X11/bin/startx
258 v01 S     0:00          \_ xinit usr/X11R6/lib/X11/xinit/xinitrc -
260 v01 S     0:00              \_ twm
262 v01 S     0:00                  \_ /usr/bin/X11/oclock -geom
                                       100x100+0+6
263 v01 S     0:00                  \_ /usr/bin/X11/xterm -ls -geom
                                       80x24+3+37
```

```
266 pp0 S    0:00            |   \_ -bash
264 v01 S    0:01            \_ /usr/bin/X11/xterm -ls -geom
                                80x48+264+
265 pp1 S    0:02            \_ -bash
303 pp1 R    0:00                \_ ps -f
```

If you need to view all the processes running on the entire system (kids, don't try this at home, unless you *really* want a lot of information, most of it of questionable value), use:

```
gilbert:~# ps -e
```

To get a fuller view of the whole of the whole system, you can use:

```
gilbert:~# ps -ef
```

or

```
gilbert:~# ps -el
```

Depending on the size and number of users on your system, you may regret using this option.

For our purposes, the most important column is the first one, which lists the IDs of running processes. When the kernel launches a new process, it assigns an ID number to the process. (As we saw above, **init** is numbered *process 1*.)

This number is important because it allows you to manipulate the process via the ID number. For instance, there are times when you may want to kill a process because it's using too many precious system resources or not performing in the manner you anticipated. If the process is running in the foreground, you can press the **Delete** or **Break** keys (depending on your keyboard) to stop the process. (If **Delete** or **Break** doesn't work, try **Ctrl-C** or **Ctrl-D**.) If a process is running in the background or has been launched by another user at another terminal, however, you must **kill** the process via the kill command:

```
gilbert:~# kill PID
```

using the PID returned by the **ps** or other commands. This sends a *signal* to the process, telling it to cease and desist. Most processes don't know what to do when they receive a signal, so they commit suicide. Not all processes respond to the straight **kill** command; for instance, shells ignore a **kill** command with no options. To kill a shell or other particularly stubborn processes, use **kill** with the *-9* option:

```
gilbert:~# kill -9 PID
```

This sends an unconditional **kill** signal to the process. If you have many processes to kill, you can wipe them all out with:

```
gilbert:~# kill 0
```

This kills all the processes in a current process group, which oversees all processes created by a common ancestor, usually the login shell.

More on the Foreground and Background

As the Linux operating system keeps track of these many processing, it must set priorities; after all, computing resources are typically a finite resource (yes, we'd all love to have the power of a Cray for our tasks, but we make do with our under powered multiuser systems), and some tasks are simply more important than other tasks when it comes to your attention. If a job doesn't require input from you, go ahead and run it in the background. This means that the process will run out of sight (and out of mind, too often), popping up only when the command is completed. While the command runs in the background, you're free to work on other tasks with other commands.

As you've already learned earlier in this book, running a process in the background is a matter of adding an ampersand (**&**) to the end of the command line:

```
$ command options &
```

For instance, you should run CPU-intensive commands, such as **sort**, in the background. There's no reason for you to interact with the **sort** command as it goes through large files; your role in the process is to issue the command and then stay out of the way. The **sort** command requires no input from you, and it doesn't write to the screen as it performs the sort. The same goes for programmers who need to compile programs; their damage is done when creating the source code, not when compiling said code.

The temptation, of course, is to assume that all commands can be run in the background. Yet this isn't true; as a matter of fact, there's a rather limited number of commands that you should run in the background. For instance, any command that relies on continued input from you, such as text editors and anything to do with electronic mail, shouldn't be run in the background.

Swap Space and Performance

When you installed Linux, you were prompted about the installation of swap space, which extends your system's random-access memory (RAM) to a physical hard disk. The notion of a swap space should be familiar to you if you've worked at all with UNIX on any sort of hardware platform, especially as you notice your hard drive thrashing when you switch between memory-intensive applications.

Linux uses *paging* to swap portions of memory (in this case, a page of 4,096 bytes) between your RAM and the hard disk. When you consider how memory-intensive *any* PC-based version of UNIX is (compounded by the memory requirements of the X Window System), it's amazing Linux achieves the performance that it does. Of course, there are a few tricks used along the way: If the page from RAM derives from a read-only file, then that page is actually tossed aside and re-read from hard disk when needed again. Similarly, Linux can share pages between applications; when you load two separate instances of an application at the same time, each instance of the application is actually reading from the same page of memory.

When you installed Linux, you had the option of installing a separate partition for swap space. Before that, we'll go into Linux's memory-management tools and then let you decide if you really need to install more swap space.

I'm Free!

The Linux **free** command lists the amount of free RAM in your system, as well as how much RAM is being used:

```
gilbert:~$ free
             total  used    free   shared   buffers
Mem          14648  3448   11200     1936   1268
-/+ buffers:         2180   12468
Swap:            0     0       0
```

The **free** command lists the total amount of RAM in blocks; a block is equivalent to 1,024 bytes, which makes the total available memory on this machine 14.99 megabytes (no, we didn't use a Pentium-based PC for this computation!). Where's the rest of the memory, since there's actually 16 megabytes installed? The **free** command literally lists the free memory; the rest is under control of the kernel and can't be accessed at any time.

Since there's not a lot happening on this machine (the **free** command was run immediately after the machine was booted), it's no surprise that only 3 megs or so of RAM is actually used, while over 11 megs are free. In addition, 2 megs are shared between processes. Contrast this to Figure 7.13, run after XFree86 is running.

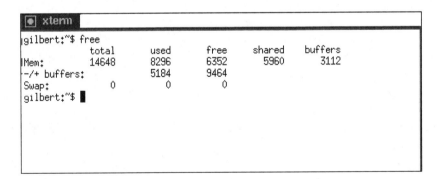

Figure 7.13 Running the free command under X.

The numbers change quite a bit after loading X Window—all of a sudden there's only a little over 6 megabytes free, with over 8 megabytes in use, and over 6 megs shared between processes.

The numbers in the *buffers* column refers to memory set aside by the system to use for common disk operations; instead of going to disk for every little task, Linux sets aside a portion of discretionary memory for these tasks (meaning that if RAM gets low, this memory will be freed for other purposes).

In this example, no swap space was set up when Linux was installed; hence the zeroes.

Deciding Whether to Use Swap Space

If you've got 16 megabytes of RAM in your PC, as was in the case in the previous example, you probably won't need swap space, unless you're performing some computational-intensive task, like programming. In these cases, you'll probably want to set up some swap space. However, if you didn't set up a separate swap partition when installing Linux, you're out of luck unless you want to use **fdisk** to repartition your hard drive and then reinstall Linux.

If the owner of the machine used as an example in the previous section wanted to install some swap space and not reinstall Linux, the only option would be to set up a swap file. Installing a swap file is actually very similar to the routine for setting up a swap partition in Chapter 2, though it can be a tad involved.

 It's best to perform this task logged in as **root**; otherwise, you'll probably run into file-permission problems.

Your first step is to actually set aside the space for your swap file on your hard disk, which means you'll use the **dd** command. Before you use it, however, you'll need to figure out how much hard-disk space you want to set aside for a swap file, as well as what you want to name it (no, it's a little less involved than naming a child; you're best off just calling it **swap** and leaving it at that). For instance, the following command would set up a 10-megabyte swap space:

```
gilbert:~# dd if=/dev/zero of=/swap bs=1024 count=10240
```

The **dd** command writes data from a special device file called **/dev/zero** (don't worry; you don't need to know anything about this file past its existence in this circumstance) into a new file called **/swap**. We set the block size as 1,024, and we set aside a total of 10,240 bytes—which ends up being 10 megabytes of RAM. We chose 10 megabytes because it's a nice, round number.

You've created a swap file, but you need to now format it. Do so with the **mkswap** command (a command you should recall from the Linux installation information). In this case, you can use to format the **/swap** file to a size of 10,240 bytes:

```
gilbert:~# mkswap -c /swap 10240
```

To make sure that the new swap file and the rest of the file system are set up correctly, use the **sync** command:

```
gilbert:~# sync
```

You're not through yet! You still need to tell Linux that it has a swap file available. In this case, you'll use the **swapon** command, specifying the name of the swap file:

```
gilbert:~# swapon /swap
```

After doing all of this, we can see from running the **free** command again (as shown in Figure 7.14) that there is indeed swap space available.

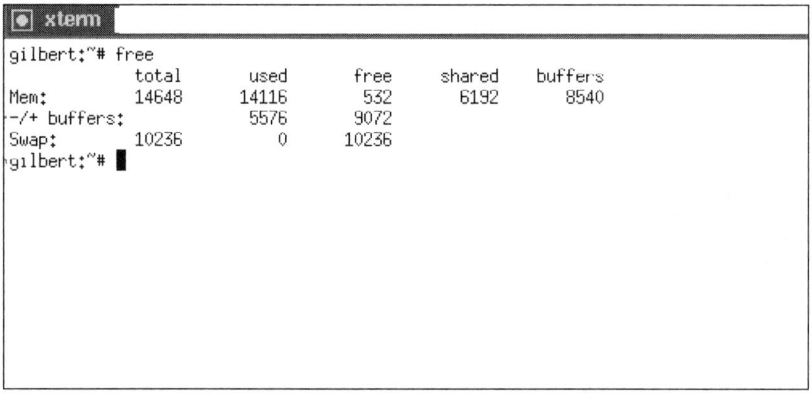

Figure 7.14 Running free after installing swap space.

After you've installed the swap space and you want the space to be permanently loaded on your Linux every time you boot, you'll need to add a line to the **/etc/fstab** file. This is the file that maintains the mounting of file systems when Linux boots. It's a somewhat confusing process, but essentially the **/etc/rc.d/rc.S** file contains the following line:

```
swapon -a
```

that searches the **/etc/fstab** file for any swap spaces. If none are present, then installation continues as normal. If there is a swap file or partition noted in **/etc/fstab**, then it is automatically mounted as Linux loads. Therefore, to make sure this swap file loads every time Linux boots, you'll need to add to **/etc/fstab** a line like the following:

```
device    directory    type    options
/swap     none         swap    sw
```

To disable the swap partition, use the **swapoff** command:

```
gilbert:~# swapoff /swap
```

Don't delete the swap file before using the swapoff command.

If you're not going to be using the swap file again, you can go ahead and remove it from your system, using the **rm** command. You'll also need to edit the aforementioned **/etc/fstab** file and remove the swap-file line from the file; if Linux searches for a swap file and doesn't find it, you'll generate a few errors and run the danger of risking memory integrity.

Games

All work and no play makes you a mighty boring Linux user. When you get tired of coding applications or creating documents with Linux, there are plenty of diversions included with the Linux operating system, including a host of games scored in the **/usr/games** directory.

DOOM

There's little we can add to a discussion of this highly popular game, where your goal is to kill as many sentient bad guys as possible.

Additional Linux Tools Not Included on the CD-ROM

If you do a directory listing of the entire CD-ROM, you'll notice that it's pretty crammed—in fact, there's not a lot of room on the CD-ROM for anything else. The amazing thing about the burgeoning Linux world is that a single CD-ROM (containing 660 *megabytes* of data) doesn't even come close to providing all of the useful software out there. This is why we encourage you to get your own Internet connection (see Chapter 9 for details), so you can grab the megabytes of useful Linux software that pops up every day.

We can't devote space to additional Linux tools not found on the CD-ROM (indeed, that would take up more space than the entire book!), but we can alert to two pieces of software that we didn't include on the CD-ROM, but that you may find of interest.

This important software is actually very similar in nature: They're all emulators of some sort, allowing you run non-Linux software on your Linux system. One program allows you to emulate DOS under Linux, another allows you to run Microsoft *Windows* applications under Linux, while yet another allows you to run Macintosh programs on your Linux system. In addition, there are emulators for Apple II and CP/M (!) software.

Of course, the more important packages allow you to run *Windows*, DOS, and Macintosh software, because this is where the action is. (No offense to those *WordStar* for CP/M users still out there.) The *Windows* and DOS emulators are not complete when we write this; you use both of them at your own risk, which can be considerable, because there are problems with both. In addition, the Macintosh emulator is a trial version of commercial software.

Most of this software can be found at **sunsite.unc.edu**, in the **/pub/Linux/system/Emulators** directory. Table 7.12 lists an index of the software from this directory, current as of the writing of this book.

In addition, there's a subdirectory named **dosemu**, which contains DOS emulators. The contents of this directory are listed in Table 7.13.

Table 7.12 A directory listing of /pub/Linux/system/Emulators.

File	Explanation
68k-simulator.tar.gz	MC-68000 Simulator for the X Window System
apple2.tar.Z	Apple IIe emulator for X & Linux
apple2_videx.tar.Z	Another part of the Apple emulator
bsvc-1.0.2.tar.z	Microprocessor simulator (Motorola 68000, Hector 1600)
cpm-0.2.tar.gz	Z80 and CP/M emulator
executorlinux199k.tar.gz	Executor Macintosh emulator (demo)
x48-0.4.0.tar.gz	HP48 calculator software emulator

Table 7.13 A directory listing of /pub/Linux/system/Emulators/dosemu.

File	Explanation
dosemu-60.1-mouse-patch	Fixes problems in **dosemu** mouse support
dosemu-HOWTO-52.3.ps	**Dosemu HOWTO** for version 0.53.3 (PostScript format)
dosemu-HOWTO-52.3.txt	**Dosemu HOWTO** for version 0.53.3 (ASCII format)
dosemu0.60.1.tgz	Source code for **dosemu** 0.60.1
garrot02.tar.gz	Returns **doseme** idle time to system
xdos0.4a.tgz	DOS emulator designed for the X Window System

Emulating DOS under Linux

If you're hot to run DOS programs under Linux, you'll want to check out **dosemu** or **xdos** (they're the same software, essentially, with one difference—**xdos** will run in an X Window window with mouse support, which **dosemu** does not). Dosemu is found on the CD-ROM in the contrib directory (**dosemu-0.6.0.1+gz**)

NOTE Strictly speaking, neither **dosemu** nor **xdos** is a DOS emulator even though they're referred to as such in documentation (the *emu* in **dosemu** refers to *emulator*). **Dosemu** runs a virtual DOS machine on the Intel-based PC architecture (much in the same manner that OS/2 handles DOS sessions).

Emulating Microsoft Windows under Linux

If there's one area where Microsoft *Windows* is superior to Linux, it's in the vast amount of software that runs under *Windows*. That's why a team of volunteers is working on WINE, the *WINdows Emulator* (or, by some other accounts, *Wine Is Not an Emulator*; both are correct, apparently). It allows you to run Microsoft *Windows* binaries under Linux.

For more information on WINE, you can set your WWW browser to **http://daedalus.dra.hmg.gb/gale/wine/wine.html**, or else you can grab it directly via FTP from **ftp://sunsite.unc.edu/pub/Linux/ALPHA/wine**. Be warned, however, that WINE is still alpha software, which means you use it at your own risk.

Summary

The chapter begins with an extended discussion of the **emacs** text editor. Part of the GNU Project, **emacs** is a full-featured text editor that runs both in character mode and under the X Window System. While **emacs** may take some getting used to for some users, it's both easy to use and powerful at the same time—a combination you don't find every day in the Linux software world.

Linux contains a number of text processors, which take the output from a text editor and turn it into something a printer can understand. Primary amongst these tools are **groff**, the GNU version of **troff**; TeX, the high-end text-processing tool from Donald Knuth; and **texinfo**, the formatting tool also from the Free Software Foundation. In addition, **sed** was covered as a text processor, although it contains elements of both text editors and text processors.

Printing straight text is one thing, but printing graphics and text under Linux is quite another. Luckily, there are tools for editing and printing PostScript-formatted document, in the form of Ghostview.

Linux contains a number of tools for compressing and archiving files, including **gzip** and **gunzip**, as well as the UNIX **tar** command (as implemented by the FSF, of course). These tools can be handy when grabbing software from the Internet, as well as when you want to create some system backups to prevent against disaster.

Linux also feature a number of tools specific to the PC architecture. These commands, called the Mtools, allow Linux to access DOS-style parts of the PC, such as the floppy drive that contained a DOS-formatted floppy, as well as perform some basic DOS functions, such as creating and deleting directories. These commands, by and large, are for use with the floppy drive.

If you've gotten this far in this book, you're probably the system administrator of your system—or the equivalent, anyway. This chapter covers quite a few system-administration tools, including adding and deleting users and groups. In addition, the system administrator also has quite a few tools available for scheduling tasks, such as **at** and **cron**.

Linux's multiprocessing capabilities are explored in this chapter, as well as the tools needed to manage them, such as **ps** and **kill**.

When you installed Linux, you were asked about creating a swap partition to extend your system's RAM. Linux also gives you the choice of setting up a swap file for an additional extension. Setting up this swap file—as well as eliminating it—is covered in this chapter.

The Slackware distribution of Linux also features more than a few games, including the popular DOOM and the golden oldie Tetris (in both character-mode and X Window versions).

The chapter ends with a discussion of various emulators found via the Internet: **dosemu** and **xdos**, which emulate the MS-DOS operating system, and WINE, which runs Microsoft *Windows* applications.

Section III

Linux Communications and Networking

No operating system is an island, which is why Linux contains so many tools for dealing with the outside world:

Chapter 8 covers serial telecommunications tools like **seyon** and **minicom**, which allow you to dial into online services and bulletin-board systems.

Chapter 9 covers Linux TCP/IP networking and the Internet. As any good UNIX, Linux has TCP/IP networking built in. The chapter contains an overview of TCP/IP networking, as well as an overview of the Internet tools contained on the accompanying CD-ROM.

Serial Communications Under Linux

This chapter covers:

- Serial communications and Linux
- Using **seyon**
- The many options to **seyon**
- Using **minicom**
- Options to **minicom**
- Using **term**
- Setting up **term**
- Further sources of information regarding **term**
- Using **rzsz**
- Getting more information about the **rzsz** commands

Expanding Your Reach via Modem

Even if you're using Linux as a standalone system, you're not limited to your little neck of the woods. Linux and its many accompanying tools allow you connect via modem to other parts of the world, whether it be bulletin-board systems (BBSes), online services, or the Internet. Thanks to its reliance on good UNIX software, it also contains several tools for connecting to character-based systems like CompuServe or local bulletin-board systems. (Alas, until WINE gets finished, you won't be able to connect to graphical online services like America Online.)

In this chapter we cover the many tools Linux features for serial communications, beginning with a very functional telecommunications program, **seyon**, followed by discussions of the **minicom** and **term** packages, ending with a discussion of older UNIX comm tools like **rzsz**.

Seyon: Telecommunications from Linux

The **seyon** telecommunications program, developed by Muhammed M. Saggaf (as immortalized in Figure 8.1), is a surprisingly functional terminal-emulation package for the X Window environment.

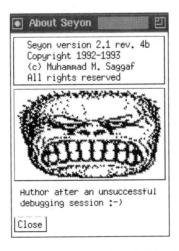

Figure 8.1 The "About Seyon" dialog box.

Seyon supports many features that can be found in popular telecommunications packages like *Procomm*, including a dialing directory, support for several protocols (including Zmodem), various emulation modes (including DEC VT102, Tektronix 4014, and ANSI), and translation modes (for communicating with PC-based services).

To use **seyon**, you need to have a modem and a connection to a telephone line. When you installed Linux, you were prompted about the location of your modem on your PC—in other words, the COM port connected to your modem (if your PC was typical at all, this would have been COM1 or COM2). This information was then translated into a device file called **/dev/modem**, which is used by input for **seyon**.

Therefore, to launch **seyon**, use the following command line:

```
gilbert:~$ seyon -modems /dev/modem
```

If you're smart, you'll set up an alias for this rather cumbersome command line. If you merely launch **seyon** with no options, you'll get an error message. After you load **seyon**, you'll see two windows created, like what's shown in Figure 8.2.

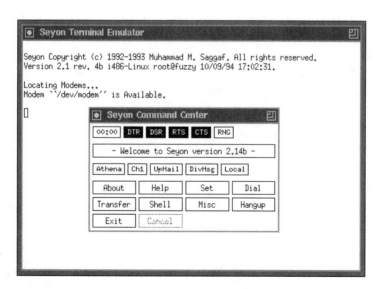

Figure 8.2 Seyon at startup.

The Command Center is where you'll spend most of your time in **seyon**. The top row of status buttons returns information from the modem (DTR, DSR, RTS, and CTS are standard telecomm indicators, while RNG tells us that a call is going through, while the number indicates the time of the call; very handy information if you're paying an online service by the minute).

The next large box is a status indicator, telling us whether **seyon** is active, awaiting a call, or making a call. If **seyon** is inactive for any period of time, various messages—most of which are on the cutesy side—will be displayed.

The next row of buttons doesn't do a heck of a lot, as the buttons have no actions associated with them. However, the remaining buttons are what catch our interest, as they form the guts of functionality of **seyon**:

About displays the humorous dialog box shown in Figure 8.1.

Help displays the online-manual page for **seyon**. **Seyon** is capable of some pretty advanced maneuvers not covered here.

Set opens a dialog box (shown in Figure 8.3) that contains various system settings:

- **Strip 8th** strips the eighth bit—useful for connecting to non-UNIX systems.
- **BS->DEL** turns the **Backspace** key into **Delete** key. The **Backspace** key is not universally supported in the UNIX world, and if you're communicating a lot with other UNIX hosts, you'll want to turn this feature on.
- **Meta->Esc** translates the **Meta** key into the PC **Esc** key. You'll want to leave this setting alone.
- **XON/XOFF** refers to the software flow-control setting. The default is to have this setting disabled. However, some remote hosts require **XON/XOFF** control; hence the need for this setting.
- **CTS/RTS** is another flow-control setting. Again, the default is disabled, but some remote hosts require it to be enabled.
- **AutoZmodem** tells **seyon** to automatically enable a Zmodem file transfer when prompted by the remote host. This is a matter of convenience.

- **IdleGuard** sends a string to the remote host if the session has been idle. The goal is to keep the session from being terminated due to inaction, as most remotes have auto-logoff capabilities.

- The **Baud** dialog box (actually a misnomer; you're setting the bits per second, not the baud rate) sets the session speed. Unfortunately, the fastest session is 38400 bps. Generally speaking, you'll want to set the session speed higher than the actual session. When using a 14,400-bps modem, you'll want to set the session speed to 19,200 bps.

- **Bits** refers to, well, bits. Generally, this setting should be 7 or 8.

- **Parity** can be none, even, or odd.

- **Stop bits** can be 1 or 2.

- **Common** is a shortcut to setting the bits/parity/stop bits separately; most remote hosts require a setting of 8-N-1 or 7-E-1.

- **NewLine** allows you to set an outgoing UNIX newline to be translated to a newline, a carriage return, or a newline/carriage-return combination. Most PC-based online services prefer the new line/carriage-return combination.

- **Port** sets the modem port. Of course, if you couldn't specify this when starting **seyon**, you couldn't get to that point anyway.

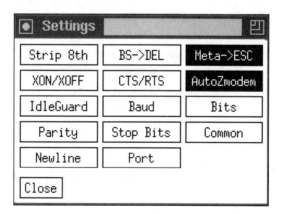

Figure 8.3 The Set dialog box.

The **Dial** button brings up a list of telephone numbers. When you first use **seyon**, you'll be presented with a long list that contains the same telephone number. This is the example **seyon** dialing directory, which you'll want to adapt for your own usage. This is not a difficult task (select **Edit** from the Dialing Directory dialog box), and you can use the many examples found in the example file. An edited Dialing Directory dialog box is shown in Figure 8.4.

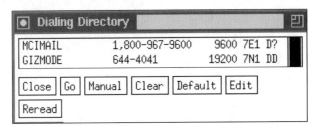

Figure 8.4 The Dialing Directory dialog box.

This dialog box also allows you to manually enter a phone number, using the current **seyon** system settings.

The Transfer dialog box (shown in Figure 8.5) allows you to send and receive files. These are actually external protocols, although the various Zmodem iterations are part of the default **seyon** installation. The Help files describe how to install other protocols within **seyon**.

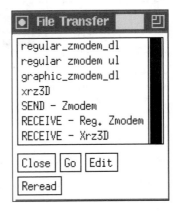

Figure 8.5 The File Transfer dialog box.

The Shell dialog box allows you to run a **shell** command from within **seyon**.

The Miscellaneous dialog box contains a set of various capabilities, including text capture, a text editor, and a file viewer. It's shown in Figure 8.6.

Figure 8.6 The Miscellaneous dialog box.

The **Hangup** button hangs up the current connection. The **Exit** button exits **seyon**. Finally, the **Cancel** button cancels the current operation.

This overview of **seyon** should give you a pretty good idea about its capabilities. But there's a lot more to **seyon**; for example, **seyon** features a slew of command-line options—too many to cover here. However, if you're serious about using **seyon** regularly, you should check out its scripting mechanisms, which are akin to a formal programming language (featuring if/then statements and the like). Again, by summoning the Help files from the Command Center, you'll get a complete overview of the **seyon** scripting mechanisms.

Using Minicom

Seyon is an X Window-based application. However, you may not want to do everything from within X, therefore you might want a character-based telecommunications package. This exists in the form of **minicom**, written by Miquel van Smoorenburg.

Minicom is a full-screen telecommunications package. It works similarly to other PC-based telecommunications packages, offering a menu (accessible by pressing **Ctrl-a z**) as shown in Figure 8.7. Every command is accessible with the **Ctrl-a** combination, by the way.

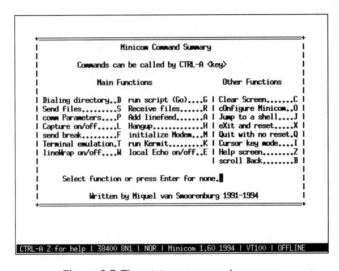

Figure 8.7 The minicom command summary.

To get working quickly in **minicom**, you can press **d** from this command summary. At this point you can manually enter a telephone number, or else you can press **Enter** for your dialing directory. From this menu you can also add new phone numbers, edit existing numbers, or delete unwanted entries.

To change communications parameters, type **Ctrl-a p**, which brings you to a dialog box with comm parameters, as shown in Figure 8.8.

As **minicom** is a character-based Linux program, it relies heavily on keyboard combinations. Most of these combinations are accessible from the menu shown in Figure 8.7. However, since you might not want to go to this screen for every little action, we list the key combinations for you in Table 8.1.

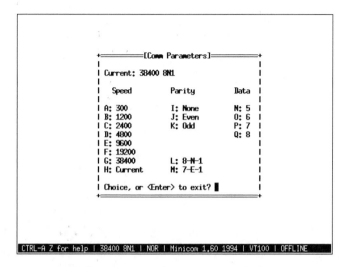

Figure 8.8 Setting comm parameters in minicom.

Table 8.1 Key combinations in minicom.

Key	Result
a	Adds a linefeed to each line
b	Scrolls back through the terminal window, into the buffer
c	Clears the screen
d	Displays the dialing directory
e	Turns echo on and off. Useful if you're seeing two characters where you should only see one, or if you're not seeing any characters when you should see some
f	Sends a break to the remote host
g	Runs a script
h	Hangs up the modem
i	Sets the cursor-key mode
j	Jump to the shell while leaving **minicom** in memory
k	Starts a **kermit** session

Table 8.1 Key combinations in minicom. (continued)

Key	Result
l	Turns capture on, saving the current session to file (**minicom.cap** is the default, although you can enter a new filename)
m	Initializes the modem
o	Configures **minicom** (a task for when you're logged in as root, by the way)
p	Sets comm parameters, such as bps rate, stop bits, and parity
q	Quits **minicom** without resetting the modem
r	Receives a file from the remote host. The supported protocols are Zmodem, Ymodem, Xmodem, and Kermit
s	Sends a file. The supported protocols are Zmodem, Ymodem, Xmodem, and Kermit.
t	Changes the terminal emulation among VT100, Minix, and ANSI
w	Turns the line-wrap on and off
x	Exits **minicom** and resets the modem
z	Summons the command-summary screen

One nice feature of **minicom** is its scripting capabilities. While the script itself can be a shell script (the documentation explains how to implement this), **minicom** allows you to set up a password with the script, preventing unauthorized usage of the script within **minicom**. Having said this, there are some other acknowledged security issues with **minicom**, mostly relating to its running in superuser mode. If security is an issue in your Linux system, you may want to rethink **minicom**.

The online-manual page for **minicom** is quite extensive and can probably answer any questions you may have.

Using Term

The **term** program allows you to make multiple connections via your telephone line and a dialup shell account on a networked UNIX host. The same capability allows you to run X applications over a serial line. In this sense, **term** is taking advantage of the remote host to do more than one thing over the serial line. In this manner it's like a SLIP or PPP connection, but there's one difference: whereas a SLIP or PPP connections means that your local machine gets its own IP address, **term** runs totally from the remote host.

This also means that the remote host must also be running **term**, which involves compiling and installing **term** both on your machine and on the remote host. This can be a drawn-out process, involving group permissions and running the **make** command. (It's not necessarily difficult, but it is a lot of busy work.) You'll definitely want to check through the documentation before actually sitting down and installing **term**.

You must have TCP/IP support in your kernel to use **term**. If you installed Linux without this support, you must either recompile the kernel or totally reinstall Linux.

One advantage to **term** is that many popular Linux communications tools already have support for **term**. In addition to the **term**-specific commands listed in the documentation, popular software like NCSA Mosaic for X Window, support **term** off the bat.

The accompanying CD-ROM contains the **TERM-HOWTO** from Bill Reynolds, which describes (in some depth) how to set up **term** on a system.

Using Rzsz

If you're a PC user and have dabbled in telecommunications, you've probably worked with software packages that did everything—managed the dialup and login process, oversaw the file transfers, and essentially centralized all manners of serial communications. However, Linux being the good UNIX workalike that it is, features different tools for accomplishing the same thing. Dipping into the UNIX software chest, we can come up with a few commands that allow serial communications without needing any fancy programs—or even an interface, for that matter.

The UNIX **cu** command is used to call another computer system. If you're working on a standalone system, you'll probably want to use **minicom** or **seyon** instead, but if you're working on a network that has UUCP already configured, you can use the **cu** command (which is a UUCP command) for making the initial connection.

Once you're connected to a remote system, you can use the **rzsz** set of commands for uploading and downloading documents. Essentially, these commands implement the Zmodem, Ymodem, and Xmodem protocols from the command line, assuming that a valid connection has already been made. In addition, the remote host must also support the protocol you want to use. As the Zmodem protocol is already popular among most online services and bulletin-board systems, it's useful to have.

There are actually six commands in the **rzsz** distribution. As they differ slightly from other **rzsz** distributions (the **man** pages and the online help messages don't match), we'll list them here and then further explain each of them:

- **rz** or **lrz** receives Zmodem files from a remote host.
- **rb** or **lrb** receives Ymodem files from a remote host.
- **rx** or **lrx** receives Xmodem files from a remote host.
- **sz** or **lsz** sends Zmodem files to a remote host.
- **sb** or **lsb** sends Ymodem files from a remote host.
- **sx** or **lsx** sends Xmodem files from a remote host.

To get the skinny on each of these commands, use the —*h* option to the command (additionally, this Linux distribution does feature online-manual pages for the **rz** and **sz** commands, shown in Figure 8.9). For instance, **sb -h** on the command line gives you the following:

```
gilbert:~# sb —h
Send file(s) with ZMODEM/YMODEM/XMODEM Protocol
        (Y) = Option applies to YMODEM only
```

```
          (X) = Option applies to XMODEM only
Usage:  lsz [-2+abdefkLlNnquvwYy] [-] file ...
        lsz [-2Ceqv] -c COMMAND
        lsb [-2adfkquv] [-] file ...
        lsz [-2akquv] [-] file
```

and much more....

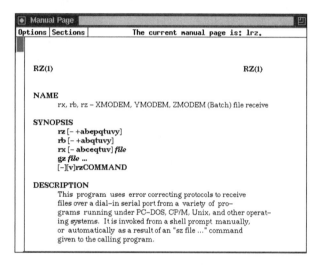

Figure 8.9 Online-manual page for rz/lrz.

How you actually use these commands will partially depend on the remote host, of course; some, especially UNIX-based hosts, require that you first start **rz** on the remote host and then run **sz** locally if you want to upload a file. Other hosts, particularly PC-based ones, have their own methods for handling a file upload.

Other Linux Telecommunications Tools

If none of these serial telecommunications tools strikes your fancy, you can also peruse wider offerings on the Internet for some more appropriate tools. Always popular, yet difficult to use and set up, is C-Kermit (available from the official **kermit.columbia.edu** FTP site, in the **/kermit/c-kermit** directory). Be warned that you'll need to use a **makefile** to create a version for Linux.

Another option is the **pcomm** telecommunications package. This package is essentially a Linux workalike to the popular DOS/*Windows Procomm*, featuring a dialing directory, interactive usage, and more. You can grab it from the **ftp.cecer.army.mil** FTP site, in the **pcomm** directory.

Summary

This chapter covers serial communications under the Linux operating system, focusing on packages like **seyon**, **minicom**, **term**, and the **rzsz** utilities.

The next chapter covers the many tools for Internet usage.

The Internet and Networking

This chapter covers:

- Linux and the Internet
- Linux and TCP/IP
- SLIP and PPP
- Electronic mail
- The World Wide Web
- Web browsers
- The UUCP commands
- Using **ftp**
- The **telnet** command
- Using the Usenet

Getting on the Worldwide Network

The Internet has been the recipient of a ton of hype recently, and with good reason—it's one of the most exciting development's in the computer world in quite some time. As both a computer user and a Linux user, you'll greatly benefit from the many possibilities offered by the many offerings of the Internet.

How you connect to the Internet depends on your specific circumstances, however. If you're using Linux in a corporation that's already connected to the Internet, you can merely piggyback from that connection. If you're working on a standalone Linux workstation, you can set up your own Internet connection.

Both of these possibilities exist because of Linux's built-in networking capabilities, centered around the TCP/IP protocol. The concept behind TCP/IP networking is actually pretty simple. Each machine on the network as an individual TCP/IP address, and every other machine on the network can access this machine (if only be denied access, of course; there are some security measures involved if need be). The extent of the network depends on your needs; some companies purposely restrict their TCP/IP networks to a very confined set of machines; other allow full access to the global Internet.

In this chapter, we'll first discuss the basics of TCP/IP connectivity for Linux, followed by a discussion of the Internet and the Internet tools included on the CD-ROM and available from various Internet sites around the world.

TCP/IP and Linux

TCP/IP (Transmission Control Protocol/Internet Protocol) has become the *lingua franca* for networking in the UNIX world. Because UNIX-based systems were instrumental in forming the Internet and its predecessors, TCP/IP became the dominant protocol for communications on the Internet. TCP/IP is the major tool for networking UNIX-based computer systems, as most UNIX implementations contain support for TCP/IP. Other operating systems, such as DOS and OS/2, can also connect to TCP/IP networks, although this requires special add-on software.

Linux comes with full support for TCP/IP (provided you installed it when you installed Linux; if not, you'll need to look at reinstalling Linux or recompiling your kernel). This support comes in the form of the NET-3 set of protocols and programs. On your end, connecting to a UNIX network via TCP/IP is merely a matter of making sure your PC is correctly hooked up to the network via Ethernet card and cabling.

In Chapter 1 we covered supported Ethernet cards. If you need more information about setting up your Ethernet card, check out the **ETHERNET-HOWTO** contained on the accompanying CD-ROM, in the **docs** directory.

Linux also allows you to make a TCP/IP connection via telephone line, using the SLIP or PPP protocols. If you want to connect to the Internet via a dial-up connection, you'll need to use these tools.

Before you try using any of these tools, you should have some background in TCP/IP. We advise checking out Olaf Kirch's *Linux Network Administrator's Guide*, which has been printed by various sources (including the Linux Documentation Project and SSC).

In addition, the CD-ROM contains a very useful, detailed guide to TCP/IP networking and NET-3 in the form of **NET-2-HOWTO**, in the **docs** directory.

These guides should form the basis of your networking expertise. However, we'll provide a short overview of TCP/IP networking here before we move on to a discussion of the Internet.

TCP/IP Basics

Under a TCP/IP network, every computer on the network is assigned an *IP address*, including your computer. If your Linux workstation is permanently connected to a TCP/IP network, this address will remain constant. If you're using a dialup connection to the Internet through a service provider, your IP address will be dynamically assigned when you login the service. This address comes in four fields, such as 255.255.0.0. This breaks down to:

subdomain.subdomain.domain.domain

You will find detailed information on IP addresses, how they're structured, and how you can acquire them on the accompanying CD-ROM.

From your end, IP addresses are important for connecting to another computer on the network. However, in many situations you don't need to know the specific IP address to make a connection, which you've probably discovered when you see lists of Internet addresses (such as those found in Appendix A) without any IP addresses listed. Why's that? Because early in the Internet's development the decision was made to allow a *Domain Name Server* (DNS) to handle these dirty details. Your TCP/IP network (or your service provider) has a named DNS somewhere on the network. When you enter an Internet address like *ftp.x.org* or a mail address like *reichard@mr.net*, a lookup is performed on the DNS, which then makes sure that the mail or the request is routed to the proper machine. If you've installed TCP/IP on your system, you'll be running a daemon named *named* that handles the connections to the DNS.

The **fwhois** command connects to the DNS and returns information about a specific user or a domain name:

```
gilbert:~$ fwhois mr.net
Minnesota Regional Network (MR-DOM)
        511 11th Avenue South, Box 212
        Minneapolis, MN 55415

        Domain Name: MR.NET

        ....
```

Record last updated on 16-Nov-93

Domain servers in listed order:

NS.MR.NET   137.192.240.5
RSO.INTERNIC.NET   198.41.0.5
RIVERSIDE.MR.NET   137.192.2.5
SPRUCE.CIC.NET   35.42.1.100

gilbert:~$ fwhois dfazio@mr.net
Fazio, Dennis (DF202)   dfazio@mr.net
Minnesota Regional Network (MR-DOM)
        511 11th Avenue South, Box 212
        Minneapolis, MN 55415

Record last updated on 16-Dec-91

The **fwhois** command also lists users on your Linux system, even if you're not connected to the Internet.

Setting up TCP/IP Information

The files that control TCP/IP configuration are stored in the **/etc** directory. When you first set up Linux and are asked about machine names and domain names, this information is then sent to the **/etc/hosts** file. While you don't absolutely need to mess with this file if you're connected to the Internet (it does many of the same things that a Domain Name Server does), it's a good thing to place the names of essential servers in this file. And if you're not connected to the Internet but are maintaining a small network, this is the place to store the IP addresses for the workstations on your system. (Again, this could be done via a DNS on your local system, but it's a lot easier to use the **/etc/hosts** file.)

Another file to check is the **/etc/networks** file, used to configured different networks in the TCP/IP subsystem. This file is summoned when the system launches, and its functions are handled by DNS servers if you're working on the Internet. Again, if you're not connected to the Internet but want to have subnetworks and such (you really don't; we're speaking hypothetically here if you're working on a small network), you'd use this file instead of a DNS.

You'll also want to run the **ifconfig** command, which essentially tells the kernel about your Ethernet card and the IP addresses if you've not done so already. To see the current state of your system, use the command with no options:

```
gilbert:/$ ifconfig
lo     Link encap:Local Loopback
       inet addr:127.0.0.1  Bcast:127.255.255.255  Mask:255.0.0.0
       UP BROADCAST LOOPBACK RUNNING  MTU:2000  Metric:1
       RX packets:0 errors:0 dropped:0 overrun:0
       TX packets:40 errors:0 dropped:0 overruns:0
```

Linux's SLIP/PPP Tools

If you don't have a permanent TCP/IP connection to the Internet, you can use Linux's SLIP and PPP tools to connect to the Internet via a service provider of some sort. SLIP (Serial Line Internet Protocol) and PPP (Point-to-Point Protocol) allow you to connect to another TCP/IP machine.

Linux contains the **dip** command, which handles these connections to a service provider. To run it, use the following command line:

```
gilbert:/$ dip -t

dip>
```

The *-t* option tells **dip** to accept commands.

Since dial-up Internet connections are so individualistic (we've dealt collectively with both static and dynamically allocated addresses), we're going to leave it up to you to configure **dip**. You'll want to read carefully through the online-manual pages for **dip**, as they contain plenty of examples for your usage. They also contain example scripts, which you can adapt to automatically log you on a remote connection.

Internet Tools

After you work out your connections to the Internet, you can take advantage of the network tools available under Linux.

We'll begin with a discussion of Internet mail, followed by other Internet goodies.

A new program, **SLIRP**, is run in a remote UNIX shell accountand makes it act like a SLIP/CSLIP account. We compiled it on an Ultrix machine and connected to it with DIP. It works great! The source for it is on the CD-ROM in **/contrib**.

Using Electronic Mail

The ability to send electronic messages to individuals, groups of people, or everyone in the company is not one of the flashiest features of the Linux operating system, but it is certainly one of the most used. Other networking systems, particularly from the MS-DOS world (like Novell NetWare) lack basic electronic-mail (or e-mail) capabilities, while other operating systems featuring built-in electronic mail lack the other extensive capabilities featured in Linux.

The **mail** program has been an important part of UNIX almost since the very beginning. As UNIX evolved, so has **mail**—to an extent. The actual electronic-mail mechanisms are similar to the original **mail** mechanisms; changes mainly concern how a user interacts with a **mail** program. The procedures described here may not appear exactly the same on your system, as there are a large number of mail programs, both UNIX- and X Window-based, that vary in how they present information to the user.

Linux gives you a few options for reading and sending mail, starting with the **mailx** command and ending with programs like **elm** and **pine**, which ship on the accompanying CD-ROM.

Receiving Mail

Linux informs you of incoming mail when you login the system. You'll see a message like:

```
You have mail.
```

Unless you read your mail at this point, this message will reappear periodically, as the shell is automatically set up to remind you of unread mail.

To view this mail, type:

```
gilbert:/$ mail
```

You'll see something like what's shown in Figure 9.1.

```
gilbert:/# mail
Mail version 5.5 6/1/90.  Type ? for help.
"/var/spool/mail/root": 4 messages 4 unread
>U  1 root                  Thu Sep 15 02:23 132/4321   "Register with the Lin"
 U  2 volkerdi@mhd1.moorhe  Thu Sep 15 02:53  66/2758   "Welcome to Linux!"
 U  3 root                  Thu Sep 15 02:23 132/4321   "Register with the Lin"
 U  4 volkerdi@mhd1.moorhe  Thu Sep 15 02:53  66/2758   "Welcome to Linux!"
& []
```

Figure 9.1 Incoming mail.

The shell responds with a list of your mail messages, listed in the order they were received by your system, newest mail first. The first field lists the sender of the message, the second through fifth fields denotes the time and date the message was received, the sixth field records the number of lines in the message and the size of the message (in bytes), and the final field indicates the subject of the message.

Press **Enter** to read the first message on the list. If it's a long message, the entire message will scroll by. If you want to stop scrolling the message, type **Ctrl-S**; to start it again, type **Ctrl-Q**.

There are two types of messages waiting for us: messages from **root** and messages from **volkerdi@mhd1.moorhead**. If you're connected to the Internet and have your own network with other users, your electronic mail can come from two sources: Your own system, and from other systems. Mail from other systems, sent on the Internet or the Usenet, has its own unique addressing scheme (more on that in the next section). Mail from your own system use the same login names as described in Chapter 1; these names are contained in the **/etc/passwd** file.

While not illustrated here, the first and older scheme of addressing mail via the Usenet and UUCP mail is called a *bang path*, first popularized on the Usenet, which makes up part of the Internet. Essentially, you're telling the mail system the exact route it must take to send your mail. This can be a gigantic pain, especially if there are many, many machines a message must go through before it is delivered. Luckily, this manual addressing of electronic mail is on the wane, which is why you see so few electronic-mail addresses dotted with exclamation marks.

Still, there's a need for bang paths when it comes to electronic mail. Many users now take advantage of *gateways*, which forward mail to other connected machines. If you have access to a gateway (check with your system administrator; chances you do if you have ability to send and receive electronic mail from the Internet), you can just send mail to the gateway, denoting the system name and the user name:

```
$ mail kevinnet!concubine!kevin
```

where *kevinnet* is the name of the gateway (as it happens, *kevinnet* is a fictional gateway; kids, don't use this address at home), the system name is *concubine*, and *kevin* is the user name. The bang character, or exclamation point (!), separates the entries.

The newer addressing scheme, and one that is growing in popularity (mainly because of the growing popularity of the Internet), is called *domain addressing*. Structured as the exact opposite of a bang path, a domain address couples the name of the user with an address. This scheme grew out of the need for international standardization of electronic-mail addresses and provides a hierarchical structure to addressing. Essentially, the world is split into country domains, which are then divided into educational domains (indicated by the suffix .edu in the address) and commercial domains (indicated by the suffix .com in the address). There are hundreds and hundreds of commercial and educational domains, with the number growing each day.

Reading a domain address is quite simple. In the address of:

```
reichard@mr.net
```

reichard refers to the user, while *mr.net* refers to the domain. The user and domain names are separated by the at (@) symbol. As a user, you don't need to know the specific path a message must take, nor do you need to know the name of a gateway. With a domain address, sending a message is simple:

```
gilbert:/$ mail reichard@mr.net
```

The idea of the Internet is fairly amorphous and abstract. The Internet is technically a collection of many networks that somehow manage to talk to each other. As a user, all you need to know is a recipient's electronic-mail address; the system administrator handles the basic details of linking a system to the Internet.

If you're on the Internet, you can also receive electronic-mail from afar. To find your machine address, type **uname -n** at the prompt:

```
gilbert:/$ uname -n
gilbert
```

where *gilbert* is the name of your UNIX system, also called the *hostname*. To list all the systems you can directly communicate with, type **uname**:

```
gilbert:/$ uname
othersystem1
othersystem2
othersystem3
```

where *othersystem* refers to the other systems.

> The **uname** command doesn't support this option on all systems. If this is the case, you can look in the file **/etc/hosts**, covered earlier in this chapter, to get a good idea what other systems your computer networks with.
>
> In a large regional or nationwide network, the list of other systems can be quite large. If you want to find a specific system and don't want to wade through a huge list of names, use **uname** in conjunction with **grep**:
>
> ```
> $ uname | grep othersystem121
> othersystem121
> ```
>
> If the name of the other system is returned, you can send electronic mail to someone with an account on that system. In addition, you can send messages to people on the Internet if you are connected to the Internet, provided you know the exact address of the recipient.

Let's look at the first message from **root**, shown in Figure 9.2.

```
                                    rxvt
//PERSON
# This is about yourself, the sender of this message
country:
# ISO 3166 two-letter country code of where you live
email:
# Your E-mail address
may-publish:
# YES if you agree that information about you can be published
# If not given, nothing but statistical information will be published
name:
# Your name
started:
# Month and year you started using Linux, like "nov 93"
usage:
# The place where you use Linux. Home, school, work or combinations of these


//END
The END command is only required if you have a mailer that adds stuff
below the last line of the message.
& []
```

Figure 9.2 An incoming electronic-mail message.

At the beginning an e-mail message is a *header*. With the Internet, mail may go between one or more systems on its way to you. You can't count on a direct link between systems, and because of these uncontrollable paths it make take some time for a message to reach the recipient; delivery times of 15 hours to 24 hours are not uncommon, but neither are delivery times of 10 seconds.

Creating Mail

It's very easy to create mail. (*Too* easy, some would say, as they survey mailboxes full of irrelevant mail messages.) To create a short message at the keyboard, simple combine mail with the name of the recipient, followed by a period on its own line. The resulting mail is shown in Figure 9.3.

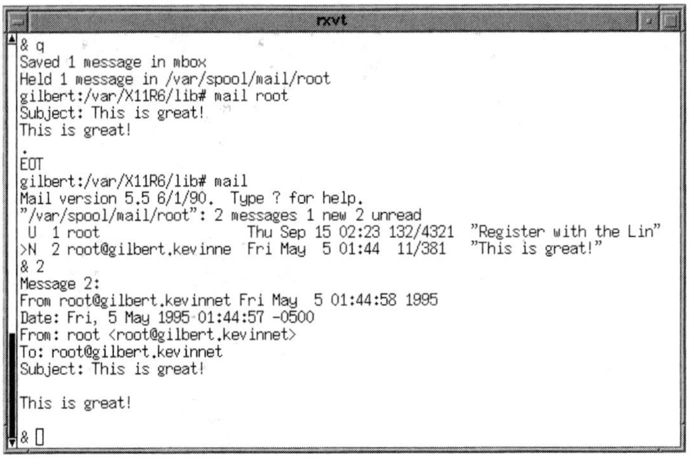

```
rxvt
& q
Saved 1 message in mbox
Held 1 message in /var/spool/mail/root
gilbert:/var/X11R6/lib# mail root
Subject: This is great!
This is great!

.
EOT
gilbert:/var/X11R6/lib# mail
Mail version 5.5 6/1/90.  Type ? for help.
"/var/spool/mail/root": 2 messages 1 new 2 unread
 U  1 root                 Thu Sep 15 02:23 132/4321  "Register with the Lin"
>N  2 root@gilbert.kevinne Fri May  5 01:44  11/381   "This is great!"
& 2
Message 2:
From root@gilbert.kevinnet Fri May  5 01:44:58 1995
Date: Fri, 5 May 1995 01:44:57 -0500
From: root <root@gilbert.kevinnet>
To: root@gilbert.kevinnet
Subject: This is great!

This is great!

& []
```

Figure 9.3 Incoming mail.

As always, end input from the keyboard by typing **Ctrl-D**. Some e-mail programs also accept a single period on its own line to terminate the message, instead of **Ctrl-D**. The procedure would be the same if you were sending a message to a user on a remote machine:

```
gilbert:/$ mail reichard@mr.net
```

You can send the same message to multiple users with the *-t* option:

```
gilbert:/$ mail -t johnsone@camax.com reichard@mr.net
```

```
This, too, is a test.
.
```

The resulting message will contain multiple *To:* fields in the header.

Sending an existing file as the text of an electronic-mail message is almost as simple. After creating an ASCII file using **vi** or **emacs**, save the file and then redirect it as input on the command line:

```
gilbert:/$ mail johnsone@camax.com < note
```

What Do I Do with My Messages?

After you read a message, the shell presents you with a different prompt:

```
&
```

asking for a response related to the **mail** program. There are many actions you can take at this point; the handiest options are listed in Table 9.1.

Table 9.1 A selection of mail commands.

Command	Result
RETURN	Prints next message
-	Prints previous message
d	Delete current message
dN	Deletes message number *N*
dp	Deletes current message and go to the next message
dq	Deletes current message and quit
u N	Undeletes message *N*
s *filename*	Saves message to **filename**. If **filename** is not specified, message is saved to **$HOME/mbox**
w *filename*	Saves message without header information to *filename*. If *filename* is not specified, message is saved to **$HOME/mbox**
?	Lists mail commands

Saving Messages

As we saw in Table 9.1, saving a message is simply a matter of typing:

```
? s filename
```

If you don't get many messages, it's no big deal to save them all to the same file. But if you get a lot of messages on a wide variety of topics, it's a good idea to introduce some organization to your mail habits.

Let's say you're working on a project with user *erc*, and you want to keep all of his mail messages in the same file. You do so with the s option at the **?** prompt:

```
? s erc
```

where *erc* is the name of the file containing his mail messages. When you do this the first time the shell creates a file named **erc**. Subsequent uses will append mail messages to the existing **erc** file.

To read this file, use **mail** with the *-f* option:

```
gilbert:/$ mail -f erc
```

 Don't make the mistake of assuming your electronic mail messages are private. Since mail messages normally appear in unencrypted text files, anyone with super user privileges, such as your system administrator, can read your mail. To bring the matter more to home, few businesses have policies regarding the privacy of electronic mail communications. When in doubt, assume that your boss can read your mail.

Other Mail Packages

As you can tell, **mail** sports an exceedingly primitive interface. Over the years, a crop of new mail programs have appeared, some commercial software and some free, each of which aims at making life easier for the user. Some of the free ones are being included with Linux.

Xmh is an X Window front-end to **mh**, as shown in Figure 9.4.

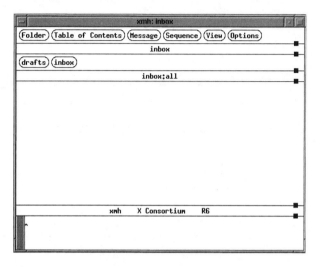

Figure 9.4 Xmh in action.

Pine is another popular electronic-mail program, shown in Figure 9.5.

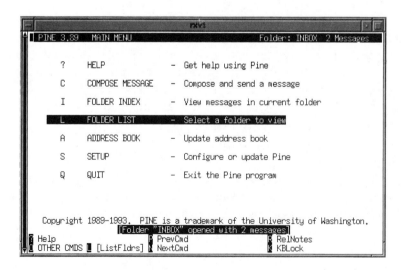

Figure 9.5 Pine in action.

Finally, there's **elm**, which is one of our favorites. **Elm** stands for *el*ectronic *m*ail and it works by providing an easy-to-use interface over the standard **mail** program.

The basic **elm** screen looks like that shown in Figure 9.6.

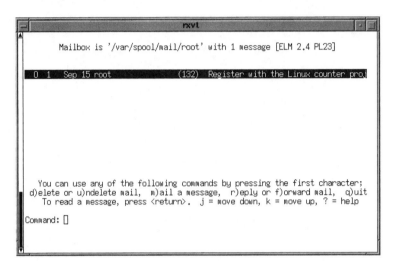

Figure 9.6 The elm mail program.

You can use the arrow keys on your keyboard to select a message. Pressing **Return** reads the message. **Elm** is so simple, so fast and so easy that we think you'll soon be a convert. The online help, available by typing a question mark (**?**), should get you going in no time. (Like many users, we're often too busy to read the manual. In fact, we've never read the **elm** manual—the program is that easy.)

NOTE If you've been observant, you've noticed that all of the programs shown in this section work from the same mail file. This is no accident; to prevent multiple mail files from popping up all over your Linux system (as well as the entire UNIX system, if you're networked), the mail packages work from the same incoming-mail file.

Using a Web Browser

Electronic mail, of course, is a rather unglamorous function of the Internet. Most of the hoopla surrounding the Internet concerns *web pages*, accessed via *web browsers*. To understand these terms, a little background is in order.

By the end of the 1980s, most of the infrastructure that was to become the Internet was already in place—primarily, the nationwide linkage of computers that could almost instantaneously access other computers on the network. Before that, things like mail and newsgroups were passed along from computer to computer (mostly overnight, when phone rates were lower). When the Internet finally took shape, it became possible to access any other internetworked computer directly.

Armed with these capabilities, CERN researchers, lead by Tim Berners-Lee (now head of the WWW Consortium at MIT), developed an information-exchange structure, called the World Wide Web, that would take advantage of these instantaneous links. A computer on the Internet has a distinct address, and a piece of software (called a *web browser*) would use that address for instant connectivity. Pages on that internetworked machine are formatted in the HyperText Markup Language, or *HTML* (itself a subset of the complex Standard Generalized Markup Language, or *SGML*). This formatting would specify things like headlines, body text, and hypertext links to other Web resources.

It's up to the local web browser to actually render this web page on the local computer. For instance, the web browser will contain a tag for a headline; the web browser uses a local font to create this headline. The same goes for body copy and hypertext links.

Popular Web Browsers

Mosaic from NCSA was the first popular web browser, and for many users it still epitomizes the power of the Internet. Of late, however, *Netscape Navigator* has garnered a lot of attention as being the cutting-edge Web browser.

We're not going to play favorites here; you'll need to go out and grab whichever web browser you want. Here, we'll use Netscape Navigator in our examples (as shown in Figure 9.7), but there's nothing that wouldn't apply equally to NCSA Mosaic. In fact, there's a whole list of freeware web browsers that have been compiled for use under Linux; you can grab them via **ftp** (which we'll describe later in this chapter) from **sunsite.unc.edu/pub/Linux/system/Network/infosystems**. They include:

- **Mosaic** (which has been compiled for Linux in several different versions; you'll want to check them out before committing to the download time, which can be considerable)
- **Lynx** (a freeware text-only browser)
- **tkWWW** (a freeware web browser written in Tcl/Tk)
- **Chimera** (a freeware browser)

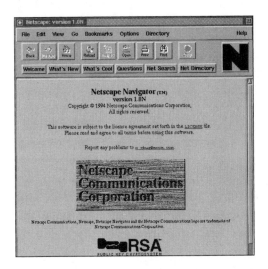

Figure 9.7 Netscape Navigator.

By and large, the World Wide Web is a graphical beast; most of these web browsers (the big exception is Lynx) run under the X Window System.

Page Limits

At its core, the World Wide Web is actually an ingeniously simple thing. A web browser, such as Mosaic or Netscape, sends a request over the network to a web server; the request can be one of five formats (as listed in Table 9.2 presented later in this chapter). The server then honors the request by sending a text file formatted in the HyperText Markup Language (HTML), which inserts "tags" in the text. The text file is then rendered by the local web browser, which matches the tags to resources on the local machine—for instance, a tag for TITLE would be rendered in a font and point size set up through the web browser.

The HTML language also allows graphics and hypertext links to be embedded in the document. Most graphics files are in the GIF and XBM file formats. The hyperlinks are noted with their own tag and are usually set off in a different color within the rendered document. For instance, under a heading titled *Other Resources*, there may be a line colored blue that says *Sun Microsystems Home Page*. To the web browser, however, there's an embedded web address (in this case, *www.sun.com*). Double-clicking on *Sun Microsystems Home Page* initiates a request to the web server *www.sun.com*. You don't need to know the *www.sun.com* address; you only need to know how to use a mouse.

You can start Netscape with the following command in an **xterm** window:

```
gilbert:/$ netscape
```

When Netscape launches, it connects directly to a Netscape Communications home page (*www.mcom.com*). (By the way, this is a good way to test if Netscape is configured properly; if you or your system administrator has misinstalled Netscape, it will report that a connection to *www.mcom.com* has failed.)

Chances are pretty good that you won't want to spend much time wandering around the Netscape home page. The beauty of the World Wide Web is that it allows you to jump from web site to web site, either those linked to your current page or a page totally unrelated.

A page on the World Wide Web is formatted in the HyperText Markup Language (HTML). If you were to view the document in text mode—which is possible with many web browsers, including Netscape—you'd see that the text seen in Figure 9.8 is scattered with "tags," like *<H2>*. There's no mentions of point sizes, colors, or the like. The beginning of the file shown in the Netscape illustration in Figure 9.8 looks like this:

```
<TITLE>Netscape Handbook: Graphical Elements</TITLE>

<A NAME="RTFToC0">
<B>
<FONT SIZE=+3>G</FONT><FONT SIZE=+2>raphical elements</FONT>
</B></A>

<ol>
<A HREF="../online-manual.html">Netscape Handbook: Table of
Contents</A>
<li><a href="graphics.html#RTFToC1">Netscape window</a>
<li><a href="graphics.html#RTFToC2">Point and click navigation</a>
<li><a href="graphics.html#RTFToC4">Content area and text
fields</a>
<li><a href="graphics.html#RTFToC9">Security information</a>
<li><a href="graphics.html#RTFToC5">Window controls</a>
<li><a href="graphics.html#RTFToC3">Toolbar buttons</a>
<li><a href="graphics.html#RTFToC6">Directory buttons</a>
<li><a href="graphics.html#RTFToC7">Newsgroup list buttons</a>
<li><a href="graphics.html#RTFToC8">Newsgroup article buttons</a>
</ol>

<HR ALIGN="right"WIDTH=85%>
<A NAME="RTFToC1">
```

```
<FONT SIZE=+3>N</FONT><FONT SIZE=+1>etscape window</FONT>
</A>
<P>
```

This section on graphical elements describes what you see in the
Netscape window. Most of the tools and text fields that help you to
navigate the Internet are visible, though you have the option of
hiding some tools in order to give more space on the screen to the
content area.

```
<p>
```

On the page describing point and click navigation, you'll find a
description of each type of graphical element: colors/underlining,
status indicator, progress bar, toolbar buttons, content/text fields,
window controls, and menus. Subsequent pages go into more detail on
how toolbar buttons, text/content fields, and window controls work. An
entire section of pages is devoted to menu items, including those that
let you set important options and preferences effecting the look,
performance, and functionality of the Netscape window.

```
<p>
```

You can open multiple Netscape windows to view multiple pages of
information. The title bar of the window shows the title of
currently loaded page.

```
<P>
<HR ALIGN="right"WIDTH=85%>
<A NAME="RTFToC2">
<FONT SIZE=+3>P</FONT><FONT SIZE=+1>oint and click
navigation</FONT>
</A>
<P>
```

The rendered page is shown in Figure 9.8.

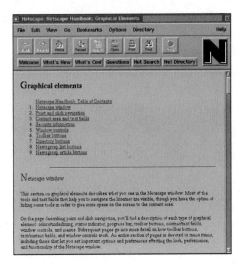

Figure 9.8 Netscape with a rendered page.

This is because the work of rendering the home page is done at the local level, matching local resources to the specifications of the web page. You'll notice that there are a few different point sizes and typefaces on the home page. The web document makes a reference to <TITLE>; the web page then matches a local font and point size to the text.

A graphic is also rendered locally. When the document downloads, the graphic is sent separately, in the GIF format, which makes for quicker file transfers. (Even so, some GIF documents can be *very* large and take a long time to download, even at a high-speed network link.)

URL Formats

You tell a web browser where to look by entering a *Uniform Resource Locator*, or *URL*. The WWW community has standardized on a number of URL formats, as listed in Table 9.2.

Table 9.2 URL formats and their meanings, from the WWW FAQ.

Format	Represents
file://wuarchive.wustl.edu/mirrors/msdos/graphics/gifkit.zip	File at an FTP site
ftp://wuarchive.wustl.edu/mirrors	FTP site
http://info.cern.ch:80/default.html	WWW site
news:alt.hypertext	Usenet newsgroup
telnet://dra.com	Telnet connection to Internet-connected server.

This means that you can connect to many Internet resources via a web browser. Most web browsers have a menu selection or dialog box that allows you to enter a URL; the Netscape mechanism is shown in Figure 9.9.

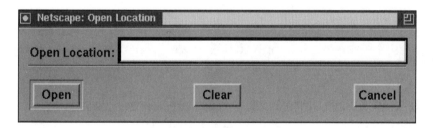

Figure 9.9 The Netscape URL dialog box.

Communications with the UUCP Commands

In many respects, the Internet is the "new wave" of UNIX communications. However, there are many UNIX and Linux users who might want to take advantage of other communications methods.

One older method is **UUCP**. Originally, UNIX-to-UNIX Copy Program (**uucp**) was written to communicate between systems via ordinary telephone lines. The **uucp** program allows you to copy files from one system to another. Today, these connections can take place between those same telephone lines via modem (at all speeds, from 2400 bits per second to 19.2 kbps), direct wiring, a local-area network, or a wide-area network connected via dedicated phone lines. Although the connection mechanisms have changed, the basic UUCP system has not and remains mechanism-independent, which makes your life much simpler. As a user, you don't need to know the specifics of the connection mechanism; all you need to know is how to access the utilities that make communications possible.

Dealing with **uucp** and the networking utilities on a configuration level is an advanced topic best left to system administrators and those with iron stomachs, suitable for dealing with the complex task of networking Linux machines.

There's no one great *uber*program that oversees Linux connections to the outside world. Much like everything else in the Linux and UNIX worlds, the communications utilities are quite small and serve limited purposes by themselves; only when strung together do they actually make up a powerful communications system.

Why connect to the outside world? Some companies directly link far-flung offices via dedicated phone line to ensure instantaneous communications among employees. Others connect via modem over phone lines to the UUCP Network, a series of UNIX computers that pass along electronic mail and files all around the world.

In a rather confusing situation, UUCP refers both to a specific command (**uucp**) and a series of related commands (most of which begin with **uu**). In this chapter, **uucp** will refer to the specific **uucp** command, while UUCP will refer to the general command set.

To make things even more confusing, there's more than one implementation of the UUCP utilities on the market. In this chapter, we'll be covering the HoneyDanBer UUCP, named for its three creators (Peter *Honey*man, *Dan* A. Nowitz, and *Brian* E. *Red*man). This implementation is supported in the version of Linux on the accompanying CD-ROM.

A UUCP Primer

At its core, the UUCP commands allow machines to communicate directly via network links or telephone connections. They are limited in scope and are geared toward the rudimentary purposes of sending along files, electronic mail, and (sometimes) Usenet news.

In this chapter, we'll focus on the few commands you're likely to use. (If you want information about *all* of the UUCP commands, check Appendix A for a list of further reading material.) We'll also avoid configuration issues, which are best left to a system administrator.

Before you use **uucp**, you'll need to know what machines are connected to yours. The **uuname** command does just this:

```
gilbert:/$ uuname
geisha
spike
```

Why is this information important? Because you'll need to specify machine names with the **uucp** command.

Using Uucp

The **uucp** command is used to copy files from one machine to another. At first glance, in this age of Internet and the Information Superhighway, you may think that this is incredibly retro technology. And, conceptually, it is.

Realistically, however, the **uucp** command has its widest application in the corporate world, where interconnected computers are very common. In these situations, the corporate systems may not be tied to the outside world, but only connected to other corporate systems. In these cases, the **uucp** command is a handy way of transferring a file from your system to the corporate headquarters in Sioux City, Iowa.

The best way to understand the **uucp** command isn't to think of it as a strange and unfamiliar networking command—just think of it as an extended version of the common **cp** command, which you've used earlier in this book. Instead of downloading and uploading files from a local directory, you're using **uucp** to download and upload files from another machine.

There's also one added advantage to the **uucp** command: All in all, it's a rather secure method of transferring files, when everything is set up correctly. (Ah, again, there's the issue of security popping up again.) The **uucp** command, as well as the UUCP utilities, can enact very specific guidelines on where files can be uploaded to or downloaded from.

Let's look at a typical **uucp** command line:

```
$ uucp chap9.txt spike!/usr/spool/uucppublic/chap9.txt
```

While this may seem to be a long command line, a closer look will show that it's actually rather simple.

The **uucp** portion of the command line, obviously, refers to the **uucp** command. This is followed by the name of the file to be copied (**chap9.txt**).

The next portion is potentially the most confusing portion for novice users, as it represents the destination of the file by name of the machine and the directory. In this case, **spike** refers to the name of the machine; the **uucp** command knows this because the name of the machine ends with an exclamation mark (**!**).

If the exclamation mark looks familiar, it should; remember, the Usenet method of electronic-mail addressing with bang paths makes heavy use of exclamation marks.

The exclamation mark is immediately followed by the destination directory. The **usr/spool/uucppublic** directory is a common destination for UUCP sites.

Please be aware that none of the machine names in this chapter are real. Don't use these specific examples on your own system.

Generically, the **uucp** command would look like this:

```
gilbert:/$ uucp sourcefile destinationfile
```

The **uucp** command can also be used to grab files from another machine, as long as you have the proper permissions (again, a configuration issue that we'll duck). In this case, you'll alter the **uucp** command line used earlier in this chapter. The principle is the same: use the **uucp** command to list the source file and then its destination. In this case, the remote file is the source file, and a local directory is the destination:

```
gilbert:/$ uucp spike!/usr/spool/uucppublic/chap9.txt\
/usr/spool/uucppublic
```

When using the **uucp** command to download a file, all you need do is specify the destination directory; the command assumes that the filename will remain the same, and that the destination directory exists on your local machine.

Potential Problems with the Uucp Command

As many frustrated users can attest to, the **uucp** command, as well as the greater UUCP command set, is not foolproof.

Perhaps the greatest frustration is that the **uucp** command isn't interactive, and there's no way to monitor the status of a file transfer. You can tell **uucp** to send you a receipt via electronic mail when the file transfer is completed:

```
gilbert:/$ uucp -m chap9.txt spike!/usr/spool/uucppublic/chap9.txt
```

However, if you don't receive the electronic mail confirmation, then you can assume that the transfer has failed. Finding out why, however, isn't that easy a task.

It is made somewhat easier, however, by the presence of a logfile that **uucp** maintains as part of the transfer process. To get at this file, use the **uulog** command:

```
$ uulog
```

This will provide a lot of output—probably too much for your troubleshooting purposes. It's probably better if you combine the **uulog** with the name of a machine:

```
$ uulog -sspike
```

Yes, *-sspike* is correct. In an oddity, the *-s* option to **uulog** must be *immediately* followed by the name of the machine (in this case, *spike*).

You'll then need to read through the arcane information from **uulog** and try to make some sense of it. Successful file transfers will end with *REMOTE REQUESTED* or *OK*.

What Can Go Wrong?

When a **uucp** connection fails, there are can be many potential culprits. The **uulog** command can be handy to discover that a connection was denied by the remote system (something like *ACCESS DENIED* will appear in the logfile; unfortunately). In this case, the login name or the password required by the remote machine may have been changed; in either case, this is a task for the system administrator to tackle.

If this isn't the case and *ACCESS DENIED* still appears in the logfile, it could be a simple case of a mistyped command line. If you type the wrong filename or directory, the connection will succeed, but the transfer will fail. Again, by a careful read of the logfile, you can determine this.

Your transfer may also be the victim of your own impatience. Not all **uucp** requests are instantaneous; many system administrators chose to queue requests and then make the transfers after hours, when long-distance rates are cheaper.

Free Software and Ftp

Linux also features **ftp**, a command that allows you to link directly to another computer using the network TCP/IP. Essentially, if you have a TCP/IP connection to the Internet, you can use **ftp** to connect to any public site on the 'Net. In this section, we'll guide you through an **ftp** session.

Using Ftp

The **ftp** command can be used to connect to any other computer on your network running **ftp**. If your system is connected to the Internet, you can use **ftp** to access files from other Internet computers worldwide. These machines with which you network may or may not be running the UNIX or Linux operating systems; this operating-system independence is what makes **ftp** so widely used.

Ftp is interactive software, which means it asks you for information at specific times. Start it with the following:

```
gilbert:/$ ftp
ftp>
```

You'll be presented with the **ftp** prompt, where you enter special **ftp** commands. To get a list of available commands, type a question mark (?) or *help* at the prompt:

```
ftp> ?
```

or

```
ftp> help
```

A list of the most common **ftp** commands is listed in Table 9.3.

Table 9.3 Common ftp commands.

Command	Result
ascii	Use ASCII as the file-transfer type
bell	Ring the bell when file transfer is complete
binary	Use binary as the file-transfer type
bye or quit	Terminate **ftp** session
cd	Change directory on the remote machine
close	End **ftp** connection to remote computer, but keep local **ftp** program running
delete *filename*	Delete filename on remote computer
get *filename*	Get filename from the remote machine
get *filename1 filename2*	Get *filename1* from the remote machine and save it locally as *filename2*
help	List available commands
mput *filename*	Copy the local *filename* to the remote machine
pwd	List the current directory on the remote machine

It's simple to download files from a remote machine with **ftp**. Let's say we want to grab some files from the machine named *mn.kevin.com*. (No, this isn't a real machine.) Assuming that this is a machine on the Internet that supports anonymous **ftp**—and our fictional machine does, of course—you would merely specify its name on the command line:

```
gilbert:/$ ftp mn.kevin.com
```

If the connection goes through, you'll receive a verification message, along with a login prompt. Since this is *anonymous* ftp, use *anonymous* as a login name:

```
Name: anonymous
```

You'll then be asked for a password. Some systems require you to supply your electronic-mail address, while others require *guest*. Use either. You'll then be presented with an **ftp** prompt.

The remote system has been set up to give you limited access which means that your maneuverability is very limited, and the files you want are usually close at hand. If you need to change to another directory, do so with the UNIX **cd** command.

NOTE Before embarking on the great file quest, you should know something about the files you're downloading. If they are straight C files in uncompressed, ASCII form, you can download them using the default file-transfer settings. Most larger files, especially binary files, are stored in compressed form so that they take less time to transfer.

These compressed files end with **.Z**, **.z**, **.tgz**, or **gz**. so they are instantly recognizable. To download compressed files, you must change to binary mode, since you're downloading binary files. Do so with:

```
ftp> binary
```

Once you are placed in the correct directory containing the file to be downloaded, start the download process with the **get** command:

```
ftp> get filename
```

As you download the file, there will be a prompt on the system, and you won't be able to enter any keystrokes.

After the file has been transferred successfully, you'll be given a message similar to the following:

```
Transfer complete
```

You may also be told the size of the file, as well as the transfer time.

Since you're through with your file needs, close the connection with the **bye** command:

```
ftp> bye
```

What Do I Do With the File?

If you download an ASCII file, you can view it using any editor, including **vi** or **emacs**. If it's a source-code file, you can compile it for use on your own system; we explain the process in Chapter 10. If you've downloaded a compressed binary file, you will have to uncompress it (and perhaps unarchive it) at the command line using **uncompress**, **unpack**, **tar**, or **gzip**—things you learned about in Chapter 7.

Other Networking Commands

In addition to **ftp**, which is used to transfer—copy—files from system to system, there are a number of other common networking commands. These commands work to aid the connection among your computer and others on the same link. Generally, if you work at a site with multiple UNIX computers, these computers will be networked together, usually using the Ethernet network protocol. Your systems may also be networked with the worldwide Internet, which as you already know is a collection of connected networks. (Say *that* three times fast.)

Using the Rlogin Command

The **rlogin** command allows you to remotely login to another computer on your network (remember that if you're on the Internet, you're on a worldwide network). You must, of course, have a valid user account on any machine to which you want to login. To use **rlogin**, you need the name of the machine to login to. To login a machine named *nicollet*, you'd use a command line like the following:

```
gilbert:/$ rlogin nicollet
Password:
```

At the *Password* prompt, you may need to enter in your password on machine *nicollet*, which may or may not be different than the password you use on your current machine. Once logged in, you're computing on the remote machine and can run any standard UNIX command. You also log out the same way you normally logout:

```
gilbert:/$ logout
Connection closed.
$
```

Note that after you logout from a remote machine, you're back to the command prompt at your original machine. This tends to get confusing, so be careful.

The basic form of **rlogin** is:

```
rlogin hostname
```

where *hostname* is the name of the machine to login.

Using the Telnet Command

The **telnet** command works much the same as **rlogin** does, allowing you to connect directly to a remote machine. Because the **telnet** command is considered part of the toolkit used by the Internet surfer, it's actually gained in popularity over the years.

Telnet allows you to either run a command directly on a remote machine while displaying the results on your own, or run a specific command on a remote machine (many sites that allows **telnet** put restrictions on what users can run, due to security concerns). With **telnet**, you only need to know the address of the machine you're connecting to, such as **sunsite.unc.edu**, as illustrated by the following:

```
gilbert:/$ telnet
telnet> open sunsite.unc.edu
Trying 198.86.40.81
Connected
*************** Welcome to SunSITE.unc.edu ***************
SunSITE offers several public services via login. These include:

NO MORE PUBLIC gopher login!
Use lynx the simple WWW client to access gopher and Web areas
For a simple WAIS client (over 500 databases),  login as swais
For WAIS search of political databases,        login as politics
For WAIS search of LINUX databases,            login as linux


For a FTP session, ftp to sunsite.unc.edu. Then login as anonymous
```

```
For more information about SunSITE, send mail to
info@sunsite.unc.edu

UNIX (R) System V Release 4.0 (calypso-2.oit.unc.edu)

login: swais
```

In this case, **sunsite.unc.edu** offers a variety of services to the general computing public, here centering around WAIS databases. Other **telnet** sites may not offer such a wide variety of services; a site like **archie.rutgers.edu** offers only **archie** searches.

Unfortunately, Linux does not offer **archie** as of now, so you'll need to use a public **archie** server to perform a search.

NOTE

Sunsite.unc.edu is a public Internet site. If you're using **telnet** within your corporation, the rules will be slightly different. Here, **sunsite.unc.edu** offers public access; you don't need an account on **sunsite.unc.edu**, nor do you need a password. However, **sunsite.unc.edu** does put restrictions on what can be done by a visitor; for example, you can't use the standard Linux command set, and your options are limited to the login selections. For a private system, you'll need an account on the remote system before you can login, and you may be subject to the same sorts of restrictions. Remember: security.

The Usenet and Newsgroups

The Internet's roots can be traced to the Usenet, a worldwide messaging system. The Usenet, while technically comprising a portion of the Internet, is know best for electronic-mail and newsgroup distribution.

UNIX "insiders" brag of being on the *net*, but what actually constitutes the *net*—Internet or Usenet—depends on the user and his or her system. Though the two are linked, there are crucial differences, and anyone (essentially) can get on the Usenet.

Thousands of computers are linked—worldwide—in the loose network we call the Usenet, a public network of linked UNIX and non-UNIX machines, dedicated to sending information to companies, schools, universities, the government, research laboratories, and individuals.

The Usenet performs a variety of services, but perhaps the most popular service involves *newsgroups*. A newsgroup is a discussion of various topics, ranging from computing to sociology to boomerangs to Barney the Dinosaur. In fact, there are thousands of Usenet newsgroups. Some are trivial and a waste of bandwidth, others are of interest to only a small set of users, and others would interest a host of users. (Take a gander at *alt.sex.bestiality.barney*, and you'll see the validity of this point.)

These newsgroups are divided into classes, to better allow users to figure out what to read in the plethora of information arriving daily. Table 9.4 covers the major newsgroup classifications.

Table 9.4 The major Usenet newsgroups.

Name	Subject
alt	alternative hierarchy, not subject to other rules
biz	business-related groups
comp	computing
misc	miscellaneous subjects
news	news about the Usenet
rec	recreational activities
sci	science
soc	social issues
talk	talk

Not only is this computer-dweeb heaven, but the Usenet provides valuable information on everything from vegetarian recipes to buying a house. There are Usenet newsgroups for just about every topic you can imagine—and then some, from *rec.sport.football.college* to *soc.culture.bulgaria*. (*Alt.buddha.short.fat.guy* was definitely a surprise the first time we saw it.) In addition, there are regional newsgroups; those of us in Minnesota have access to a wide range of newsgroups that begin with *mn*, such as *mn.forsale*.

While the Usenet can be a powerful information source, you'll also find a lot of inaccurate information, as nearly anyone can get on the Usenet. So take what you read with a grain of salt. Generally, the more technical the group, the more accurate the information you'll get. The group *comp.compilers* (information on writing compilers for computer languages) certainly contains more unbiased information than *comp.sys.next.advocacy* (advocates—an unbiased group if there ever was one—of Next workstations).

However, there are many Usenet newsgroups that you'll find useful. Being technical types ourselves, we regularly peruse the newsgroups relating to UNIX, the X Window System, and related topics (electronic-mail packages like **elm** and **pine**, software like **emacs**). Appendix A lists Linux-related newsgroups.

These classifications are broken down into specific newsgroups. The syntax of a newsgroup name is simple: The name of the classification followed by a descriptive suffix. For instance, the name of the newsgroup devoted to questions concerning the UNIX operating system is *comp.unix.questions*. Note the use of periods to separate the elements. A listing of some popular newsgroups is listed in Table 9.5.

Table 9.5 A sampling of frequently accessed Usenet newsgroups.

Newsgroup	Topic
comp.databases	Database-management issues
comp.lang.c	C-language issues
comp.source.unix	UNIX source code
comp.text	Text-processing issues

Table 9.5 A sampling of frequently accessed Usenet newsgroups. (continued)

Newsgroup	Topic
omp.unix.questions	Questions about the UNIX operating system
misc.jobs.offered	Job openings
rec.music.gaffa	The music of Kate Bush
sci.space.shuttle	Space exploration issues associated with the NASA space shuttle

Newsgroups can also be *open* or *moderated*. Open newsgroups mean that anyone can post to them, while moderated newsgroups have someone to review the postings before they're passed out to the general public. As you might surmise, moderated newsgroups tend to be more reliable and useful.

WARNING

The Usenet newsgroups are aggressively egalitarian. News can be posted by just about anyone. Using it as a source of information requires some skepticism on your part. On the one hand, it's a great place to find very technical, specialized, information—the more technical and specialized the better. Many leading figures in the computing industry regularly post information in the newsgroups. And since there's nothing new under the sun, chances are that the problem that plagues you has already been solved by someone else in the Linux world.

On the other hand, every opinion is not created equally, and a lot of ill-founded opinions can be found in most newsgroups. Veterans refer to the *signal-to-noise* ratio; newsgroups with a lot of ill-founded opinions and bickering are said to be filled with noise. As with any other source of information, treat what you see on the Usenet newsgroups with a healthy dose of skepticism.

Reading and Writing the News

Although all the news items are text files and could in theory could be read with **vi** or **emacs**, there are so many of them in so many separate files that it's not really feasible to read each file. A full Usenet *newsfeed*, that is, all the incoming message files from all the worldwide newsgroups, adds more than 30 megabytes of files to your disk each day. (Remember when we said earlier that UNIX files seem to propagate proportionally? Well, there's your example.) This is how a type of software, called *newsreaders*, evolved. Newsreaders help you sort out, with varying degrees of usefulness, what to read from the hundreds of new files that appear daily. The basic idea is to read those messages you're interested in and skip the rest. There's simply no way to read every incoming message, even if you spend all day in front of your computer.

We are not going to cover the many news readers in depth—Linux features several, and you're encouraged to check them all out. They include:

- **trn**, a reader with expanded search capabilities (shown in Figure 9.10)

- **inn, a basic reader**

- **tin**, a threaded reader that arranges messages by topic (as shown in Figure 9.11)

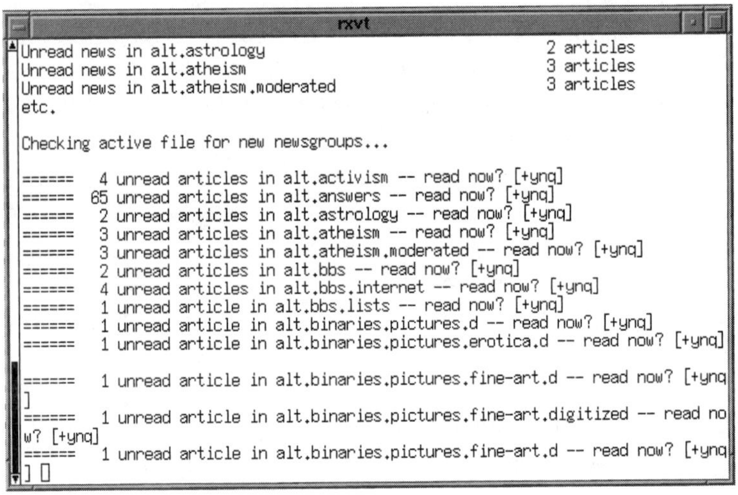

Figure 9.10 The trn newsreader.

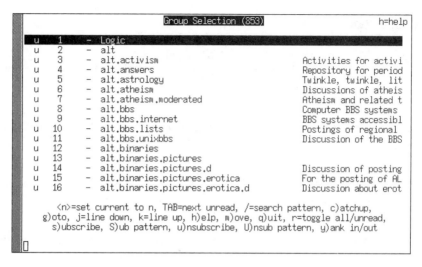

Figure 9.11 The tin newsreader.

How Do I Find a File for Download?

If you're on the Usenet, you'll be surrounded with information regarding free software and how to get it. The trick is knowing where to look for it.

Some universities and corporations maintain archive sites that support anonymous **ftp**. These locations are referred to regularly in the newsgroup *comp.sources.*

In addition, many computer-related newsgroups will contain news items labeled **FAQ**, or Frequently Asked Questions. One of the frequently asked questions will (undoubtedly) concern the existence of archival sites.

And, finally, you can post a plaintive plea in a newsgroup, asking for information about a particular program. You may receive some rude comments from people who tire of answering questions from innocent beginners, but undoubtedly some kind person should answer your request with useful information.

Summary

This chapter covers Linux's many tools for connecting to other computer systems and to the Internet using TCP/IP features. These include TCP/IP connections to an existing network, or dial-up access using Linux's SLIP and PPP tools.

Once connected, Linux offers many commands for networking Internet access and usage, including **ftp** (which lets you transfer software from remote sites), **rlogin**, and **telnet**. Also, you can peruse Usenet newsgroups thanks to several news readers.

In addition, Linux offers several **mail** options, including the mail command and the **xmh**, **pine**, and **elm** newsreaders.

The Usernet is a service of newsgroups. Linux features several newareading programs. Unfortunately, a web browser is not one of the tools included with Linux. You'll have to get this on your own—but with the other tools listed in this chapter, you'll be able to grab one easily.

In the next (and final) chapter, we cover programming and Linux.

Section IV

Linux Programming

The book ends with **Chapter 10**, an overview of Linux programming. In this chapter, you'll find explanations of Linux's programming tools (including the GNU C compiler), as well as X Window programming tools for Linux.

Programming in Linux

This chapter covers:

- The GNU C compiler
- C programming
- The **cc** command
- Using **make**
- Programming under the X Window System
- Using shared libraries
- Using **imake**
- Using Tcl/Tk
- A short introduction to using Perl
- Using **gawk**, the GNU Project version of **awk**
- Using LessTif to mimic OSF/Motif

Programming under Linux

This chapter is not going to turn you into an instant Linux and X Window programmer. We will, however, show you how to program in the Linux environment. We'll cover a lot of the odd things that you're just supposed to know when programming on Linux, including where the X libraries are, and some interesting tidbits about how Linux uses shared libraries.

For the programmer, Linux offers all the freeware utilities and compilers you'd expect for software that relies heavily on offerings from the Free Software Foundation. Starting with the GNU C compiler, you can develop C, C++, and Objective-C programs on your Linux system. In addition to these mainstream languages, Linux supports Tcl, Perl, Smalltalk, and a host of other programming languages and utilities. In addition, we've thrown freeware called **LessTif** on the accompanying CD-ROM, for those of you who want Motif compatibility but don't want to pay for commercial software.

Your main worry is whether you've installed the proper disk sets for your compiler and associated tools. (If you haven't heard of one before, a compiler is a tool that converts a program in text form into an executable Linux command.) Being programmers ourselves, we always recommend this; if you haven't, you can always go back and use the Setup program to reinstall the proper disk sets..

If you're not a programmer, chances are that you'll be lost in much of this chapter. Even so, you'll find some interesting Linux utilities mentioned here. In addition, many free Linux programs come in source-code-form only, so you'll need to learn to compile them, so it might be important to know about the process of compiling and linking C programs.

The Linux C Compiler: GNU CC

The main C and C++ compiler on Linux is the GNU **gcc**. **gcc** is an all-encompassing program, being able to compile a number of programming languages: C, C++, and Objective-C. **Gcc**, or **cc**, which is linked to **gcc**, compiles C and C++ programs just like you'd expect. The command-line parameters are all standard **cc** parameters as well as the traditional **gcc** parameters. If you're used to programming on UNIX, you'll find Linux works as you'd expect.

For those newer to C programming, we'll provide a short introduction. If you're really new at this, you'll likely want to get a C programming book to help you out.

C Programming

C programs–and in fact, most programs in general–usually start in plain old text files. (Linux makes extensive use of simple text files, as you've seen throughout this book.) These text files are created with text editors like **vi** or **emacs**. Once created, C programs must be compiled with a C compiler, **cc** or **gcc** (which are one and the same on Linux). This C compiler converts the text file, which the programmer wrote, into object, or machine, code for the Intel platform. Then, object modules (files of object code) are linked together to make an executable program, a brand new Linux command. Once the process is successfully completed, you can execute this program like any other command you type at the command line. Being able to create your own command is a neat thing.

In addition to creating C or C++ programs, you can also use shell scripts or write code in a number of interpreted languages such as Perl or Tcl, which we cover later on in this chapter. From the plethora of Linux program-creation tools, you need to choose what is the appropriate tool for any given task.

The first step is identifying what types of files you're dealing with. Table 10.1 lists the most common Linux file types and their common file extensions.

Table 10.1 Program file types.

File Suffix	Meaning
.a	Library
a.out	Executable (no one uses the a.out name)
.c	C program
.C	C++ file (note the uppercase C)

Table 10.1 Program file types. (continued)

File Suffix	Meaning
.cc	C++ file
.cpp	C++ file
.cxx	C++ file
.c++	C++ file
.f	Fortran program
.for	Fortran program
.h	C include file
.o	Object module (compiled from a .c file)
.s	Assembly code
.sa	Shared library stubs linked with your program
.so.n	Run-time shared library, version number is n
.tcl	Tcl script
.tk	Tcl script

Most C programs are stored in one or more files that end with .c, for example, as **neatstuff.c** and **myprog.c**. When you compile a C file, the C compiler, **cc**, creates an object file, usually ending with .o. The linker (called linkage editor in Linux parlance), **ld**, then links the .o files together to make an executable program. The default name for this program is **a.out**, although no one really uses **a.out** for their program names. Instead, programs end up with names like **ls**, **cp**, or **mv**. All of this is controlled by the **cc** command.

The Cc Command

The **cc** command executes the C compiler which can compile and link C programs into executable commands. To test out your Linux C compiler, we'll use the following short program:

```
#include <stdio.h>

int main()
```

```
{    /* main */

    /* This is a comment */

    printf("Linux is my favorite O.S.\n");
    return 0;

}    /* main */
```

Enter the above code into a text file named **chap10.c**, using your favorite Linux text editor.

It's a good idea to always name C program files with a .c extension. This isn't required, but following conventions like this make Linux easier to use.

After you type this short program in, you can follow through the simple steps below to create a working executable program from this C file.

The program you typed in was simply a text file. There's nothing in it to make it an executable command. To do so, we need to compile and link the program. Both steps are accomplished by the following **cc** command:

```
$ cc -o chap10 chap10.c
```

The above command runs the C compiler, **cc**. The *-o* option tells **cc** to build a program named **chap10** (the default name without the *-o* option is the awkward **a.out**). The *chap10.c* part of the command tells **cc** to compile the file named **chap10.c.** The **cc** command both compiled and linked the program.

You should now have an executable program named **chap10**. You can execute this program by typing **chap10** at the command line. When you do, you'll see the following output:

```
$ chap10
Linux is my favorite O.S.
```

Now you're a real C programmer and ready for a new lucrative career.

Compiling the Long Way

When we used the **cc** command, above, **cc** first compiled the program into an object module. Then, **cc** linked the object module to create an executable program, the file named **chap10**. This is very important if you have more than one file to compile together into your program. Most C programs require a number of .c files, all of which must be compiled and then linked together to form one program. One of the main reasons for separating C programs into multiple files is simply sanity: reading a 1-megabyte program in one file is ludicrous. And yes, C programs get to this size and even much bigger than 1 megabyte. Some C programs which we've worked on include well over a million lines of C code.

To use the long method of compiling and linking, we split the tasks into two steps. First, you compile all the .c files you require. Then, you link the resulting .o files (we'll get into this later) into your executable program. Since we have a very small C program typed in already (you did type it in, didn't you?), we'll start with that.

To compile **chap10.c** into an object module, a .o file, with the following command:

```
$ cc -c chap10.c
```

If successful, you should see a file named *chap10.o* in your directory. The .o file is called the object file (or object module), and it contains unlinked machine code.

The next step is to link the object files (usually there's more than one) into an executable file. To do this, we again use the -o option to **cc**, but this time we pass a .o file at the end of the command line, rather than the .c file we used above:

```
$ cc -o chap10 chap10.o
```

This command links together the file **chap10.o** into the executable program **chap10**. You can place more than one object filename on the command line, as in the following example:

```
$ cc -o chap10 chap10_a.o chap10_b.o chap10_c.o
```

Normally you'll want to pick more descriptive filenames than the ones we've used, though.

Working with CC

In normal operation, the **cc** command executes a number of other commands under the hood. Once such command is **cpp**. The **cpp** command is the C preprocessor. This reads a C program file, a *.c* file, and expands any # directives. In the short program above, the *#include* directive means to include the file **stdio.h**. That is, **cpp** reads in **stdio.h** and inserts the contents right at the *#include* directive. Most C programs use one or more include files.

These include files are normally stored in **/usr/include**. If you use the angle brackets, (<) and (>), around an include filename, like **<stdio.h>**, this means that **cpp** looks for a file named **stdio.h** in the standard places, of which **/usr/include** is the default (the *-I* command-line parameter can add more directories to the include file search path; see Table 10.2 below). You can also use quotation marks (") around the filename.

All C programs are built around the section labeled **main()**. **The main()** section (called a *function* in C parlance) is executed when the program starts. Our **main()** function has three C program statements, all of which call the **printf()** function, which prints out the text between the quotation marks to your screen. As you can tell, this is not a sophisticated program.

The \n character passed to **printf()** in the program above means that a new line character is printed. This starts a new line. If you're used to a DOS machine, then you'll note that UNIX uses a new line character where DOS uses a carriage return and then a new line. The backslash, \, is used as a special character in C programs. Usually, a backslash is combined with another character to make a non-printable character, such as \n for a new line or \a for a bell.

Using the CC Command

The **cc** command uses a number of command-line parameters to tell it what to do and to allow you to fine-tune the process of building executable programs from C language text files. Table 10.2 lists commonly used **cc** command-line parameters:

Table 10.2 Cc command-line parameters.

Parameter	Meaning
-Idirectory	Searches the given *directory* for include files, as well as **/usr/include**
-c filename.c	Compiles the file *filename.c* and build the object module *filename.o*. This does not create an executable command
-o progname	Names the executable program *progname*. The default name is **a.out**
-g	Compiles with debugging information
-O	Optimizes the program for best performance

Most UNIX compilers don't allow you to mix the *g* (include debugging information) and *O* (optimize) options, but the GNU C compiler used by Linux allows this.

There's a huge number of **cc** command-line options; use **man cc** to see them.

Linking with Libraries

For C programs, a *library* is a collection of commonly used routines that you can reuse in your programs. Most C programs require more than just the standard C library. If you look in **/usr/lib**, you'll see most of the libraries supported by Linux. Table 10.3 lists the major locations for Linux libraries.

Table 10.3 Locations for Linux libraries.

Directory	Libraries
/usr/lib	Main system libraries
/usr/openwin/lib	Open Look libraries like the Xview library
/usr/X11R6/lib	Most X Window libraries
/usr/interviews/lib	InterViews libraries

To link with a given library, you use the *-l* command-line option to **cc**. To link with the X11 library, use *-lX11*. This is shorthand notion for linking in the library named **libX11.a** (or it's shared-library equivalent, **libX11.sa**).

Linux Shared Libraries

Linux supports a great concept called *shared libraries*. Because so many Linux programs link in very large libraries, particularly X Window libraries, the program size tends to grow. When you run these programs, they take up more memory (real and virtual). To help alleviate this problem, Linux supports shared libraries. The whole purpose is that many programs can reference a single copy of the library loaded into memory. For X Window programs, this saves a *lot* of RAM.

The problem with Linux shared libraries is that they are very tightly linked to their version numbers. Thus, if you upgrade your version of the X Window System from Release 5 to Release 6, you'll have to relink every X application to use the new shared libraries. If you don't, it's likely that the old programs won't continue to run. We mention the X libraries in particular because many Linux users got burned by the upgrade to Release 6. In this instance, you must keep the old shared libraries around until you get all your X programs updated. For some programs, such as DOOM or NCSA Mosaic for the X Window System, you may have to wait until someone else compiles a new version.

Programming with X

Linux comes with a number of X Window libraries, ready for both you to program with and for you to use when compiling freeware X Window applications. Unfortunately, Linux does not come with the Motif libraries, necessary to compile a number of neat utilities including the Mosaic Internet browser. (You can purchase the Motif libraries from a number of third parties, though; see Appendix A for details.)

When compiling X programs, you normally don't have to do anything special to link, other than adding the X libraries to your **cc** command line. The X Window include files should be in the proper place, **/usr/include/X11** (actually a symbolic link to **/usr/X11R6 /include/X11**, but good enough for the compiler).

To compile and link an X program with X11 Release 6, you can use the following command line:

```
cc -o foo foo.c -lXaw -lXt -lXext -lX11 -lSM -lICE
```

Programmer's Tools

In addition to the basic compiler, Linux comes with a large number of utility programs and tools to help make programming easier. The first and foremost tool is a program called *make*.

Building Programs with make

Most C programs require more than one *.c* file of source code. When one of these files change, at least one (and maybe more) of the files must get recompiled to have the executable program reflect the changes. Tending to be lazy, programmers don't want to recompile *all* the files if just one changed. Furthermore, these lazy programmers don't want to have to keep track of all the files that changed. This is where the tool called **make** comes in.

Make is a command that helps build or "make" UNIX programs from the C language source-code files. **Make** uses a set of rules, stored in a file called **Makefile** to tell it the most efficient way to rebuild a program. You keep a **Makefile** in each directory where you develop C programs.

The **Makefile** contains a set of rules, using a rigid syntax, that describe how to build the program. Most of the rules declare what parts of the program depends on other parts. Using these dependency rules, **make** determines what has changed (based on the file modified date) and what other things depend on the file or files that changed. Then, make simply executes the commands in the **Makefile** to build each thing that needs to be rebuilt.

The basic **Makefile** syntax is deceptively simple. (Linux includes the GNU **make** program, which accepts a number of rule short-cuts. For this chapter, though, we'll just cover the basics.)

You start out with a so-called *target*. The target is something you want to build, such as our program **chap10** from the example above.

To create a target in the **Makefile**, begin with a new line, you name the target–what you want to build, then place a colon (:), a tab, then list the files the target depends on. Starting on the next line, begin with a tab, then place the UNIX command used to build the target. You can have multiple commands, each of which should go on its own line and every command line must start with a tab.

In the abstract, the **Makefile** rules look like the following:

what_to_build: what_it_depends_on

　　command1_to_build_it

　　command2_to_build_it

　　command3_to_build_it

　　...

　　lastcommand_to_build_it

In the abstract, this looks confusing. Here's a more concrete example, using the **chap10** program we provided above.

The target we want to build is the **chap10** program. The **chap10** program (the target) depends on the object module **chap10.o**. Once we have the object module **chap10.o**, then the command line to create the **chap10** program is:

```
chap10:    chap10.o
    cc -o chap10 chap10.o
```

The above **make** rule states is that if **chap10.o** has a more recent date, then execute the **cc** command to build the **chap10** program from the object module **chap10.o**.

This is just part of task, as we still have to compile **chap10.c** to create the object module **chap10.o**. That is, the file **chap10.o**, is said to depend on the file **chap10.c**. You build **chap10.o** from **chap10.c**. To do this, we use another **make** rule.

This time, the object module **chap10.o** depends on the text file **chap10.c**. The command to build the object module is:

```
chap10.o:   chap10.c
    cc -c chap10.c
```

With this **make** rule, if you edit **chap10.c**, you'll make the file **chap10.c** have a more recent date/time than the object module **chap10.o**. This causes **make** to trigger the **cc** command to compile **chap10.c** into **chap10.o**.

You've discovered the secret to **make's** rules. Everything depends on the date/time of the files, a very simple–but clever–idea. The idea is that if the text of the program *.c* file is modified, then you better rebuild the program with **cc**. Because most users are impatient, if the *.c* file hasn't been changed, there's simply no reason (at least in our example) to rebuild the program with **cc**.

A Make Example

To try out **make**, enter in the following text into a file named **Makefile**:

```
#
# Test Makefile
#
# The program chap10 depends on chap10.o.
chap10:     chap10.o
    cc -o chap10 chap10.o

# The object module chap10.o depends on chap10.c.
chap10.o:   chap10.c
    cc -c chap10.c
```

The above **Makefile** should be in the same directory as your sample C program file, **chap10.c**. To use **make**, we need to tell it what to **make**, that is, what target we want to build. In our case, we want **make** to build the program **chap10**. The following command will build this program:

```
$ make chap10
        cc -c chap10.c
        cc -o chap10 chap10.o
```

We should now have the **chap10** program ready to run. If we try **make** again, it–being very lazy–tells us that there's no new work to do:

```
$ make chap10
`chap10' is up to date.
```

Why? Because the **chap10** program was built and nothing has changed. Now, edit the **chap10.c** file again, or use the **touch** command to bump up the date/time associated with the file:

```
$ touch chap10.c
```

When you call **make** again, it knows it now needs to rebuild the **chap10** program, because presumably the **chap10.c** file has changed since the last time **chap10.c** was compiled with **cc**. Since **touch** only updates the date/time associated with the file and doesn't change the internals of the file in any way, we've just fooled **make**. **Make** doesn't bother checking if a file is different; it merely checks the time the file was last written to, blindly assuming that no one would ever write to a file without modifying its contents. Normally, though, you don't want fool **make,** but use its simple rules to make your life easier.

Make supports a number of useful command-line parameters, as shown in Table 10.4.

Table 10.4 Make command-line parameters.

Parameter	Meaning
-f *makefile*	Uses the named file instead of **Makefile** for the rules
-n	Runs in no-execute mode. Only print out the commands, don't execute them
-s	Runs in silent mode; doesn't print out any commands make executes

As you compile Linux freeware, you'll notice that there are a lot of conventions with **make** and **Makefiles**. For example, most **Makefiles** contain a target called all, which rebuilds the entire program when you execute:

```
$ make all
```

In addition, most **Makefiles** also contain a clean target that removes all .o files and other files created by the compiler, and an install target that copies the built executable file to an installation directory, such as **/usr/local/bin**.

Imake

In addition to **make**, there's a another tool called **imake**. **Imake** is used to generate **Makefiles** on a variety of systems. **Imake** uses an **Imakefile** for its rules. These rules then help generate a **Makefile**. This **Makefile** is then used by make to build the program. Sound convoluted? You bet it is. The main reason **imake** exists is because of radically different system configurations, especially where the X Window System is concerned.

You'll find **imake** especially popular with programs for X Window. The problem with X is that there's so many options that every UNIX platform is configured slightly differently. There's simply no way you could write a portable **Makefile** that could work on all such platforms. **Imake** uses an **Imakefile**, along with configuration files that are local to your system. Together, the **Imakefile** and the local configuration files generate a **Makefile** that should work just dandy on your system. (In addition to **imake**, there's an even handier package called GNU **Configure**. Unfortunately, **imake** is very common among X Window programs and **configure** is not.)

If you need to compile programs for the X Window System and you see an **Imakefile**, here's what you should do. First, run the **xmkmf** shell script. This script is merely a simple front-end to **imake**:

```
$ xmkmf
mv Makefile Makefile.bak
imake -DUseInstalled -I/usr/lib/X11/config
```

The above commands should make a backup of any **Makefile** you have (to **Makefile.bak**) and then create a new **Makefile** based on the commands in an **Imakefile**.

Imake isn't easy to grasp, so if you have problems with **imake**, you should check with your system administrator, or look up **imake** in a book on the X Window System (such as *Using X*, MIS: Press, 1992; see Appendix A for a list of books on using the X Window System).

Debuggers

Since Linux remains firmly in the GNU program-development world, it provides the **gdb** debugger, as well as the X Window front end, **xxgdb**, as shown in Figure 10.1.

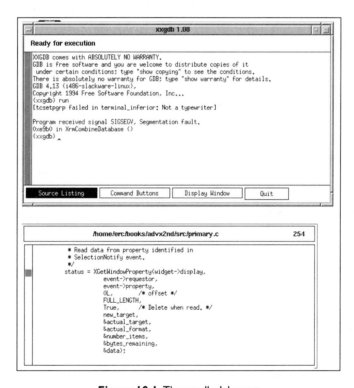

Figure 10.1 The xxgdb debugger.

X Window Tools

If you're developing X Window applications, a few extra utilities may help. The **xman** program (mentioned in Chapter 6) provides a graphical front-end and nice formatting for UNIX online manual pages.

For critical X programs, you'll find **xcmap** very useful. This simple X application displays the current color map. For color-intensive X applications, this can help you track down obscure X problems.

Similarly, the **xev** application helps you see what events the keyboard keys are really sending to the X server.

For selecting fonts, **xfd** and **xfontsel** both help you choose a good-looking font for your applications.

For C++ development, there's a neat X Window tool called **iclass** in the InterViews package that displays class libraries (as shown in Figure 10.2). To get this tool, you need to load in the optional InterViews package fron the CD-ROM.

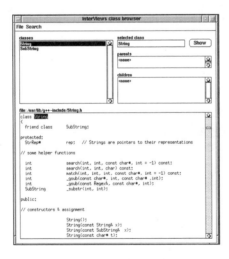

Figure 10.2 The iclass C++ class browser.

Parsers and Lexers

If you're used to building your own parsers, you'll find the GNU **bison** (a port of UNIX **yacc**—Yet Another Compiler Compiler) and **flex** (a fast **lex**). Linux even includes **flex++** for developing C++ scanners.

Other Tools

We list some more useful tools for the programmer in Table 10.5.

Table 10.5 More useful programming tools.

Tool	Usage
ar	Collects object files into libraries
diff	Compares differences between files
gprof	Gathers timing statistics about your programs for performance tuning
hexdump	Displays ASCII, decimal, hexadecimal, or octal dump of a file
objdump	Display information on object files
ranlib	Generates an index in an **ar**-created archive (library)
rcs	Source-code Revision Control System
strace	Displays system calls from your program

There's even a tool called **ansi2knr** that converts ANSI C to old-style Kernighan and Ritchie-style C (without function prototypes). With Linux, you don't really need this, as **gcc** fully supports ANSI C.

There's more than what we listed above in Table 10.5. Chances are just about every UNIX freeware tool is available on Linux.

Other Programming Languages

C is by and large the programming *lingua franca* on UNIX and Linux, with C++ (an object-oriented extension to C) fast gaining in popularity. In addition to these languages, Linux provides a host of other opportunities to program.

First, the GNU C compiler also supports the Objective-C extension to the C programming language. Objective-C is very popular under the Nextstep environment.

Linux also provides GNU Smalltalk (those GNU folks have done a lot for programmers, haven't they?) should you like a pure object-oriented programming language. For artificial intelligence fans, there's Common Lisp (under the name **clisp**). Additional programs include Fortran, Ada, and Pascal.

In addition to the programming languages above, Linux offers even more, including a number of scripting languages. A scripting language is a lot like the language that comes with the UNIX shell. The main difference between a programming language and a scripting language is that scripting languages are usually interpreted instead of compiled and scripting languages usually make it easier to launch Linux commands from within your programs—called scripts when you use a scripting language. As you can tell, the line between programming languages and scripting languages is blurry.

Of the scripting languages available on Linux, the two hottest languages are Tcl and Perl, while **gawk** continues to attract a lot of attention.

Tcl

Tcl, short for the Tool Command Language, is a very handy scripting language that runs on most UNIX platforms as well as Windows NT. Combined with Tcl's X Window tool kit, called Tk, you can build a lot of neat X Window graphical programs without a lot of coding.

In addition, Tcl is made to be embedded in C programs, so you can use Tcl as a standard extension language for your spreadsheet, game, or other software you write.

We mostly use Tcl to create programs that have a friendly user interface, look like Motif programs and that can run on a wide number of systems. Tcl and the Tk tool kit present something akin to the Motif look and feel—not close enough for purists, but close enough for most users. This is a great benefit because the Motif libraries don't ship with Linux, while Tcl does.

Tcl is a scripting language, much like the languages built into **sh** and **ksh**, the most common Unix command shells. The language has some nice features for handling strings and lists (of strings—just about everything is a string in a Tcl program).

The Tk tool kit then acts as an add-on to Tcl, allowing you to easily build widgets and create an X Window user interface. The whole concept of widgets, though, is likely to be daunting unless you've programmed with one of the many X tool kits, such as OSF/Motif. Each widget acts as a part of your user interface, for example, a list of files, a pushbutton to exit the program and so on. If you have worked with OSF/Motif or the Athena widgets, you'll catch on to the concepts of Tk pretty fast. Even if you haven't worked with the OSF/Motif or Athena libraries, we found the basics of Tcl very easy to grasp. (There are some frustrating parts to Tcl, though.)

The Tk add-on to Tcl provides most of the standard set of widgets you'd expect. These widgets mirror most of the main widgets in the OSF/Motif tool kit, except for the handy option- menu, combo-box, and notebook widgets. Tcl exceeds OSF/Motif in a number of areas, too, especially with the canvas widget, which allows you to place graphic "objects" such as lines, rectangles, Bezier curves, and even other widgets inside the canvas.

Programming with Tcl

Like most scripting languages, Tcl uses a dollar sign, $, to get the value of a variable. This is because everything in Tcl is a text string, so it needs a special character to differentiate a string from the value held within a variable. Thus:

```
variable
```

is just the literal string variable, while

```
$variable
```

returns the value stored in the variable named, appropriately enough, *variable*. This is the same as most shell scripting languages. (There are some tricky aspects to this, though. We found that simple typos—forgetting the $—were responsible for most of our Tcl errors.)

For example: if you have a directory name in the variable *dir* and want to use the **cd** command to change to that directory, you issue the following Tcl command:

```
cd $dir
```

The basic syntax for Tcl seems like a cross between Lisp and C. The basic function, called *proc*, looks much like a C function, for example:

```
proc add_one { value } {

    return [expr $value+1]
}
```

The braces give it a definite C feeling. The Lispishness comes from the use of the set command, instead of assignment. That is, instead of a C statement like:

```
a = b;
```

in Tcl you code this as:

```
set a $b
```

(Remembering all the while that the $ can trip you up at first.)

One nice thing about Tcl is the ability to use variables at any time, without predeclaring them except for arrays, which you need to indicate are arrays before using with widget commands.

Working with Tcl

To try out some Tcl programs, you should run the Tcl interpreter, called **wish**, which allows you to enter Tcl commands as if you were in a Tcl-based shell, which is what **wish** is.

The most interesting use of Tcl is to create graphical programs including widgets such as push buttons. To create a pushbutton in Tcl, use the **button** command:

```
button .b1 \
  -text "My first button" \
  -command { exit }
```

Since Tcl is a scripting language, you can use the backslash character, \, to extend a command on one line over many lines. This makes your programs easier to read.

The above command creates a button widget named *.b1* (the leading period is important). Just like Linux uses the / character to mark the root directory, Tcl uses the period (.) to mark the root widget (your application's main window). We're then creating a button widget that sits like a sub directory beneath the root widget.

The *-command* sets the Tcl command that will run when the button gets pushed. In our case, the **exit** command exits **wish** and our Tcl script.

It's important to note that the code for the *-command* gets evaluated only when the button is pushed, usually sometime after the button is created and usually when the Tcl program is in another procedure. Because of this, local variables no longer have their values at execution time.

This can be very difficult to debug. We show some workarounds in the sample code below.

To get a widget to appear, we must pack it. The **pack** command takes a lot of parameters, including the name of the widget or widgets to pack:

```
pack .b1
```

Tcl widgets don't appear until you pack them.

Making Script Files for Tcl

You can put together a set of Tcl commands into a script file, just like C and Bourne shell scripts. The program to execute the script is again wish. Our script below assumes that **wish** is located in **/usr/bin** (as it is for Linux).

To turn our first example into a working script, we do the following:

```
#!/usr/bin/wish -f
#
# example1.tcl
#
# Create a button.
button .b1 \
    -text "My first button" \
    -command { exit }


pack .b1


# end of file example1.tcl
```

To show you more of a flavor of Tcl scripting, we put together the following file. In it, Tcl commands create a set of buttons that allow you to launch useful Linux programs like **xman** and **xterm**. The toolbar appears at the bottom of the screen and uses the override-redirect mode that prevents a window manager from placing a title bar around the window. Also, in honor of Windows 95, we place the current time at the end of the toolbar.

In our script, we create a number of procedures, called *procs* in Tcl. The *exec_cmd* procedure executes a text string as a UNIX command. We use the **eval** statement to deal with text-string issues and evaluate any Tcl variables within the command. Try this Tcl script without the **eval** in the *exec_cmd* procedure and you'll see why we need it. (It has to do with evaluating the arguments as one string or as a command line. This is one area where Tcl is not intuitive.)

The *update_time* procedure gets the current time, using the UNIX **date** command. *update_time* then changes the text displayed in a widget (you pass *update_time* the widget name) and uses the **after** command to set up a callback, the *update_time* procedure, to get called after a particular amount of time.

The main part of the Tcl script creates a frame widget to hold all the buttons, and then creates a set of buttons. The logo button quits the script when pressed. We use the words *Linux* as well as your machine's hostname for the text in the logo button.

The **Manuals** button calls up **xman** to display UNIX online manuals. The **Mail** button calls up a shell window (**xterm**) and runs our favorite mail program, **elm**. The **Shell** button launches an **xterm** window. And the **File Manager** button launches the **xfm** file manager program.

Our script appears below:

```
#!/usr/bin/wish -f
#
# toolbar.tcl
# Tcl script that puts a toolbar to launch
# programs at the bottom of the screen.

#
# Executes a command as a UNIX process.
#
proc exec_cmd { command } {

    # Execute as a UNIX process in the background.
    # We use eval to handle the messy details of
    # separating the command into its elements.
    # (Try it without eval and you'll see why.)
    #
    eval exec $command &
}


#
# Tcl/Tk procedure to place the
# current time in a widget.
#
set title_interval  40000
set time_command    "/bin/date \"+%I:%M %p\" "

global title_interval time_command
```

```
proc update_time { butn } {
    global  title_interval time_command

    # Get current time.
    set timestr [ eval exec $time_command ]

    $butn config -text $timestr

    # Set up command to run again.
    after $title_interval " update_time $butn"
}

#
# Global commands to execute when
# toolbar buttons get pushed.
#
set cmds(man)   "/usr/bin/X11/xman -notopbox -bothshown"
set cmds(mail)  "/usr/bin/X11/xterm -ls -e elm"
set cmds(term)  "/usr/bin/X11/xterm -ls"
set cmds(file)  "/usr/bin/X11/xfm"

# Make cmds array global.
global cmds

#
# Main program.
#
#   Set window manager values.
wm geometry        .    +0-0
wm overrideredirect . true

#
# Frame to hold everything.
#
set back lightgray
```

```
frame .frame -relief raised -bd 2 -bg $back
.frame config -cursor top_left_arrow

#
# Logo/Name widget.
#
set title [format "Linux: %s" [ exec hostname ] ]

button .frame.logo -text $title \
  -command { exit } -bg $back \
  -relief flat -padx 8

pack .frame.logo -side left -fill y

#
# Create other widgets
# that make up our toolbar.
#
button .frame.man -text "Manuals" \
 -command { exec_cmd $cmds(man) } \
 -relief flat -padx 8 -bg $back

button .frame.mail -text "Mail" \
 -command { exec_cmd $cmds(mail) } \
 -relief flat -padx 8 -bg $back

button .frame.term -text "Shell" \
 -command { exec_cmd $cmds(term) } \
 -relief flat -padx 8 -bg $back

button .frame.file -text "File Manager" \
 -command { exec_cmd $cmds(file) } \
 -relief flat -padx 8 -bg $back
```

```
# Pack all the buttons, in order.
pack .frame.man .frame.mail \
  .frame.term .frame.file \
  -side left -fill y


# Set up timer label.
label .frame.time -bg $back
update_time .frame.time
pack .frame.time -side left -fill y


pack .frame


# end of file toolbar.tcl
```

When you run this script, you'll see a toolbar like the one shown in Figure 10.3.

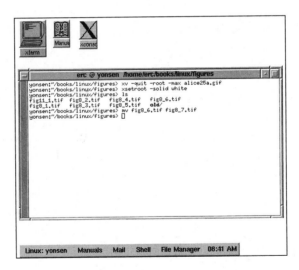

Figure 10.3 The toolbar Tcl script in action.

You can use this script as an example to help you delve into Tcl programming. There's no doubt you'll need more information on Tcl to really get into it.

Perl

Perl is a freeware scripting language developed to handle a number of system administration tasks. **Perl** stands for Practical Extraction and Report Language. The whole point of the language is to make it easier for you to extract data from UNIX and output reports on things such as Usenet news disk usage and a list of all users on your systems, sorted in order of largest disk usage. (**Perl** tends to exceed at tasks that revolve around reporting system information.)

To make sure you've installed **perl** when you install Linux, type in the following:

```
gilbert:/$ perl -v
```

If you have **perl** on your system, you should see the version number for **perl**. If not, you need to run the Setup program again. (The Setup program installs **perl** 4.0p36 from the **d** series. **Perl** 5.001 can be found on the CD-ROM in the **contrib** directory.)

A First Perl Script

Perl, like most Tcl and most other UNIX scripting languages, uses the # as a comment marker. Any line with # is ignored from the # onward. To **print** out data in a perl script, use the print statement:

```
#! /usr/bin/perl
print "Linux runs perl!\n";
print "Oh, joy!\n";
```

When you run this script, you'll see the following output, as you'd expect:

```
Linux runs perl!
Oh, joy!
```

The \n stands for a newline, or linefeed character and is typical UNIX parlance as we described above in the section on C programming.

You can also prompt for data in **perl**, using the odd syntax below:

```
#! /usr/bin/perl
# Prompting for input in perl.

print "What is your first name: ";

# <STDIN> stands for standard input: the keyboard.
$first_name = <STDIN>;

# Remove trailing linefeed.
chop($first_name);

printf "What is your last name: ";
$last_name = <STDIN>;

chop($last_name);

print "Your name is $first_name $last_name.\n";
```

When you run this script, you'll see the following prompts:

```
What is your first name: Eric
What is your last name: Johnson
Your name is Eric Johnson.
```

Perl provides a lot of support for arrays, UNIX process control, and string handling. **Perl** offers a string set of array operations, which allow you to have a set of data treated as one unit, for example:

```
(1,2,3,4,5,6)
```

The above array has the values 1 through 6. You can also intermix text and numeric values, as shown below:

```
(1, 2, 3, 4, "Linux is out the door")
```

You can assign this array to a variable and then access any element in the array. A great strength of **perl** is its associative arrays, where you can use a key value for an array index and associate this with a data value. For example, you can have a **perl** array for a first name, last name and street address. You could then access the street address as shown below:

```
#! /usr/bin/perl
# Associative arrays in perl.

# zippy is an associative array.

$zippy{"firstname"} = "Zippy";
$zippy{"address"} = "1600 Pennsylvania Ave.";

# Print the data.
print $zippy{"firstname"};
print "'s address is ";
print $zippy{"address"};

# End with a carriage return.
print "\n";
```

The example above stores a first name and an address in the associative array named *zippy*. Associative arrays form a very powerful feature and can be used effectively in a lot of system administration tasks.

The output of the above script looks something like the following (and predicts the results of the next election):

```
Zippy's address is 1600 Pennsylvania Av.
```

In addition to associative arrays, **perl** has a lot of commands to format text to allow you to create reports (the original reason for **perl's** existence). **Perl** is intimately tied in with UNIX and provides a number of shortcuts for common UNIX activities, like accessing the password file, as we show below:

```
#! /usr/bin/perl
# Accessing the password file.

# Get Eric's password entry and print it.

@erc_entry = getpwnam("erc");

($username, $realname, $homedir) = @erc_entry[0,6,7];

print "User $realname has";
print " a home directory of $homedir";
print " and a username of $username.\n";
```

When you run this script, you'll see output like the following:

```
User Eric F. Johnson has a home directory of /home/erc and a
username of erc.
```

Naturally, you'll want to use a username that is available on your system.

There's a lot more to **perl**, which fills more than one book on the subject. If you're interested in learning more about **perl**, see Appendix A.

Gawk

Developed by three Bell Labs researchers (Alfred *A*ho, Peter Weinberger, and Brian *K*ernighan—hence the acronym *awk*), **awk** is a programming language (with some strong similarities to the C programming language, discussed earlier in this chapter), but used much in the same manner as other UNIX scripting tools. Hence its inclusion in this chapter.

Technically speaking, **awk** doesn't ship with Linux; instead, the GNU version, **gawk**, does ship with Linux. (By now you shouldn't be surprised that Linux features any other software from the GNU Project.) Since **gawk** is virtually identical to other implementations of **awk** (there are a few extensions to **awk** in **gawk**, but you can ignore them if you choose), most users with experience with **awk** will have no problems with **awk**.

Gawk's primary value is in the manipulation of structured text files, where information is stored in columnar form and information is separated by consistent characters (such as tabs, spaces, or other characters). **Gawk** takes these structured files and manipulates them through editing, sorting, and searching.

Let's use a data file named **workers** as an example:

```
Eric      286    555-6674    erc       8
Geisha    280    555-4221    geisha    10
Kevin     279    555-1112    kevin     2
Tom       284    555-2121    spike     12
```

Let's sink into the trap of abstraction for a minute and compare our example file output to a two-dimensional graph. Each row across is called a *record*, which in turn is made up of vertical *fields* or *columns*, almost like a database. **Gawk** allows us to manipulate the data in the file by either row or column. Using the **gawk** command is not a complicated process. The structure of the **gawk** command looks like:

```
$ gawk [option] 'pattern {action}'
```

(The only options available with **gawk** are -*F*, which allows you to specify a field separator other than the default of white space; -*f*, which allows you to specify a filename full of **gawk** commands instead of placing a complex pattern and action on the Linux command line, and -*W*, which runs **gawk** in total compatibility with **awk**.) Here we should define our terms. A *pattern* can be an ASCII string (which **gawk** treats numerically; instead of seeing the character *e* as an *e*, it sees it as the ASCII equivalent), a numeral, a combination of numerals, or a wild card, while *action* refers to an instruction we provide. So, essentially, **gawk** works by having us tell it to search for a particular pattern; when it has found that pattern, then **gawk** is to do something with it, such as printing the pattern to another file.

The simplest **gawk** program merely prints out all lines in the file:

```
gilbert:/$ gawk '{ print }' workers
Eric    286    555-6674    erc      8
Geisha  280    555-4221    geisha   10
Kevin   279    555-1112    kevin    2
Tom     284    555-2121    spike    12
```

Continuing our above example, let's say we wanted to pull all records that began with the string *geisha*. We'd use the following:

```
gilbert:/$ gawk '$1 ~ /Geisha/ {print $0}' workers
```

Here's what the command means, part by part:

- *$1*: Tells **gawk** to use the first column for the basis of further action. **Gawk** will perform some action on a file based on either records or fields; a number beginning with a $ tells **gawk** to work on a specific field. In this case, *$1* refers to the first field.
- ~: Tells **gawk** to match the following string.
- */Geisha/*: The string to search for.
- *{print $0}*: Tells **gawk** to print out the entire record containing the matched string. A special use of the $ sign is with the character 0, which tells **gawk** to use all the fields possible.
- *workers*: The file to use.

In our case, **gawk** would print the following to the screen:

```
Geisha    280    555-4221    geisha    10
```

Not every action need to be the result of matching a specific pattern, of course. In **gawk**, the tilde (~) acts as a relational operator, which sets forth a condition for **gawk** to use. There are a number of other relational operators available to **gawk** users that allow **gawk** to compare two patterns. (The relational operators are based on algebraic notation.) **Gawk** supports the same relational operators as found in the C programming language; they are listed in Table 10.6.

Table 10.6 Gawk relational operators.

Operator	Meaning	Usage
<	Less than	*$1* < *"Eric"* returns every pattern with an ASCII value less than *"Eric"*.
<=	Less than or equal to	*$1* <= *"Eric"* .
==	Equals	*$1* == *"Eric"* returns every instance of *"Eric"*.
!=	Does not equal	*$1* != *"Eric"* returns every field not containing the string *"Eric"*.
>=	Greater than or equal to	*$1* >= *"Eric"* returns every field equal to or greater than *"Eric"*.
>	Greater than	*$1* > *"Eric"* returns every field greater than *"Eric"*.

We could increase the sophistication of **gawk** searches in a number of ways. Firstly, we could incorporate the use of compound searches, which uses three logical operators:

- &&, which works the same as the logical AND
- | |, which works the same as the logical OR
- !, which returns anything NOT equaling the original

For instance, let's say we wanted to know how many workers had a value in the fifth field that is greater than or equal to 10:

```
gilbert:/$ gawk '$5 >= 10 { print $0 } ' workers
Geisha   280      555-4221      geisha  10
Tom      284      555-2121      spike   12
```

We can also combine tests, to print out, for example, all workers who have the fifth field less than 10 and the second field greater than 280:

```
gilbert:/$ gawk '$5 < 10 && $2 > 280 { print $0 } ' workers
Eric     286      555-6674      erc     8
```

While these examples are obviously contrived, you can use **gawk** to help pull out all entries that share certain postal (ZIP) codes, or all employees who have a salary in a certain range. We're just scratching the surface with **gawk**.

Gawk can also be used to return entire sections of data, as long as you can specify patterns that begin and end the section. To return the records of Eric and Kevin and all between, use the following:

```
gilbert:/$ gawk '$1 ~ /Eric/,/Kevin/ {print $0}' workers
Eric     286   555-6674   erc       8
Geisha   280   555-4221   geisha    10
Kevin    279   555-1112   kevin     2
```

If we don't want to print the whole record, we can print just a few of the fields, as in the example below, which prints out fields 2 and 1:

```
gilbert:/$ gawk '$1 ~ /Eric/,/Kevin/ {print $2, $1}' workers
286 Eric
280 Geisha
279 Kevin
```

As with other UNIX commands, **gawk** can be used in pipes, and its output can be directed to other files or directly to the printer. For example, if we were looking through a large file and expecting many matches to a particular string (such as salary ranges or employment starting dates), we might want to direct that output to a file or to a printer.

For example, to use **gawk** with the UNIX **sort** utility, we can sort the output of the last example:

```
gilbert:/$ gawk '$1 ~ /Eric/,/Kevin/ {print $2, $1}' workers | sort
279 Kevin
280 Geisha
286 Eric
```

(Note that this is sorting on the leading number.)

Gawk also provides some summary abilities as well. The **NR** symbol in an **gawk** command returns the number of records, for example.

We can combine this with **gawk**'s ability to total fields in an **gawk** program.

Gawk Programs

You're not limited to what fits on the command line with **gawk**. You can also store a series of **gawk** commands in a file and then use **gawk** to execute the file.

For example, we can store our simplest **gawk** command, {**print**}, in a separate file and use the following **gawk** command:

```
gilbert:/$ gawk -f gawk.1 workers
Eric     286     555-6674      erc     8
Geisha   280     555-4221      geisha  10
Kevin    279     555-1112      kevin   2
Tom      284     555-2121      spike   12
```

In this case, we're assuming the file **gawk.1** contains our very simple **gawk** program:

```
{ print }
```

You can combine this with the **gawk BEGIN**, **END**, and **NR** commands to make a more complex **gawk** program. When working with this, it's good to remember that **gawk** applies each **gawk** command to every record; that is, every line of text, in the input file. A program like {**print**} says that for each line in the input file, print it.

The **gawk BEGIN** command lists what to do before reading each line of text. For example:

```
BEGIN { print "Workers for Spacely's Sprockets"; print "" }
{ print }
```

The above **gawk** program will print out the text "Workers for Spacely's Sprockets" before printing each line in the **workers** file. One the command line, this will look like the following (if we stored the above **gawk** program in a file named **gawk.2**):

```
gilbert:/$ gawk -f gawk.2 workers
Workers for Spacely's Sprockets

Eric     286     555-6674      erc      8
Geisha   280     555-4221      geisha   10
Kevin    279     555-1112      kevin    2
Tom      284     555-2121      spike    12
```

The **print** "" prints a blank line.

The **END** statement similarly lists commands to execute after data is all read. Here's where the **NR** command, number of records (or lines) comes in handy, as in the following example:

```
BEGIN { print "Workers for Spacely's Sprockets"; print "" }


{ print }


END { print "There are ",
      NR,
      " employees left after the latest wave of layoffs." }
```

The above example uses cleaner formatting for the **END** statements. This makes no difference in the output if we had instead placed the entire **END** command on one line. We can name this file **gawk.3** and then execute the following command:

```
gilbert:/$ gawk -f gawk.3 workers
Workers for Spacely's Sprockets

Eric     286     555-6674      erc      8
Geisha   280     555-4221      geisha   10
Kevin    279     555-1112      kevin    2
Tom      284     555-2121      spike    12
There are  4  employees left after the latest wave of layoffs.
```

This brief explanation covers **gawk** in the simplest terms. For instance, **gawk** includes most of the trappings of a full programming language, including loops, variables, string operations, numeric operations, and the creation and manipulation of arrays. If you're interesting in a useful programming language that can be mastered relatively quickly, we would recommend further reading on **gawk**; our recommendations can be found in Appendix A.

Using LessTif

Everyone wants to use the OSF/Motif libraries until they find out that they're an added-cost feature for Linux. Unfortunately, the OSF/Motif library is commercial software, which means that you have to pay extra to either get the OSF/Motif library source code or a set of binaries for your platforms. Add to this hassle the frustrating nature of the overly complex OSF/Motif license for software developers, where it's almost impossible to tell if you can actually distribute your applications, and you're ready to scream.

However, we've run across a great programming effort called LessTif, which is gaining more and more OSF/Motif functionality each day. While it's not in completed form, we thought you might want to take a look at it, so we included it in the CD-ROM's **contrib** directory, under the name **lesstif-Apr25-0550.tar.gz**.

LessTif is a workalike clone of the OSF/Motif libraries. That is, it is a set of programming libraries that look and acts like the OSF/Motif libraries (Xm and Mrm). Under the hood, the code is entirely different. From a programmer's perspective, though, LessTif has the same API as the OSF/Motif libraries and supports a number of OSF/Motif widgets, supporting more OSF/Motif widgets with each release. It uses public header files of the same name as their OSF/Motif counterparts.

For your programs, LessTif should allow your OSF/Motif programs to be recompiled under LessTif with no source code changes—at least that's the theory. We've had to make a few changes so far to get around the fact that LessTif is incomplete as we write this. Luckily, since LessTif is undergoing what looks like constant development, the problems we face today should gradually go away.

Distributed under the GNU license, you can use LessTif in free applications. You'll probably want to check over the GNU licenses before using LessTif for commercial software.

Installing LessTif

LessTif comes in source-code format. All you need to do is run **xmkmf** and then make in the standard way to build X programs:

```
xmkmf
make
```

With Linux, you should use the X11 Release 5, not Release 6, header files and X libraries to compile LessTif. If you run into any problems, there's a file named **INSTALL** with the distribution.

Problems with LessTif

The developers of LessTif clearly let you know that LessTif is not a complete OSF/Motif clone by any means. This is only natural at this early stage in LessTif's development. Even so, there's quite a few things present in LessTif that will appeal to OSF/Motif programmers.

LessTif, as incomplete free software, is not without its problems, though, as you'd expect. We point these out not to attack the very nice authors of LessTif, who are devoting a lot of time writing code to give away, but to allow you to make a choice whether you can start with LessTif now, or need to wait for further development.

To see how far LessTif is developed now, we used version number 1256 and tried to compile a set of example programs that run the gamut of common OSF/Motif usage.

In our case, we used the example programs that ship with our book *Power Programming Motif* (MIS:Press 1994), which provided us with a set of programs that used most OSF/Motif widgets and concentrated on the code needed for commercial software development, including heavy use of window-manager functions. We found that a surprising number of programs compiled and ran on different platforms. Each program looked very close to the versions compiled with the true OSF/Motif libraries. Unfortunately, quite a few also dumped core when run. The key for your effective use of LessTif will be to test out your programs. And, since the source is available, you can track down bugs if you'd like. We're sure the LessTif authors would appreciate extra help.

Many of the resource and value defines used in our sample OSF/Motif programs are undefined in LessTif, including: XmCR_FOCUS, the *currInsert* field of the XmTextVerifyCallbackStruct, XmNfocusCallback, XmNallowResize, XmVaPUSHBUTTON, _XA_MWM_MESSAGES, and XmNiconPixmap.

This just shows the incomplete nature of LessTif. Of these undefined symbols, XmNallowResize, which you use to allow your top-level shell widgets to be resized, hit virtually all of our OSF/Motif test programs.

LessTif does not yet support the XmD\rawnButton widget, either (this is not a commonly used widget, though). On the plus side, LessTif does seem to support most of the other OSF/Motif 1.2 widgets.

Editres Support

Editres is an X application and protocol that allows programs compiled with the X Toolkit Intrinsics (Xt) library to export information on widget attributes to an outside program, namely editres itself.

With **editres**, for example, you can change the font, colors and text displayed with any widget, presuming an application supports the **editres** protocol. To do this, an application must set up an event-handling function and pass the special **editres** library call, _XEditResCheckMessages, as the handler. For example, the following code sets this up for a OSF/Motif application:

```
#include <X11/Xmu/Editres.h>

Widget      toplevel;
void        _XEditResCheckMessages();

/* ... */

XtAddEventHandler(toplevel,
  (EventMask) 0,
```

```
True,
_XEditResCheckMessages,
NULL);
```

With this set up, your OSF/Motif application will properly respond to the *edirs* protocol.

The reason we mention this is that LessTif calls `XtAddEventHandler` automatically for you from the *Vendor* shell widget. Thus, all LessTif programs will support **editres**. But, there's a slight problem with this. `_XEditResCheckMessages` resides in the X miscellaneous utilities library **(libXmu.a)** and you must be sure to link this in.

To link with LessTif, you need to link in at least the following libraries, as shown in the command below:

```
cc -o foo foo.c -1Xm -1Xmu -1Xt -1X11
```

We mention this because it's likely you're not linking in the Xmu library now. It's nice that LessTif supports **editres** from the start, but you need to remember to link in the Xmu library.

All in all, for free software, it's hard to complain about LessTif. LessTif isn't ready for prime-time usage yet, but it has made great strides in recent months. (As a small sample, we noticed notes on previous versions) You'll probably want to track its progress and conduct some tests before using it. Better yet, you may want to volunteer to help the effort.

Finding out More about LessTif

You can look up the LessTif home page on the World Wide Web by accessing *http://www.cs.uidaho.edu:8000/hungry/microshaft/lesstif.html* or send E-mail to *hungry@uidaho.edu* to get more information on LessTif. (You're also encouraged to grab a more recent version of LessTif.) If you're interested in issues regarding the development of LessTif, you can subscribe to a mailing list. Send the following message (as part of the message body, not the summary line), to *majordomo@pain.csrv. uidaho.edu:*

```
subscribe lesstif
```

Summary

We realize that many of you are potential and practicing programmers, so we spent a great deal of space on the many programming tools available with Linux. Even so, we've barely touched the surface of the Linux programming environment, both for traditional character-based programs and those running under the X Window System.

The chapter begins with a discussion of the GNU C compiler, **gcc**, which ships with Linux. With **gcc**, you can create and compile C, C++, and Objective-C programs, as explained in this chapter. You learned about compiling the long way and the short way, with the **make** command.

The chapter then moves to programming under the X Window System, and the programming libraries you'll need. In addition, you learned about the **imake** command, which is used by many X Window applications for compiling on various operating systems.

The Tcl/Tk combination allows you to create OSF/Motif-like interfaces through the use of a relatively easy-to-master scripting language. We provide an example script that throws a toolbar on the screen.

Perl is a hot scripting language, made hotter by its widespread use on the Internet. But you should be able to take advantage of its many uses, even if you never go near the Internet.

In what should come as a shock to no one, Linux features yet another command from the GNU Project, **gawk**, which is the functional equivalent of the **awk** programming language. **Gawk** works best on structured commands, although it does have extended programming capabilities.

Finally, we end the discussion with a look at LessTif, which acts as a substitute for the commercial OSF/Motif programming libraries. While LessTif is clearly a work in progress, it's interesting enough for us to include on the accompanying CD-ROM—and it should be interesting enough for you to look at if you're at all interesting in OSF/Motif programming.

For More Information

Books

This book focused on the Slackware distribution of Linux on the accompanying CD-ROM. Should you wander away from this distribution, you may want to check out alternative sources of Linux information. Also, since this book doesn't cover the UNIX operating system or the X Window System in any depth (it takes entire forests to cover these topics in any depth), you may want to look for another UNIX/X book or two. The following listings should fill most of your needs.

Other Linux Books

Running Linux, Matt Welsh and Lar Kaufman, O'Reilly & Assoc., 1995. This nonspecific Linux primer covers both Linux and some general UNIX commands. It's not tied to any specific distribution of Linux, so some of the information won't apply to the accompanying CD-ROM. Still, Welsh is a Linux expert (and a rather graceful writer, also) and he deals with some advanced topics not covered in this book.

Linux Network Administrator's Guide, Olaf Kirch, SSC, 1994. This technical overview of Linux networking should cover whatever you need to know about Linux on the network. Although this book is written from the viewpoint of a technically sophisticated user, it's still useful for anyone who needs to deal with Linux on the network.

Linux: Unleashing the Workstation in Your PC, Stefan Strobel and Thomas Uhl, Springer-Verlag, 1994. This technical overview of Linux is a terse overview of the main Linux characteristics, written from a computer-science point of view.

Using Linux, Jack Tackett Jr., David Gunter, and Lance Brown, Que Books, 1995. This book by committee also covers a much older Slackware distribution of Linux.

UNIX Books

Teach Yourself UNIX, third edition, Kevin Reichard and Eric F. Johnson, MIS:Press, 1995. OK, so we're biased. This book provides an overview of the UNIX operating system, with topics ranging from system configurations and shell scripts to the Internet. Some computer experience is assumed.

UNIX in Plain English, Kevin Reichard and Eric F. Johnson, MIS:Press, 1994. This book covers the major commands in the UNIX command set—and most of the information should be directly applicable to Linux.

UNIX Fundamentals: The Basics, Kevin Reichard, MIS:Press, 1994. This book is for the true UNIX neophyte, who know little or nothing about UNIX—or computing, for that matter. It's part of a four-book series covering UNIX fundamentals (the other titles are *UNIX Fundamentals: UNIX for DOS and Windows Users; UNIX Fundamentals: Communications and Networking;* and *UNIX Fundamentals: Shareware and Freeware*).

X Window Books

The UNIX System Administrator's Guide to X, Eric F. Johnson and Kevin Reichard, M&T Books, 1994. This books focuses on topics related to UNIX and X, including configuration and usage. There's also some information about XFree86. An accompanying CD-ROM contains all of the UNIX/X freeware detailed in the book.

Using X, Eric F. Johnson and Kevin Reichard, MIS:Press, 1992. This book covers X from the user's point of view, covering both usage and configuration issues.

Motif Books

Power Programming Motif, Eric F. Johnson and Kevin Reichard, M&T Books, 1994. This second edition covers OSF/Motif programming through version 1.2.

Magazines

If you're at all serious about your Linux usage, you'll want to check out *Linux Journal* (SSC, 8618 Roosevelt Way NE., Seattle, WA 98115-3097; 206/782-7733; $19 per year; *subs@ssc.com*). This monthly magazine covers the Linux scene, offering practical tips as well as profiles of the many interesting people in the Linux community.

The number of UNIX-specific magazines has fallen to the wayside in recent years (a trend, admittedly, that baffles us). *UNIX Review* is our favorite, if only because two-thirds of the writing team contribute a monthly X Window column.

OSF/Motif and Linux

OSF/Motif, as licensed from the Open Software Foundation, is commercial software. OSF/Motif is actually many things, including a style guide, a window manager, and a set of programming libraries.

Since OSF/Motif is licensed, commercial software, it's not included on the accompanying CD-ROM. Since OSF/Motif is beginning to be a prerequisite for any serious commercial UNIX development, you may at some time need to find OSF/Motif for your Linux system, if you're looking at any professional installations.

MetroLink (4711 N. Powerline Rd., Fort Lauderdale, FL 33309; 305/938-0283; *sales@metrolink.com*) offers OSF/Motif for Linux.

Slackware Mirrors

The Slackware distribution of Linux is maintained at the **ftp.cdrom.com** site, in **/pub/linux/slackware**. At this site, you can grab the very latest version of Slackware (although you shouldn't do this too often; you should upgrade in response to specific needs, not just as a general practice).

This is a busy site, however, so you may want to check out a *mirror* site. A mirror site contains the same Linux files as does the **ftp.cdrom.com** site, and they're updated regularly. In addition, as a good Internet citizen you should use the FTP site closest to you, keeping in mind that most of these sites are maintained for the use of local users, not global Internet users. By the way, (**Ftp.cdrom.com** is in California.)

Table A.1 lists the sites known to mirror the Slackware Linux release.

Table A.1 Slackware Linux mirrors.

Country
Site
Location
Australia
monu1.cc.monash.edu.au
/pub/Linux/distributions/Slackware
/pub/OS/Linux/distributions/Slackware
Bond.edu.au (131.244.1.1)
Chile
ftp.ing.puc.cl
/pubLlinux/Slackware
ftp.dcc.uchile.cl
/Linux/Slackware
ftp.inf.utfsm.cl
/pub/Linux/Slackware
Hungary
ftp.kfki.hu
/pub/Linux/distributions/Slackware

Table A.1   Slackware Linux mirrors. (continued)

Country
  Site
    Location

Switzerland
  nic.switch.ch
    /mirror/Linux/sunsite/distributions/Slackware

United Kingdom
  src.doc.ic.ac.uk
    /packages/Linux/Slackware-mirror

Denmark
  ftp.nl.net

  ftp.dd.dk
    /pub/Linux/dist/Slackware

Canada
  pcdepot.uwaterloo.ca
    /Linux/Slackware

Mexico
  ftp.nuclecu.unam.mx
    /Linux/Slackware

Portugal
  ftp.di.fc.ul.pt
    /pub/Linux/Slackware

  ftp.ncc.up.pt
    /pub/Linux/Slackware

Spain
  luna.gui.uva.es
    /pub/Linux.new/Slackware

France
  ftp.ibp.fr
    /pub/Linux/distributions/Slackware

Czech Republic
  vcdec.cvut.cz
    /pub/Linux/local

Table A.1 Slackware Linux mirrors. (continued)

Country
 Site
  Location

Germany
 ftp.gwdg.de
  /pub/Linux/install-mount/slack102

 ftp.informatik.uni-bonn.de
  /pub/unix/Linux/Slackware

 ftp.informatik.rwth-aachen.de
  /pub/Linux/local/Slackware

 ftp.rz.uni-sb.de
  /pub/Linux/distributions/Slackware

Brazil
 farofa.ime.usp.br
  /pub/Linux/Slackware

Japan
 ftp.cs.titech.ac.jp
  /pub/os/Linux/Slackware

Taiwan
 NCTUCCCA.edu.tw
  /Operating-Systems/Linux/Slackware

Finland
 ftp.funet.fi
  /pub/OS/Linux/images/Slackware

 ftp.twi.tudelft.nl/pub/Linux/slackware

South Africa
 ftp.sun.ac.za
  /pub/Linux/distributions/Slackware

Hong Kong
 ftp.cs.cuhk.hk
  /pub/Linux/Slackware

United States
 mrcnext.cso.uiuc.edu
  /pub/Linux/Slackware

Table A.1 Slackware Linux mirrors. (continued)

Country
Site
Location

sunsite.unc.edu
/pub/Linux/distributions/Slackware
ftp.halcyon.com
/pub/Linux/Slackware
ftp.cs.columbia.edu
/archives/Linux/Slackware
ftp.ccs.neu.edu
/pub/os/Linux/Slackware

There are also some additional FTP sites that may interest you. We list them in Table A.2.

Table A.2 FTP sites related to Linux.

Site	Contents
rtfm.mit.edu	Linux FAQs
tsx-11.mit.edu	Linux software archives
sunsite.unc.edu	Linux software archives

Linux HOW-TOS

The collective wisdom of the Linux community has been distilled into a series of text documents, called HOW-TOS, that describe various portions of the Linux operating system. We've included the latest version of these documents on the accompanying CD-ROM (in the **/docs** directory), but if they don't answer your questions, you may want to see if a more recent version is available via the Internet. You can find them in many sites, but the official repository of these documents is at **sunsite.unc.edu**, in the **/pub/Linux/docs/HOWTO** directory.

Usenet Newsgroups

The Usenet newsgroups listed in Table A.3 are devoted to the Linux operating system.

Table A.3 Usenent newsgroups related to Linux.

Newsgroup	Topic
comp.os.linux.admin	Linux system administration
comp.os.linux.advocacy	Why Linux is the perfect operating system
comp.os.linux.announce	Product announcements
comp.os.linux.answers	Answers to far-ranging questions
comp.os.linux.development	Software-development issues.
comp.os.linux.development.apps	Application-development issues
comp.os.linux.development.system	System-development issues
comp.os.linux.hardware	Linux and the wacky world of PC hardware
comp.os.linux.help	Linux, the problems it causes, and how to solve them
comp.os.linux.misc	Miscellaneous Linux topics
comp.os.linux.networking	Linux and networking
comp.os.linux.setup	Installing and configuring Linux
comp.os.linux.x	XFree86 and Linux

Web Pages

Linux is a big topic on the Internet; a recent search on the CMU Lycos Web-page database yielded over 6,000 Web pages that mention Linux somewhere. We've done a little editing for you and compiled this assortment of interesting Linux-related Web pages. Naturally—this being the World Wide Web and all—most of these pages spend a lot of time pointing you to other Web pages, which in turn point you to even more Web pages. Table A.4 lists our favorite Linux-related Web pages, while figures A.1 and A.2 show a few.

Table A.4 Linux resources on the World Wide Web.

Web Page   Explanation
http://sunsite.unc.edu/mdw/welcome.html An important source of Linux information and archived software
http://www.Linux.org/ Linux.org home page
http://www.cdrom.com Home of Slackware
http://harvest.cs.colorado.edu/brokers/lsm/query.html The Linux Software Map, which lists Linux applications
http://www.uni-mainz.de/~kubla/LinuxInt/Welcome.html Linux International home page
http://sunsite.unc.edu/mdv/Linux.html Home page for the Linux Documentation Project
http://www.beckman.uiuc.edu/groups/biss/people/baba/Linux.html Where Linux mailing-list archives are stored
http://skynet.ul.ie/~hjw/Linux-sites.html Links to other Linux resources
http://ens12.univ-mrs.fr/Us/CS/Linux/Links.html More links to other Linux resources
http://www-leland.stanford.edu/~wkn/Linux/slip/slip-1.html Information about Linux and SLIP
http://www.edu.ee/Linux/Linux.html As the excerpt from Lycos states:"Slackware Linux Distribution Installeerimise lühijuhend Selline täiesti empiiriline asi, kes oskab, tehku parem." We couldn't have said it better ourselves
http://www.fokus.gmd.de/Linux/Linux-misc.html Linux in Germany
http://www.Linux.org.uk/ Home page for European Linux users
http://www.waldorf-gmbh.de/Linux-mips-faq.html Running Linux on a MIPS-based machine, a version currently under development

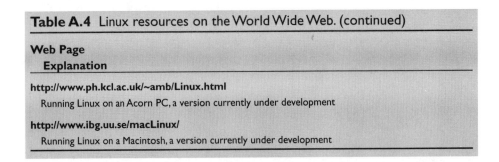

Table A.4 Linux resources on the World Wide Web. (continued)

Web Page
  Explanation

http://www.ph.kcl.ac.uk/~amb/Linux.html
  Running Linux on an Acorn PC, a version currently under development

http://www.ibg.uu.se/macLinux/
  Running Linux on a Macintosh, a version currently under development

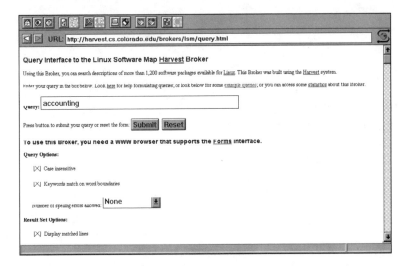

Figure A.1 The Linux Software Map.

If there's one thing about the Web, it's always changing. If you want to generate a more current listing on Linux-related home pages, check out the Carnegie-Mellon Lycos home page (*http://lycos.cs.cmu.edu/*). Lycos is a searchable database of Web pages across the world. We've always found it to be useful, even during times when the many Lycos servers were under a lot of stress.

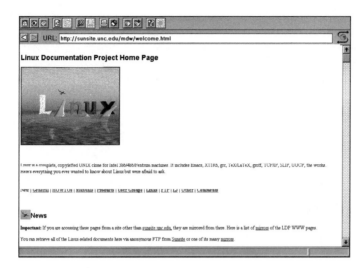

Figure A.2   The Linux Documentation home page.

Extending Your X Server

This appendix covers a frequently asked question about X on Linux: Since Linux doesn't support an X program that requires a specific X extension, how do you get an X installation to run these programs? For example, XFree86 does not come configured to run three-dimensional graphics programs requiring the PEX extension.

We show you how to reconfigure your X server, extending it for these new needs. We'll show you how to do this and then discuss memory and performance trade-offs. We'll focus on the 3D PEX extension, because it's the most-requested X extension that XFree86 doesn't support by default on Linux.

What Is an X Extension?

An X extension is a piece of program code that extends the X server by adding some significant new functionality missing from the core X protocol, such as direct support for 3D graphics.

Each extension needs to modify the X server and come with a programmer's library so that programs may make use of the extension. Some of these extensions, such as Shape, are so standard that it's hard to view them as add-ons. The Shape extension, for example, allows you to have round (and other odd-shaped) windows. The oclock program takes advantage of this, as we show in Figure B.1.

Figure B.1 Oclock using the Shape extension.

We list the most common X extensions in Table B.1.

Table B.1 Common extensions to X.

Extension	Usage
LBX	Low-bandwidth (serial-line) X
MIT-SCREEN-SAVER	Allows you to create your own screen savers
MIT-SHM	MIT shared-memory Ximage extension
Shape	Nonrectangular windows
X3D-PEX	PHIGS 3D extension to X
XTestExtension1	Testing
XIE	X Image Extension
XInputExtension	Adding new input devices, like digitizing tablets
XVideo	Video extension

To see what X extensions your system supports, run the **xdpyinfo** program from within an **xterm** window (you must be running X, of course). When you run **xdpyinfo**, you'll see a lot of output describing your X server. Part of that output will include a list of extensions, probably something like the following:

```
number of extensions:    9
    BIG-REQUESTS
    MIT-SCREEN-SAVER
    MIT-SHM
    MIT-SUNDRY-NONSTANDARD
    Multi-Buffering
    SHAPE
    SYNC
    XC-MISC
    XTEST
```

Our X server doesn't support a lot of fun extensions, such as PEX.

What You Need to Extend X on Linux

Most of the time, you'll get XFree86 (the implementation of X for Linux) in binary format. Because of this, you need a special package, called the X *link kit*, to extend the Linux X server. The link kit allows you to compile and link a new X server. The version of XFree86 that ships with this book contains the link kit; to install it, you'll need to run the **setup** program again. One of the menu choices should cover the link kit.

If you don't have this, you can get it over the Internet. Usually the file is called **X311kit.tgz** or something like that.

The link kit allows you to rebuild the X server, adding in something new—the X extension you'd like to add in. You'll also need the **gcc** C compiler (which comes with Linux if you choose to install it) and **libgcc.a**, gcc's standard C library. You should have installed both when you installed Linux.

To see which version of **gcc** you have, try entering the following:

```
$ gcc -v
Reading specs from /usr/lib/gcc-lib/i486-linux/2.5.8/specs
gcc version 2.63
```

To really make use of PEX, you'll need to load the PEX libraries, include files and fonts, part of the PEX package at install time. (This may also be found over the Internet as part of the **X311pex.tgz** or something like this.) The PEX fonts, in **/usr/lib/X11/fonts/PEX**, are required to run most PEX programs.

In the next section, we'll show how to use the link kit to rebuild the X server for PEX, the X extension that supports three-dimensional graphics. These steps are basically the same for adding in other X extensions, such as LBX, which allows you to run X programs over serial lines, or XIE, the massive imaging extension.

We choose PEX because we've seen quite a lot of questions regarding this particular X extension. Three-dimensional graphics are becoming more and more popular. The basic techniques, though, apply to any X extension you need to add.

Configuring the Server Build

Before you can build a new X server, you must edit a configuration file, **site.def**. Change to the **/usr/X11R6/lib/Server** directory. This is where most of the relevant files are kept.

In this directory, edit the **site.def** file (always make a backup first). In this file, you need to specify a number of things, including:

- which X extensions to build, e.g., PEX
- which X server to build, e.g., SuperVGA **XF86_SVGA** or S3 **XF86_S3**

In Table B.2, we list the settings we've succeeded with. Note that we disable the creation of most of the X servers, since we only need the S3 and SVGA X servers. Because of this, you'll likely want to change our settings.

Table B.2 Settings in the site.def file.

Setting	Value	Meaning
HasGcc	YES	Linux uses the **gcc** C compiler
HasGcc2	YES	Linux uses **gcc** version 2.x
XF86SVGAServer	YES	Builds 256-color SVGA X server
XF86VGA16Server	NO	Builds 16-color VGA X server
XF86MonoServer	NO	Builds monochrome VGA X server
XF86S3Server	YES	Builds S3 X server
XF86Mach8Server	NO	Builds the Mach8 X server
XF86Mach32Server	NO	Builds the Mach32 X server
XF86Mach64Server	NO	Builds the Mach64 X server
XF86P9000Server	NO	Builds the P9000 X server
XF86AGXServer	NO	Builds the AGX X server
XF86W32Server	NO	Builds the ET4000/W32 X server
XF86I8514Server	NO	Builds the IBM 8514/A X server
XnestServer	NO	Builds the Xnest server
BuildPexExt	YES	Builds the PEX extension
BuildXIE	NO	Builds the XIE extension
BuildLBX	NO	Builds the Low Bandwidth X extension

NOTE Note that with any release, these settings may change and there may be many new ones. Use Table B.2 as a guide, not as gospel. At this time, since you're rebuilding the X server anyway, you may also want to build in one of the other X extensions, such as LBX or XIE.

Most of the servers are turned on automatically. You can turn off what you don't want. For each X server, especially the SuperVGA ones, there is a list of drivers you can set. We always pick the defaults and leave the settings (**XF86SvgaDrivers**, **XF86Vga16Drivers**, **XF86Vga2Drivers**, and **XF86MonoDrivers**) alone.

If you build more than one X server, you need to uncomment the **ServerToInstall** line and put in the X server you want installed with the symbolic link from X. Otherwise, the **XF86_SVGA** gets set up as the default X server, X.

Once you've set up the **site.def** file, you're ready to starting building a new X server.

Building a New X Server

As the root user, you should perform the following steps to build your new X server:

1. Back up your current X server.
2. Build all the Makefiles.
3. Make the new X servers.
4. Quit X.
5. Install the new X servers.
6. Ensure that **/usr/X11R6/bin/X** links to the proper X server.
7. Start X to verify the new X server works.
8. Run **xdpyinfo** to see if the new X extensions are available.
9. Clean the **/usr/X11R6/lib/Server** directory with **make clean**.

Before you start, always back up your current X server. This is to allow you to continue processing in case the new build fails. Then, build all the Makefiles by running the following command:

```
gilbert:/~$ ./mkmf
```

(All these commands must be run in the **/usr/X11R6/lib/Server** directory as the root user.) This process will take a while, as it runs makedepend on a number of files.

Once **mkmf** finishes successfully, run **make**:

```
gilbert:/~$ make
```

This builds the new X servers and will take even longer than the last step. Once you've built the new X servers, you must ensure that X is stopped. It's very convenient to **su** to the root user in one **xterm** window and build the new X servers while you have all the other windows on your screen available for your work—that's what multitasking is all about. When you need to install the new X server, however, you must ensure that X is stopped. So, quit X in the usual way.

Then, change back to the **/usr/X11R6/lib/Server** directory and run (again as root):

```
gilbert:/~$ make install
```

This will copy the new X servers to **/usr/X11R6/bin** and set up **/usr/X11R6/bin/X** as a link to the default X server (the one you configured for this above). Double-check this essential link anyway and ensure that **/usr/X11R6/bin/X** links to the proper X server (see Chapter 3 for more on this).

Now comes the fun part. Try to run X as a normal user (i.e., as yourself, not the root user), using **startx**. This step is to ensure that X still works (presuming X worked before you did all this).

If you get X up and running (it came right up for us, so if it compiled and linked with no problems, this step should be easy), then run **xdpyinfo** in an **xterm** window to see if the new X extensions are available. The list should look something like the one below:

```
number of extensions:     11
    BIG-REQUESTS
    LBX
    MIT-SCREEN-SAVER
    MIT-SHM
    MIT-SUNDRY-NONSTANDARD
    Multi-Buffering
    SHAPE
    SYNC
    X3D-PEX
    XC-MISC
    XTEST
```

(Yes, we cheated and built the LBX extension at the same time we built PEX.)

Now, once you're confident that everything is built up properly, run **make clean** in the **/usr/X11R6/lib/Server** directory (again as root):

```
gilbert:/~$ make clean
```

This will get rid of all the *.o* files created when you built the X servers and free up a lot of wasted disk space.

As a final test, you may want to run one of the PEX demo programs that comes with X (you may not have loaded these programs, though), such as **beach_ball**.

Performance and Memory Issues

PEX consumes a lot of system resources, so don't load on this extension if you're short on physical memory. When we built PEX and LBX into a new X server, it grew quite a lot, as shown by the **size** command:

```
gilbert:/~$ size XF86_S3.bak
text     data    bss     dec       hex
1277952 45056   46312   1369320   14e4e8
```

Compare this with the new size:

```
gilbert:/~$ size XF86_S3
text     data    bss     dec       hex
1736704 196608  51424   1984736   1e48e0
```

On disk, the X server files grew, too, from 1492708 bytes to 1934340.

Because of this, you may not want to compile in PEX or XIE, two of the largest X servers. (LBX isn't that large compared to PEX.) If you have a low-memory system, then PEX or other large extensions like XIE (the X Image Extension) are simply not for you.

INDEX

ABOUT THE CD-ROM

The accompanying CD-ROM is formatted under ISO-9660 standards, with Rock Ridge extensions. You can read the contents both from PCs and UNIX workstations. However, long UNIX filenames (that is, anything more than the DOS eight-dot-three format) will not be totally visible to DOS users. As there are some files that must be used under DOS to create boot floppies, these floppy-creation files do follow DOS naming conventions.

For instructions on using the CD-ROM when installing Linux, see Chapter 2. You don't actually need to be using this CD-ROM with a PC to create the boot floppies, at least not initially; you could copy the files from a UNIX workstation to a DOS machine via network or floppy, for instance, and then run the floppy-creation programs on the DOS machine.